BAND SCORING

BAND SCORING

McGRAW-HILL SERIES IN MUSIC

DOUGLAS MOORE, *Consulting Editor*

BAND SCORING

Joseph Wagner
Composer-in-Residence
Pepperdine College
Los Angeles, California

McGRAW-HILL BOOK COMPANY, INC.

NEW YORK   TORONTO   LONDON

1960

BAND SCORING

Library of Congress Catalog Card Number 60-8044

67658

7 8 9 10 11 12 EBEB 7 6 5 4 3 2 1

SPECIAL ACKNOWLEDGEMENT

All copyrighted music has been quoted and reproduced in this book with the permission of each individual copyright owner.

A special word of thanks is extended to these publisher-owners for their generous assistance and cooperation in making possible a comprehensive survey of representative band music as of the mid-twentieth century:

Associated Music Publishers, Inc.; Boosey and Hawkes, Inc.; J. and W. Chester, Ltd., London; Oliver Ditson Co.; Durand et Cie, Paris; Elkan-Vogel Co.; Carl Fischer Co., Inc.; Sam Fox Publishing Co.; Percy Grainger; Edwin F. Kalmus; Neil A. Kjos Co.; Leeds Music Corp.; Edward B. Marks Music Corp.; Mercury Music Corp.; Merrymount Music, Inc.; Mills Music, Inc.; Music Publishers Holding Corp.(M. Witmark and Sons; Remick Music Corp.); Theodore Presser Co.; G. Ricordi Co.; G. Schirmer, Inc.; Shawnee Press, Inc.; Summy-Birchard Publishing Co.; Templeton Publishing Co., Inc.; Editions Suvini Zerboni, Milan.

Posthumously to

DR. EDWIN FRANKO GOLDMAN

who awakened my interest in

the concert band

PREFACE

The history of the wind band reveals a slow but steady acceptance of the wind-percussion ensemble as a worthy art medium. The contingent development of a significant repertory of symphonic music for it has emerged and has kept pace with advanced scoring techniques that are peculiarly idiomatic for the band only. At the mid-twentieth century mark the band repertory includes original works, many in the larger forms, of superior craftsmanship and notable musicality. Progress may also be noted in the quality of band transcriptions of orchestral and keyboard music. Both of these facts are now sufficiently well established to provide the basis for a new and fresh approach to the subject of band scoring, which heretofore has been decidedly restricted in scope and relatively unrewarding from an artistic viewpoint. The wind band can no longer be considered a musical stepchild !

A short exploratory survey of the band's early history, showing its gradual rise from a utilitarian status to one of artistic independence, is presented in connection with instrumentation problems peculiar to the wind band. This preliminary examination is followed by a detailed study plan for each instrument according to its notation, range, and timbre. This information is supplemented with examples illustrating each instrument's solo and ensemble capacities in the context of condensed and full scores. The illustrative examples have been selected from three kinds of music comprising the band's repertory: original works, transcriptions of orchestral scores, and music originally written for keyboard instruments. These studies are followed by a series of scoring projects devoted to four-part music for the wood-wind and the brass sections as exercises preliminary to work with the full-band ensemble.

Scoring for the full band is not practical or even possible until the three component parts of music—melody, harmony, and rhythm—have been arranged with suitable structural textures to permit idiomatic adaptation for the wind instruments. This highly technical phase of scoring is approached systematically in this text through subject matter and a series of examples standardized in the *Reference Chart of Keyboard Idioms and Patterns.* (The usefulness and importance of the *Reference Chart* becomes clearly apparent when one considers the natural tendency of the student to do his musical thinking in terms of a keyboard instrument, plus the fact that source material is ordinarily limited to music for the piano or organ.) Scoring experience of this kind is definitely applicable, since the major part of the band's repertory consists of transcriptions of various kinds. Additional chapters, devoted to the scoring of marches and transcription of orchestral music, round out the student's scoring projects. Quotations for the band, from original works in various forms, provide illustrative material for the student of composition who wishes to work in the band medium. Scoring for the modern dance band *per se* has not been included, since this is a specialized field, although an adjunct to band scoring. Pertinent references and examples are given to demonstrate dance-band playing styles and techniques for the wind and percussion instruments as they have been incorporated in contemporary scoring for the wind band. Thus, the staple categories of the band repertory are represented, thereby providing a comprehensive approach to the study of scoring techniques applicable to many forms of band music.

Music for keyboard instruments, particularly for the piano, has certain rather definite and well-established idioms and patterns which can be isolated and classified. These characteristic playing styles ordinarily contain melodic, harmonic, or rhythmic elements on the basis of which idiomatic band textures can be arranged. Furthermore, the important factors of resonance and balance—and the means of securing them—become an integral part of the work carried out in conjunction with the subject matter of the *Reference Chart.*

The band scorer's task, in all forms of transcription, is to achieve an idiomatic transference of musical values from one medium to another without a loss of stylistic detail. The *Reference Chart of Keyboard Idioms and Patterns* has been compiled to accomplish this objective through the application of a systematic, specialized study plan based upon modifications playable by wind instruments. Although many entries in the *Reference Chart* examine digital patterns as they affect music for keyboard instruments, others are concerned primarily with musical factors resulting from or in combination with these technical considerations. Thus, the idiomatic setting of each entry of the *Reference Chart* for wind instruments becomes a working model for subsequent repetitions of the same or similar subject matter. All subject matter is kept in its original musical context wherever structural textures become directly affected by its inclusion.

The study plan is intended to stimulate and direct creative musical thinking, since band scoring involves both work with multiple voice parts in various combinations of mixed colors, strengths, and intensities, and the imaginative faculties of the individual scorer. The models selected for the *Reference Chart* in condensed score form give indication of this inclusive purpose. Here, piano and organ music has been modified to meet the need for voice textures which will be suitable for wind instruments, whether scored sectionally or for the full band.

The approach to band scoring in this text is directed to the examination and illustration of existing problems peculiar to the writing and performance of music for this medium. The book surveys the backgrounds of the variable technical capacities of bands at amateur and professional levels. Furthermore, the student is acquainted, through progressive, applied experience, with the necessity for creating scores with uniformity of texture, style, and technical difficulty.

Scoring the military march, as a unique band form, and the transcription of orchestral music are given separate attention and examination. References to orchestration versus band scoring are made whenever pertinent to assist both students and experienced musicians in their quest for a practical band-scoring technique. No previous band-scoring experience is required to obtain the benefits which can be derived from a well-planned study course and practical application of this text.

The subject matter of this text is based on teaching experience over a period of many years. This experience showed conclusively that certain errors of judgment in dealing with structural textures occurred regularly and consistently, regardless of the musical background of the student. The technical data obtained from the instrumental survey may be applied with freedom and authority only after the problems of structural textures have been solved satisfactorily. Therefore, this factor has been stressed in all illustrative examples dealing with the various categories of band scoring.

A music supplement, *Workbook for Band Scoring,* has been compiled by the author to provide relevant source material which can be used in conjunction with this text. This workbook contains preliminary material dealing with instrumental transpositions and chorals, keyboard music conforming to the subject matter of the *Reference Chart,* and excerpts from marches and orchestral scores.

A special section is devoted to music without classification for use as testing material. A systematic study-work plan carried out with the exploratory data and detailed analyses of the models given for the *Reference Chart*, can provide the basis for a practical and workable technique for band scoring.

The author gratefully acknowledges the helpful suggestions of Prof. Raymond F. Dvorak of the University of Wisconsin, Felix Greissle of the Edward B. Marks Music Corporation, Lyndoll Mitchell of the Eastman School of Music, Prof. Harwood Simmons of Syracuse University, and Lt. Col. William F. Santelmann, ret., of the United States Marine Band. My special thanks are extended to Richard Franko Goldman and my wife for their assistance in proofreading the manuscript and printed copy.

JOSEPH WAGNER

CONTENTS

CHAPTER ONE

〰〰〰

A SURVEY OF THE BAND'S HISTORY

Origins of the Band - Twentieth-century Developments
Problems of Instrumentation

The term "band" has, with the passage of time, taken on several meanings which may be both confusing and misleading. It is used for military, marching, "show," concert, and symphonic bands, dance bands, and sometimes in critical reviews of symphony orchestras. For obvious and practical reasons, in this text the term refers to a group of instrumentalists who are concerned chiefly with the performance of music for wind and percussion instruments with occasional use of string and keyboard instruments, notably the string bass, for concert music.

Recorded history reveals a close association between some kind of band music and military operations. In this connection, the band could have been regarded as utilitarian, since its chief functions were to furnish music for marching, to spur troops to combat, and to serve as a builder of morale. Although the military band still continues to be part of every country's military establishment, its activities have been widened to include the rendering of concert programs for civilian audiences as well as military personnel. With this additional activity, the military band has become the prototype of the concert and symphonic band.

Many of the most notable concert bands of the nineteenth century were quasi-military organizations, some of them functioning through municipal or government patronage. A few independent bands did come into being in America toward the close of the nineteenth century and during the first decades of the twentieth century. The names of the almost legendary pioneer directors of these bands are still remembered—Gilmore, Creatore, Kryl, Conway, Sousa, and Goldman.

The second quarter of the twentieth century has been the most productive from the point of view of the band's professional and musical progress. Professional, nonmilitary bands came into being, in many instances, through civic and commercial financial

1

assistance. The concert band became a recognized musical organization, capable of performing programs which were usually semipopular in content and which were admired and enjoyed by unsophisticated audiences of music lovers the world over.

The phenomenal growth of the band movement in the schools and colleges of America during the early 1900s was also a significant development. The enthusiasm of young instrumentalists and their directors engendered extraordinary momentum. New and different conditions appeared and they have had a lasting effect. More consideration was given to the advantages of presenting indoor concerts by bands with expanded instrumentation. Serious attempts were made to standardize the instrumentation of the concert band, with due consideration given to enlarging the wood-wind section in variety and numbers. The repertory, gradually enriched by a goodly number of significant original works, gave the band unprecedented prestige in the world of music. The wind instruments were improved sufficiently to permit advanced playing techniques, often including those previously considered impractical.

Perhaps the most significant reaction to these developments has been the aesthetic reevaluation of the concert band by musicians in general and composers in particular. Composers of many periods have written sporadically for the wind band in some form. However, it was not until the second quarter of the twentieth century that some of them took up the cause of original music for the concert band with the same sense of dignity that they had for their orchestral music. Symphonic composers of stature have now come to accept the potentialities of this heretofore neglected medium as worthy of their best efforts.

The writers of band music have had to contend with some rather special conditions affecting instrumentation which result from several factors peculiar to the band. In some measure, these conditions have been due to the band's early association with the military. Here a relatively small personnel often prompted a need for scoring strong brass and percussion sections, usually coupled with a weaker and unrepresentative wood-wind section. As the concert activities of these units increased and the later concert bands were created, greater attention was given to the place and importance of the wood-wind instruments. Paralleling these developments were the many improvements and inventions of Boehm, Sax, and Sarrus, which greatly extended the scope and value of the reed instruments, especially for concert music.

One difficulty in this area, still unresolved to the satisfaction of all concerned, is related to the acceptance and use of a flexible band instrumentation. If a flexible plan were adopted, each band scorer could select an instrumentation determined by the content, texture, and form of each piece, as opposed to scoring regularly with a prescribed full instrumentation, regardless of the musical characteristics of a given piece. Progressive band directors and music publishers feel most strongly that attempts to standardize the instrumentation for all concert bands has been a serious deterrent to the growth of music of symphonic proportions and quality.

This problem manifests itself in one specific way which deserves the attention of every band scorer. Many band directors connected with educational institutions have in the past preferred band publications with parts for all of the instrumentation approved by the National High School Band Association. This instrumentation calls for a minimum of thirty parts (see Table 1). It is not difficult to understand the music educator's point of view in this instance, as the stand taken is a practical expedient. However, a minimum instrumentation imposes certain limiting, but not insurmountable, restrictions on the serious composer who is interested in devoting his talents to the creation of a badly needed repertory of symphonic music for the concert band.

This condition should be noted well in the scoring plans of most music for the band. The approach should, and can be, both realistic and artistic if scoring objectives are properly envisioned and directed. Symphonic music at its best does not necessarily require all of the instruments to be playing all of the time regardless of the medium, be it a band or an orchestra. It is just as important for the student instrumentalist to learn to count measures of rest as it is to play his part when it appears.

It is necessary for the practical band scorer to maintain reasonable and consistent levels of technical and musical difficulty, since most band music is graded by American publishers and the various state and national agencies which promote festivals and competitions. The majority of publishers grade concert music for the band in Classes A through D. (Some state competitions use gradings of 1 through 6.) Naturally, Class A bands are fewer in number than those in the Class C and D categories. The ideal policy, and the one to be used in this text, is to score each piece for only those instruments which are really needed, with important cues[1] indicated throughout. This approach is necessarily limited

---

[1] Cued notes are those other than the original written into parts so that substitution of other instruments–preferably with similar tonal color–can be made when necessary.

3

to concert music; it does not apply to the scoring of marches or other forms of music which might be considered utilitarian[1] in usage.

Another factor confronting the band scorer in America is related to the unpredictable availability of certain instruments and to the equally uncertain skill of some performers. This condition is to be noted at most levels where bands exist—school, college, civic, military, industrial, and professional. The instruments involved are those in the double-reed family and, to a somewhat lesser degree, the (French) horns.

By the middle of the twentieth century, one finds this situation somewhat improved, although the double-reed players are far outnumbered by those playing the less difficult single-reed instruments. Some well-informed band directors even fear the eventual disuse of the double reeds, especially the bassoon, since some single-reed instruments arc being used to take over these parts. Although growth in the number and improvement in the skill of horn players can be observed, they have not acquired the advanced playing techniques to be found among players of the other brass instruments. Strangely enough, this situation does not exist to the same degree in Europe or Latin America. It seems to be an unaccounted-for and unfortunate deficiency on the American instrumental scene.

What this means to the writer of band music is that his scores should be cued and cross-cued[2] to facilitate and ensure the playing of all important parts which might otherwise be omitted. Instrumental voids are not confined solely to school bands. On the contrary, they are frequently encountered in professional municipal and service bands, which are often limited to fewer players than is customary in the larger school and college organizations. The subject of cuing and cross-cuing will be discussed in detail in Chap. 29.

[1] The words "utilitarian" and/or "functional" as used in this text refer to the usage of the music, not to its quality or its scoring.

[2] Cross-cuing is carried out by writing one part into several parts other than the original.

CHAPTER TWO

THE BAND AND ITS MUSIC

Score Evolution - Orchestration versus Band Scoring
Repertory Sources - Transcribing and Arranging

Frederick Fennell in his booklet *Time and the Winds,* succinctly sums up the progress of contemporary wind playing as follows: "The development of wind playing has been one of this country's greatest contributions to music performance in the first half of the 20th century. We have unleashed a force for music making unparalleled in the whole history of musical art."

This extraordinary progress in the art of wind playing has all but eliminated some of the technical hazards to be noted in earlier band treatises. The band can now play in tune and can, when properly trained, respond to a conductor's directions with flexibility and musicality. The concert band has been freed from musical rigidity.

The writer of band music has little to gain from a survey of pre-twentieth-century library of music for this medium. There is no accumulated repertory of classics of any consequence, although some excellent music for wind instruments in various combinations dates back to the Baroque period. Gabrieli, Pezel, and Handel are a few representative composers of that period who are worth investigating. Later Classic and Romantic composers, notably Beethoven, Mendelssohn, Berlioz, and Wagner, wrote for the band but their works in this form were not always their best efforts. Here one finds some interesting scores for various wind combinations, but they were intended mostly for single players, not multiple units.

Most band directors, until comparatively recent times, conducted almost entirely from solo-cornet parts which did nothing more than give the leading melodic lines and occasional harmonic cues. The subsequent introduction of the so-called "condensed score" was a decided advance, since it gave the director a more

5

complete picture of the most important parts, although many scoring details had to be filled in as rehearsals progressed. The increasing availability of full scores of music for the concert band is an indication of the recognition currently given the band as a serious artistic medium.

The concert band repertory has, in the past, relied heavily upon transcriptions of operatic and orchestral music in practically all forms. The military march is the chief idiomatic form developed expressly for the band. Both the quantity and quality of original concert music are decidedly twentieth-century developments. Consider, for example, the scores of such monumental works as Hindemith's Symphony in B♭ and Schönberg's Theme and Variations, which would have hardly seemed possible only a few decades ago. The many fine pieces in the smaller forms written for student bands give further evidence that the movement toward better original concert music is well graduated and educationally progressive.

Perhaps no other established medium offers such challenging opportunities and possibilities as does the concert band. Only the surface has been touched during the past two decades, but the first signs of progressive change are now apparent. Ultraconservative harmony is being replaced by post-Romantic harmonic vocabularies with the same freedom as that used for other art media. Stiff, old-fashioned rhythmic formulas are being pushed aside for newer and more energetic rhythms reflecting a truer contemporary spirit. Above all else stands the composers' ceaseless quest for a scoring technique which employs the band instruments according to their maximum idiomatic potentialities. No longer will the timeworn Romantic cliches suffice.

Whether band music reaches the status of a significant art form, and whether bands develop repertories comparable to those of other art media, depend upon three unpredictable factors: the composer, the conductor, and the publisher. The composer has given indications of his interest in this new medium. The American publisher has shown a willingness to cooperate by publishing band works at all grades of difficulty. The case of the conductor is well defined by Frederick Fennell in his *Time and the Winds*: "It can only be hoped that the activity by composers of the past ten years will be sustained by the interest of those who conduct.... Unless those who conduct our many concert bands are willing to devote themselves and their organizations to the proper study and performance of what *does exist*, it is not impossible that the current activity in new music for the band by men of first rank

6

will die a-borning." And later, "The future course of an organized musical literature for the concert band is, therefore, *more in the hands of the conductor* than the composer." This booklet ends with this significant fact: "But the future course of the development of the wind ensemble as a form of musical art rests completely in the hands of the composer—for it is he who writes *The History of the Use of Wind Instruments*."

A second consequence of the band's early reliance on the orchestral repertory has been a misguided tendency to compare and evaluate the band in terms of the orchestra. This has been an inevitable but unfortunate comparison, since these two ensembles exist and function under dissimilar conditions and for different audiences. The writer of band music should now disassociate his musical thinking from many of the idiomatic techniques of orchestration, as they concern the scoring of the wind and percussion instruments. The whole concept for band scoring needs to be approached in terms of its ówn instrumentation and not that used for the orchestra. Certain inevitable comparisons between the two media—musical form, structural textures, and certain instrumental dissimilarities affecting both scoring and performance—are justifiable and sometimes necessary to clarify details likely to be unknown or misapplied.

In scoring for the band, the student should not only differentiate clearly between its instrumentation and that of the orchestra, but should likewise understand the different idiomatic ways the instruments are to be used. This cannot be dismissed with the sole observation that the band has no string section.[1] The experienced orchestrator regards this section as the orchestra's basic choir and adds wind and percussion parts as they are needed to meet his requirements. The practical band scorer does not consider a single choir as basic for all band classifications, but varies his choir emphasis in accordance with the purpose and technical scope of each piece. To illustrate, the marching band relies on the brass and percussion sections to achieve tonal solidity and volume, while the concert band attains its most distinctive results when the wood winds are treated as the basic section. These choir distinctions will be both helpful and practical when considering scoring plans for both types of band.

The exact number of wind instruments is specified in every score for the orchestra, the number of string duplications generally being determined by each conductor. In scores for the band,

---

[1] Strings (other than the bass) and keyboard instruments appear in very few published scores and are best treated as supplementary instruments.

only the divisions of the wind parts are indicated, the number of doubling players for each part being left to the director's judgment. In both instances, the conductor tries for instrumental balance with the players at his disposal. Thus, the timbre strengths and the disposition of the wind instruments in the band can hardly be compared with those of their counterparts in the orchestra. Not only are these factors different, but the conception of their idiomatic usages in the band must be revised to meet the requirements of a changed set of scoring practices.

Another difference is the relative position of the percussion section in each medium. In the concert band, the battery of percussion instruments has an importance almost equal to that of the wind instruments. (In the marching band, the percussion section actually assumes a leading role.) In concert music, the section is neither supplementary nor limited. Rather, it serves as a contributory unit with its full potential sought and applied with greater frequency than was the case in orchestration prior to the mid-nineteenth century.

Original band music, as we have seen, is a comparatively new musical venture. The greater part of the band repertory is still made up of music originally composed for some other medium— piano, organ, voice, or orchestra. Music, transferred from one medium to another, is the work of a transcriber or arranger. The terms "transcription" and "arrangement," frequently used interchangeably, are often confusing and open to interpretation. As used by the writers of instrumental music, the two terms have acquired somewhat different meanings, depending upon the category of their usage. The term "transcription" has appeared in connection with orchestral music derived from various sources. (Orchestrators of entertainment music, known as arrangers, may be cited as an exception to this generalization.) The term "arrangement" has been used quite regularly by those scoring band adaptations of various source materials. However, it is to be noted from band publications that both writers and publishers currently appear to favor the credit line "transcription" or "transcribed by." These terms will be used in this text for simplification.

There is a place for artistic transcriptions of keyboard music (harpsichord, piano, or organ) in the band repertory. Music in this form is not likely to invite comparisons with settings involving some overlapping of instrumentation. Listings of such transcriptions at the end of this text are indicative of the scope of band scoring in this area.[1]

[1] A similar listing in the author's <u>Orchestration: A Practical Handbook</u>, is even more revealing, since it discloses a number of composers as the transcribers of their own music.

8

Band transcriptions of orchestral music often arouse strong prejudices and comparisons among those who are familiar with the orchestra but who are not equally well informed about the band. These reactions, often caused by rescored band parts which differ from their orchestral counterparts, are usually unavoidable because of inherently different problems of resonance and balance in the two ensembles. Band scoring and orchestration are developed from dissimilar basic choirs; this necessarily affects scoring plans and methods.

The media of musical reproduction (recordings, radio, and television) have increased the general public's appreciation, understanding, and desire, not only for better band music, but better performances as well. No longer can poorly composed and transcribed music, indifferently performed, meet with satisfaction or approval. This enlightenment on the part of the public places an even greater responsibility upon the writer of band music, for mere adaptation will no longer suffice. Band music must now be written with the same thoroughness and craftsmanship that was previously associated with orchestration at its best.

CHAPTER THREE

∞∞∞

THE BAND'S INSTRUMENTATION

Classifications - Irregularities

Bands in the twentieth century can, for all practical purposes, be classified as follows:

1. The military band—for parades, military functions, affairs of state, and some concerts. The completeness of the instrumentation of these bands often varies considerably with different countries and military units. Some have limited personnel with the basic instrumentation; others have the full symphonic representation. The larger and less portable instruments are generally omitted when the unit is on the march. (See Tables 1 and 3.)

2. The marching and "show" bands—for out-of-door participation at the athletic events and rallies of schools and colleges. The latter type of band performs with elaborate dance steps and routines while on the march. The instrumentation for both is essentially the same as that given in Table 3.

3. The concert and symphonic bands. There is really no difference in purpose between these units; it is merely a difference in terminology. Both are intended for the presentation of concert music and represent the band's most complete instrumentation. This is most evident in the wood-wind choir (see Table 1).

4. The wind ensemble and chamber bands. These units are highly specialized organizations devoted to the performance of music for any combination of wind and percussion instruments with supplementary strings, keyboard instruments, and voices added as desired. They differ from the concert band in that relatively few doubling parts[1] are employed, which intentionally restricts the size of both groups.

From the above listing it can be deduced that the purpose and activities of bands have been determining factors affecting their size and instrumentation. Player personnel in the first three classifications may vary from 25 to 100 while the instrumentations

---

[1] The term "doubling," in this instance, refers to one or more identical instruments playing from the same part.

10

range from the essential basic grouping to full representation in all choirs. The wind ensemble, on the other hand, has a maximum of about 45 players, with relatively little doubling of parts.

The irregularities and peculiarities of the band's instrumentation have been mentioned previously. These difficulties are further emphasized by the fact that the instruments of the band differ considerably from one country to another. The writer of band music should face this situation realistically and score his music accordingly. However, in most countries a basic, minimum core of instruments provides a nucleus which enables foreign directors to perform music published in America.

A standardized instrumentation for school bands was adapted in 1943 by the National High School Band Association. Since then, still further revisions have led to the general acceptance of the instruments listed below for the various band classifications. Publications now have parts for all of these instruments,[1] even though some of them function as duplicating and/or substituting parts.

TABLE 1

STANDARDIZED INSTRUMENTATION

Wood Winds	*Brass*
C piccolo	B♭ cornets I-II-III
D♭ piccolo	B♭ trumpets I-II
Flutes I-II	F horns I-II-III-IV
Oboes I-II	E♭ horns I-II-III-IV
E♭ clarinet	Trombones I-II-III
B♭ clarinets I-II-III	Baritone or euphonium (treble and
E♭ alto clarinet	bass clefs)
B♭ bass clarinet	Tubas
Bassoons I-II	
E♭ alto saxophones I-II	*Percussion*
B♭ tenor saxophone	
E♭ baritone saxophone	Timpani - percussion

[1] The instruments ordinarily are listed on the score page in the order given here.

Optional supplementary instruments occasionally included are Bb and Eb contrabass clarinets, Bb soprano and Bb bass saxophones, English horn, contrabassoon, fluegelhorns, harp, celesta, piano, violoncello, contrabass (string bass). Of these, the string bass is found quite regularly in the instrumentation of concert music for the band.

In Table 1, the Db piccolo and the four horns in Eb are duplicating parts of the C piccolo and the horns in F respectively. Likewise, the baritone and the euphonium parts are also duplicates. It should also be noted here that the flutes are sometimes divided into three parts and that four-part divisions are fairly common for the Bb clarinets, cornets, and trombones. The F horn listed here is the one now ordinarily employed in the orchestra and favored for the horn parts of concert music for the band. Horns in Eb, often played on melophones or alto instruments, are preferred by some band directors as substitutes in marching bands.

Bandsmen and music publishers are not all agreed on the question of full representation for all family groupings of the wood winds. It would seem that the listing given in Table 1 is a good compromise, in keeping with both artistic values and economic actualities. There is a point beyond which excessive numbers, divisions, and groupings become a liability rather than an asset.

The following points can be deduced from Table 1:

1. Many of the instruments are divided into two or more parts.

2. The number of players doubling any given part is a variable factor.

3. The band has no instruments in A, as used in orchestral music.

4. Baritone and euphonium parts are published for the player in both the bass and treble clefs. The part in the full score is ordinarily given in the bass clef, although a few of the older scores show parts in both the bass and treble clefs. The use of the treble clef in this instance is a player convenience and should not appear in the full score. Baritones are rarely divided into two parts in American publications.

Those wishing to write for the newer wind ensemble will find the instrumentation in Table 2 of especial interest. It was devised by Frederick Fennell, who founded the first such organization, The Eastman Symphonic Wind Ensemble, in 1952 and became its conductor.

12

TABLE 2

WIND ENSEMBLE INSTRUMENTATION

Reeds

2 flutes and piccolo
2 oboes and English horn
2 bassoons and contrabassoon
1 Eb clarinet
8 Bb clarinets or the same num-
    ber, or fewer, of A clarinets
    divided in any manner desired
1 Eb alto clarinet
1 Bb bass clarinet
2 Eb alto saxophones
1 Bb tenor saxophone
1 Eb baritone saxophone

Brass

3 Bb cornets or 5 Bb trumpets
2 Bb trumpets
4 F horns
3 trombones
2 Euphoniums
1 Eb tuba
1 BBb tuba or 2 BBb tubas if
    desired

Other Instruments

Percussion, harp, celesta, piano, organ, solo string instruments, and choral forces as desired

Mr. Fennell comments that this instrumentation, which gives the composer complete freedom in his choice of instruments and ensures no substitutions by cuing, is a progressive step forward: "The above instrumentation has been established as a point of departure....one from which it is possible to deviate when a particular score requires more or less instruments than are considered basic to the Wind Ensemble. This instrumentation is considered in the same sense that composers have always evaluated the *tutti* orchestra, the full organ or the complete seven-plus octave range of the piano keyboard—a sonority resource to be utilized *only* when desired."

The ideal instrumentation for the band scorer would be one he would select on the basis of the musical character of each piece. If he scored in this way, it would be realistic and practical for him to add a note to the score stating that some substitutions might be made but if so, the original intent would not be fully realized.

From this survey of the American band's instrumentation and possible but unavoidable exceptions, it should be clear that certain compromises are necessary if the final results of scoring plans are to be both practical and serviceable. These scoring expedients may be arrived at in one of two ways:

1. Write the score as desired for the full standard instrumentation (see Table 1). Then cue and cross-cue all of the leading melodic and harmonic parts which are most likely to be missing.

2. Score for the basic small instrumentation used for the marching band (see Table 3). Afterward, the addition of doublings (parts in unison or octaves), fillers (added harmony notes), and/or embellishing figurations can be made as they seem appropriate.

The first scoring style has the artistic approach and is the style generally used for concert music. The second scoring style will produce good results for music, utilitarian in character, designed for outdoor performance.

TABLE 3

BASIC BAND INSTRUMENTATION[1]

Wood Winds

Piccolo
Flute (playing the C piccolo
  part)
B♭ clarinets I-II
E♭ alto saxophones I-II
B♭ tenor saxophone

Brass

B♭ cornets I-II
B♭ trumpets (playing the cornet
  parts)
E♭ and F horns I-II
Trombones
Baritone
Tuba

Percussion

Timpani and percussion may be played by a maximum of three players. In the marching band, the fourth player can take over the bells or lyre. One player can be dispensed with if the cymbals are attached to the bass drum for one player.

Many publishers market their band publications of concert music in sets for Full or Standard Band (medium size) and Symphonic Band (maximum size). Others designate even more by using the classifications Class A, B, and C (small, medium, and large). We have previously noted that band music is graded A, B, C, and D, according to technical difficulty. These two systems of classification can be of practical value as guides to the writer of band music.

[1] Some European as well as American bands add single E♭ clarinet, oboe, and bassoon parts to this list and employ this instrumentation for both marching and concert programs.

∞∞∞∞

CHAPTER FOUR

INSTRUMENTS OF THE BAND

Divisions by Timbre and Range

The instruments of the band are grouped in three categories: wood winds, frequently referred to as the reeds; brass; and percussion. Each category has intersectional divisions based upon timbre identification (tonal color resulting from vibrating characteristics) and range compasses. *Timbre divisions* unite instruments in common family units. *Range compasses* permit part distribution comparable to the divisions of the human voice—soprano, alto, tenor, and bass.

Timbre identification and classification are first steps in establishing tonal definition. The three categories are grouped as follows:

TABLE 4

DIVISION BY TIMBRE

1. *Wood Winds* (high to low)

Non-reeds: Piccolo, flute, alto flute (bass flute) [1]
Single Reeds: Clarinets—Eb, Bb, Eb alto, Bb bass, Eb and Bb contrabass
                Saxophones—Bb soprano, Eb alto, Bb tenor, Eb baritone, Bb
                bass
Double Reeds: Oboe, English horn, bassoon, contrabassoon

2. *Brass*

Bb cornet, Bb trumpet, Bb fluegelhorn, [2] Bb tenor horn, [2] French horn in F,

---

[1] The alto flute in G—sometimes erroneously called a bass flute—and the true bass flute in C are not as yet included in the instrumentation of American band publications.

[2] Optional in the instrumentation of American bands.

15

Eb alto,[3] Eb melophone,[3] trombone, baritone,[4] euphonium,[4] Eb and BBb tubas

3. Percussion

Timpani and all other percussion instruments

The instrumentation most generally regarded as standard for the concert or symphonic band (see Table 4) appears in full score as follows:

To Dr. Edwin Franko Goldman

AMERICAN JUBILEE

A Concert Overture for Band

JOSEPH WAGNER

Playing time 5 1/2 minutes

[3] Substituting or alternate instruments for the French horn.

[4] These instruments are interchangeable and use the same parts.

16

The second step in separating the instruments according to range compass provides a serviceable plan for the average distribution of voice parts. Roman numbers in parentheses indicate alternate divisions dependent upon the ranges of the voice parts. The inclusion of the fluegelhorns is to be considered optional. Table 5 is a working guide for the scoring of four-part music as shown later in Chaps. 11, 17, and 25.

TABLE 5

DIVISION BY RANGE

Soprano

C and D♭ piccolos[1]
Flutes[1] I-II
Oboes I-II
E♭ clarinet[1]
B♭ clarinet I
E♭ alto saxophone I[2]
B♭ cornet I
B♭ trumpet I

Alto

Oboe (II)
B♭ clarinet II
E♭ alto saxophone II
B♭ cornet II (III)
B♭ trumpet II
B♭ fluegelhorn I-II
F or E♭ horns I-III
Trombone (I)

Tenor

English horn
B♭ clarinet III
E♭ alto clarinet
Bassoon I
B♭ tenor saxophone
B♭ cornet III
B♭ fluegelhorn (II)
F or E♭ horns II-IV
Trombones I-II

Bass

B♭ bass clarinet
Bassoon II
E♭ baritone saxophone
Trombone III
Baritone or euphonium
Tuba[3]
String bass[3]

Considerable prescoring knowledge can be gathered from Table 5 concerning some factors of tonal balance peculiar to the band.

The band's greatest tonal strength is in the two middle registers, alto and tenor. This inescapable fact is of particular importance in planning *tuttis* (passages for the full instrumentation), as the heavier brasses will predominate over the lighter reeds in these registers.

[1] These parts are generally in a higher octave.

[2] As soprano only.

[3] These parts are generally in a lower octave.

There are comparatively few instruments (piccolo, flute, and E♭ clarinet) for the highest octave above the treble clef. The oboe and B♭ clarinet are available and practicable up to a major sixth above the staff, while the cornets and the trumpets can manage a perfect fourth in this *tessitura* for a relatively short time. However, the parts considered within the vocal soprano range can have tonal strength and depth equal to the alto and tenor registers.

The bass register presents some difficulties, especially when parts leave the range of the bass reeds, since these parts must be played by BB♭ tubas and/or the string bass. The disparity of unequal timbres in this register requires deft handling in concert music for the band.

The instruments marked with footnote numbers 1 and 2 in Table 4 do not appear in Table 5, as they are no longer regarded as part of the standard instrumentation of American concert bands. They will, therefore, be omitted from future consideration in the scoring plans of this text.

The wind instruments of the band are pitched either in C, which is often referred to as concert (sounding as written) pitch, or in the flat keys of D♭, B♭, F, and E♭. Instruments with these keyed pitches have the greatest number of open tones in flat keys which, in turn, makes fingerings easier. Some of the technicalities peculiar to the transposition of wind instruments are examined in the following chapter.

A committee was organized in Europe in 1948 to study the international instrumentation of the band. In its findings the committee recommended that all full-score parts be written as actual sounds in C (non-transposed), but with the player's parts transposed when necessary as a temporary practice. The committee also recommended that eventually all parts—in full score and in those for the players—be printed only as "real sounds" in C. These changes in notation have not been accepted or adapted as of the mid-twentieth century.

◇◇◇◇

CHAPTER FIVE

THE HARMONIC SERIES

Its Effect on Ranges and Notation - Transposition Charts for the
Wind Instruments - Consideration of Key Tonalities for
Band Music

The harmonic series serves as the acoustical basis for the construction of the wind instruments employed in the band. (Later, in Chap. 25, it will be shown how this "Chord of Nature" also serves as a practical guide for harmonic spacings and their placement.) The fundamental (lowest note in each series, referred to as a pedal tone) identifies the keyed pitch of each instrument and acts as a generating tone from which a series of overtones is set in motion. The harmonic series for one-line C is as follows:

Fig. 1

A complete chromatic cycle may be achieved by the brass instruments by altering the fundamentals by means of valves, pistons, or a slide. The same result may be achieved by the wood winds through the manipulation of a series of open and closed or keyed holes. Massed sound in the band is, therefore, a mixture of four or five fundamental pitches and their series of overtones.

Many wind instruments of the band require transposed parts, since their written and sounding notations are not the same. The use of transposed parts is a practical device, as it enables wind players to interchange instruments when they have similarities of fingerings and means of tone production. Transposed parts thus become signs for fingerings rather than signs for pitch. The realization of these parts is carried out in the full score by the band scorer, since transposition is not done by the player.

19

We have seen that the band's wind instruments include five keyed pitches: C, Db, Bb, F, Eb. Of these five, instruments in C are ordinarily non-transposing, while the only one in Db uses an irregular form of transposition. The interval of transposition for the remaining three (Bb, F, Eb) is found by placing these key pitches *below* middle C and then counting *upward* to middle C. The resulting interval will be the one used for the *written* notation of these transposing instruments. The following chart illustrates this rule. The student is advised to think and refer to transposed parts as being written higher than they sound rather than vice versa.

TRANSPOSITION CHART FOR WIND INSTRUMENTS

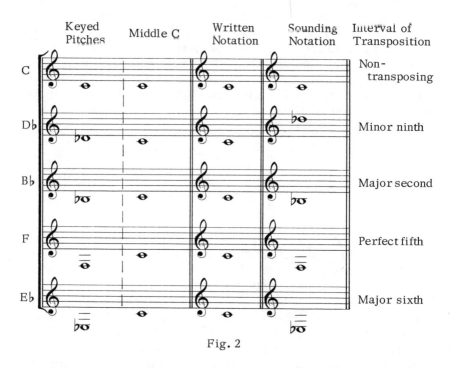

Fig. 2

The band scorer will need to know and employ these transpositions for wind instruments without range designation (tenor, baritone, or bass) when they are written in the treble clef. *Note*: Only two of the wind instruments of the band require transposition when written in the bass clef.[1]

[1] The two instruments considered as exceptional in this respect (contrabassoon and string bass) are generally regarded as optional in the band; their transposition is shown in Fig. 3.

C instruments—sound as written with a few exceptions (see Fig. 3)

Db instrument—written a minor ninth *lower* than they sound

Bb instruments—written a major second *higher* than they sound, with a few exceptions (see Fig. 4)

F instruments—written a perfect fifth *higher* than they sound

Eb instruments—written a major sixth *higher* than they sound, with a few exceptions (see Fig. 3 and 4)

A few instruments in the highest or lowest ranges, respectively, invert their usual interval of transposition as a means of eliminating excessive ledger lines. These few instruments pitched in C, Db, and Eb are shown in Fig. 3.

TRANSPOSITION CHART FOR WIND INSTRUMENTS
REQUIRING IRREGULAR TRANSPOSITION

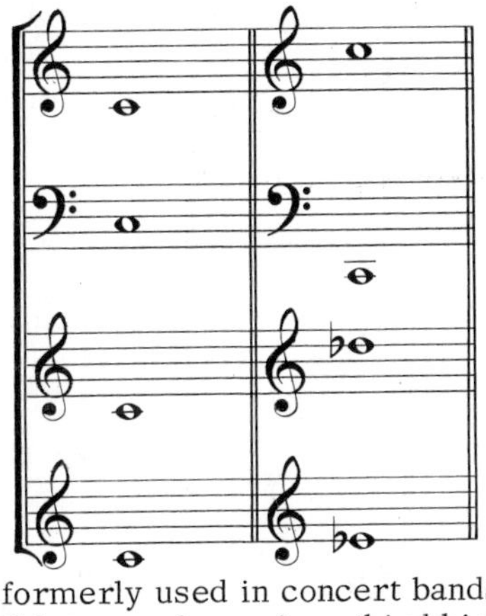

Keyed Pitches	Written Notation	Sounding Notation	Interval of Transposition
Picc. (C)			Written an octave lower than it sounds
Contrabsn. Contrabass (C)			Written an octave higher than it sounds
Picc. (Db)			Written a minor ninth lower than it sounds
Eb Cl. Eb Fl.*			Written a minor third lower than it sounds

* An Eb flute, formerly used in concert bands, has the same written range as the flute in C but sounds a minor third higher.

Fig. 3

An additional factor affecting transposition is the tonal range of certain wood winds and brasses with fundamentals in Bb and Eb. When instruments with these keyed pitches also carry the voice designations of male voices (tenor, baritone, or bass), an octave is added to their regular interval of transposition[1] for parts written in the *treble* clef. Thus a Bb bass clarinet is written a major ninth higher than it sounds.

[1] Male voices reading from the treble clef sound one octave lower than the written notation.

21

Similarly, instruments whose names include the prefix "contra," meaning low or under, along with a fundamental, ordinarily add a second octave to the regular interval of transposition. The B♭ contrabass clarinet is an example. In this case the part is written two octaves plus a major second higher than the sounding notation. (Notice that the instruments in Fig. 3 whose names include the prefix "contra," the bassoon and bass, are written an octave higher.) The E♭ contrabass sarrusophone is the exception to this rule; the irregular transposition happens here because the range of this sarrusophone is the same as that for the E♭ baritone saxophone. The following chart gives the information for transposing instruments in this category.

TRANSPOSITION CHART FOR WIND INSTRUMENTS WITH
RANGE DESIGNATIONS WRITTEN IN THE TREBLE CLEF

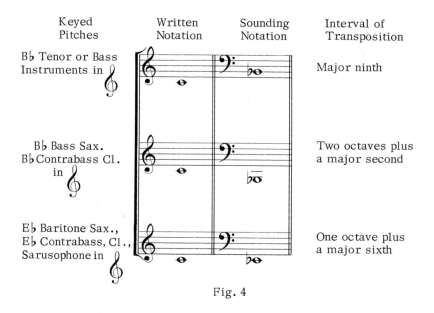

Fig. 4

The preponderance of instruments pitched in flat keys (mostly in B♭ and E♭) has two important results to be noted by the band scorer. We have already noted that these instruments provide maximum open tones and decrease technical difficulties. The matter of key tonalities is also related to the use of these instruments.

Music in keys with two or more sharps often cause awkward fingerings for transposing instruments. Although this possibility is recognized, some band directors are opposed to restricting band music to flat keys. They also believe many enharmonic changes (identical pitches with differing notations) tend to make scoring and score reading more difficult. Although both points of view deserve consideration, it would seem that the final answer lies in the selection of key tonalities which are best for the greatest number of players in the band who, after all, are the ones to perform the music.

This problem can be comprehended and studied by comparing the key signatures of all wind instruments when sounding keys go beyond G major in the sharp cycle.

TRANSPOSITIONS FOR SHARP KEYS

Fig. 5

Although the substitution of enharmonics can sometimes minimize reading difficulties encountered in keys having many sharps, little or nothing can be done to remove the basic cause of the problem. For this reason, band music is written mostly in flat keys. Further comparison of Fig. 6 with Fig. 5 will illustrate the advisability of keeping key tonalities within reasonable limits.

Fig. 6

Composers working with the band medium would do well to condition their musical thinking and planning in terms of the flat keys or to be prepared to use enharmonic notation whenever necessary. Transcribers working with keyboard music as source material have two alternatives: the music can first be written in a suitable key for the band, or the interval difference between the original key and the adapted key can be added to all instruments alike, transposing and non-transposing. The first plan is perhaps preferable, since there is less chance for error.

∽∽∽∽

CHAPTER SIX

THE WOOD-WIND INSTRUMENTS

Composition of the Wood-wind Section - Common Characteristics

Tone Production - Playing Styles - Notation for Scoring

Divided Parts

Every musical instrument has a distinguishing timbre (tone color). This results from the source or means of tone production, be it a vibrating reed, string, piece of metal, a membrane head, or the lips of a player. Each vibrating medium, plus the size and shape of the instrument, accounts for variations in sonority (full, resonant, musical sound) and timbre.

The wood-wind section of the modern concert band consists of non-reeds (piccolo and flutes), single reeds (clarinets and saxophones), and double reeds (oboes, English horn, and bassoons). Thereby three distinctly different family groupings are established, each having basic similarities in construction, manner of performance, and tone color. (Review Table 4, Division by Timbre.) These groupings account for the section's heterogeneous tonal character which, with intersectional divisions, constitutes the band's chief source of color contrast. Conversely, complete family groupings of the single and double reeds provide a homogeneity of timbre which all but equals the largest tonal spreads used in band scoring.[1] The instruments in the section are capable of being played with technical facility and good intonation; their timbres blend well together and with the brass instruments.

In the study of wind instruments, it is imperative that both the regularities and irregularities of ranges, timbres, tonal strengths and weaknesses, along with idiomatic playing styles and usages, be thoroughly analyzed and understood. These characteristics are the basis upon which the band scorer must plan instrumental selection and balance in order to secure the greatest possible effect

---

[1] This pertains particularly to the clarinets where only the very highest notes are, for practical reasons, assigned to the piccolo.

with the least possible means. The descriptive analysis for each instrument has been designed to provide the student with this information, filling in any voids due to the lack of actual playing experience.

As the instruments of the section have many technical characteristics in common, study can be facilitated by considering them collectively. This study also includes details of phrasing as it affects tonguing and notation for divided parts. This information may be correlated with the technical data given for each instrument, facilitating score reading of the illustrative excerpts which follow.

All tone production results from activating a column of air within a conical or cylindrical tube.[1] In the non-reeds, the activation is accomplished by the player's lips, which control the amount of air to be blown across the opening of the tube and also act as a reed substitution. All other wood winds use single or double reeds as the means of generating air-wave movement within the tube of the instrument.

The tonal intensity of each instrument varies with its registers.[2] As the player's control of high and low range extremes is variable, so is the quality of tone. Also, considerations of intonation and dynamics are involved here. The highest and lowest octaves for some instruments are ordinarily the more difficult to control at extremes of dynamic levels. This, of course, depends upon the player's technical skill. For these reasons, it is generally desirable to avoid range extremes, except for works consistently designed for Grade A bands or for the low extremes of those few instruments, notably the Bb clarinet and English horn, which are not so affected.

All wood-wind instruments are comparatively free from technical inadequacies. This fact in itself cannot eliminate awkward passages or compensate for unidiomatic scoring. The question here is not only can it be played, but also how will it sound? A general limit to technical difficulty should be consistently maintained in band scoring. It is unfortunate to have a few virtuoso passages inserted in a piece which might otherwise be fairly easy or only moderately difficult.

---

[1] The piccolo, flute, and clarinets have a cylindrical tube; the others are conically shaped.

[2] The high notes on some wood winds are produced by "overblowing," that is, forcing in the breath beyond ordinary limits.

26

In the matter of playing styles (*legato, staccato,* and the various gradations thereof), all wood-wind and brass instruments react in more or less the same way. Non-*legato* or detached notes are played with separate tongue attacks for each note. The specific articulation to be used is determined by the notation —*staccato, marcato,* and so forth. Some of these playing styles are shown in Fig. 7. All of them require a fresh tonguing attack for each note.

Fig. 7

Legato phrasing (smooth, connected successions of notes with *different* pitches) needs only the initial tongue attack at the beginning of each phrase, the slurs being arranged to produce the desired phrase inflections. In Fig. 8a, only one tongue attack would be used, while there would be three in Fig. 8b, and four are necessary in Fig. 8c.

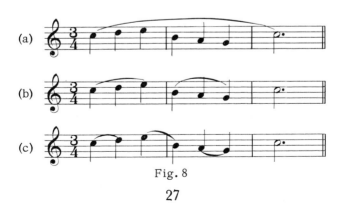

Fig. 8

27

There is one exception in connection with *legato* phrasing. Repeated notes of *identical* pitch automatically necessitate fresh tongue attacks. Many examples can be found which contain one or more repeated notes of the same pitch in one slur. In such a case, the tongue attack for the note repetition should be minimized, and the full phrase played as *legato* as possible. Fig. 9 shows a style of phrasing sometimes used to indicate how the slurring is to be done within a single phrase. This matter of repeated notes is especially important when fast, swirling scales or figurations are intended to be played *legato*.

Fig. 9

The student of band scoring should make a clear distinction between phrasing and slurring, since both use identical markings. The long, *legato* slurs used for phrasing in piano music—sometimes extending over several measures—are not idiomatic as phrasing for wind instruments. Slurring—short slurs, advantageously placed to approximate the effect of the longer ones—are preferable in most instances.

Legato and non-*legato* styles are often combined with good results for scales and figurations in lively rhythmic patterns. These two styles can also be interchanged effectively for melodic lines in all tempos, as variety in tonguing patterns helps to achieve contrast and emphasis.

Fig. 10

Slurs are also combined with dots or dashes for melodies or accompaniments, mostly in moderate-to-slow tempos. (Either combination is somewhat less practical and effective at fast tempos.) Both phrasing styles call for lighter tonguing than that ordinarily employed when single tonguing is used.

28

The slur-dot phrasing (Fig. 11) is especially appropriate for light accompaniments of intervals or chords, whereas the slur-dash combination (Fig. 12) is useful with melodic or harmonic parts when a slight pressure and spacing between the notes may be effective. The dash without the slur indicates that the affected note or notes should be played with a slight emphasis and pressure, but without accent.

Fig. 11

Fig. 12

It has been pointed out that unslurred notes are to have single tongue attacks. Double and triple tonguing styles (repetition of TK for double: TKT for triple) are employed for some wind instruments (piccolo, flute, and the brass instruments) for extremely rapid non-*legato* note clusters of two (double) or three (triple) or multiples thereof. Both tonguing styles are impractical for single and double reeds.

Although many skilled reed players develop remarkable tonguing facility, often approximating the *effect* of double or triple tonguing, it is advisable to write only those passages for reeds which can be played with single tonguing. Shostakovitch has written several measures in 2/4 for all of the winds as follows: ♩♩♩♩ ♩♩♩♩ with ♩ =176 as the unit of beat. This example comes from his Symphony No. 1, page 68 of the miniature score.

This notation calls for an extremely rapid form of single tonguing, yet it gives the effect of flutter tonguing (see page 255). This example gives an idea of a maximum speed for single tonguing, although the passage is obviously intended for highly skilled performers. Some of the score excerpts which follow illustrate these different tonguing styles in a variety of settings.

In summation, it can be said that *legato* passages are practical at all speeds when no repeated pitches occur. Also, non-*legato* passages in extremely rapid tempos are not idiomatically suited to the wood winds, other than the piccolo and flute, unless they can be played by single tonguing.

The writer of wind parts must invariably take into consideration the need for providing ample and suitable breath breaks for the player. The objective is to accomplish this without sacrificing musical characteristics or values. It will be noted in many of the following examples that band scorers have directed attention toward practical ways to relieve any strain on the player which might result from overextended wind parts. A few of these examples also display the sign (ʼ), used to indicate breath breaks for phrase endings. Wind players habitually tend to change breath after long, sustained notes, and after tied notes when they occur in extended passage work or in long melodic phrases.

All wind parts (wood winds and brasses), written on one staff and alternating between unisons and divided parts, must be clearly marked so that the copyist, director, and player will know exactly how they are to be played. Divided parts, so written, may use single stems, if the rhythmical patterns of both parts remain the same. Otherwise,. these parts must be written with upper and lower stems when necessary.

Fig. 13

Parts which cross occasionally may continue to be written on one staff with the stem direction remaining unchanged from that in Fig. 13. However, parts which cross frequently and/or have widely divergent *tessituras* and rhythms should be written on separate staves.

The student of band scoring should pay particular attention to the various means of indicating how divided wind parts can be notated. If only one part—either high or low—is to play when two parts are sharing the same staff, the notation may take any of the forms shown in the following illustration.

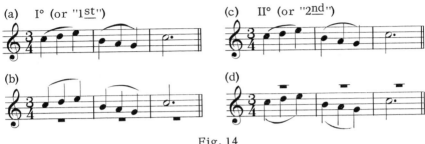

Fig. 14

If divided parts are to play in unison, they can be marked "a2," literally meaning "to two," in practice meaning "both" or "all." There also may be times when divided parts merge to play in unison for a relatively few notes. When this occurs, as in Figs. 15b and 15c, up-and-down stems are written for single notes. *Note*: In this connection, the terms *"unisono"* and *"divisi"* appear rather frequently with divided wind parts for the band.

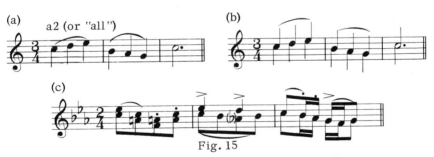

Fig. 15

Two important points of notation are to be observed in Fig. 15c. First, all cancellations or additions of accidentals in one part which carry over to another part *in the same measure* must be repeated, as shown in the first measure (A natural). Second, assumed, restored accidentals following measures with cancellations are assured, if the proper chromatic sign or signs are inserted in parentheses as in the second measure (A flat).

31

Finding phrase markings which are not only suitable but exactly right for all wind instruments is difficult for every scorer. It cannot be left to chance or haphazard application if one's full intentions are to be realized. Those who are unfamiliar with phrasing and slurring the wind instruments should sing aloud those phrases which seem problematic, noting the exact way the articulation is made and then adding the phrase markings which will ensure this articulation. It is well known that symphonic composers of stature regard this phase of their craft as one of the most difficult to perfect.

THE NON-REEDS

C Flute - Alto Flute in G - C and D♭ Piccolos

RANGES AND TRANSPOSITIONS

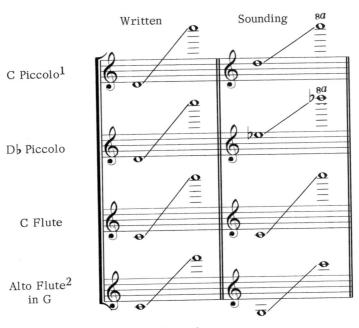

Fig. 16

THE FLUTE

The flute, originally made of wood but now available in a variety of metals, is one of the most dependable of wind instruments.

[1] The intonation of the highest note on both piccolos is insecure and playable only at *fff*.

[2] Band publications do not include parts for the alto flute.

Its excellent technical agility and general effectiveness make it well suited to a great variety of playing styles. Its tone, except in its highest octave, has less depth and carrying power than that of the reeds. For this reason, it is highly desirable to evaluate properly this instrument's three range divisions and its place both as a solo voice and as a member of the ensemble.

Range Divisions[1]

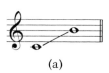

(a)

The rich, poetic tone quality of this lowest register has little chance of being heard in the band unless it is well exposed. Any kind of accompaniment here must be extremely light, spaced without conflict and with compensating dynamic adjustments; otherwise the tone is lost. *Fortissimo* passages for the flute in this register are wasted in *tuttis* for the full band. Unaccompanied solos here can be expressive without forcing.

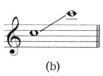

(b)

This middle octave is the neutral part of its compass. The tone quality is good but without the distinctiveness associated with the low or high registers. This range is particularly useful for secondary figurations (melodic or harmonic), for filling out chords (preferably with clarinets and/or oboes), and for solo passages of all kinds combined with other wood winds and/or doubled in octaves with them.

(c)

Once the flute ascends above the treble clef, its tone carries very well. Its brilliance has sufficient tonal strength and vibrancy to be heard in all but the loudest *tuttis*. Excluding the last three semitones, this register can be controlled and played expressively. However, these top three notes are shrill, piercing, and not safe any softer than *mezzoforte*.

The flute is well suited to all types of scale passages, *arpeggios,* broken chords, and ornamental arabesques. Melodies with large skips in an upward direction (diatonic or chromatic) are easier to play than those with a downward movement. Long, sustained notes, though possible, are less prominent than when played by the reeds. Flutes in the band form a connecting tonal link between the Bb clarinets and the piccolo. They are frequently divided

[1] Range divisions for transposing and non-transposing instruments alike are given in their written notation.

in two parts both melodically and harmonically. The following excerpts illustrate characteristic passages in varying styles and ranges.

EX. 1. *II. AIR from Water Music Suite* *

Handel
Arr. by Hershy Kay

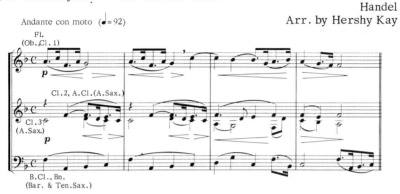

This flute melody in the low octave range, with light accompaniment, is rather exceptional. However, if played by several flutes, the tone would be firm and of nice quality.

EX. 2. *ANIMAL MAGIC*

Henry Cowell

* The numbers with titles indicate movement numbers as used by the publisher.

35

The Cowell excerpt places the flute in its high register with a rather florid style *(forte)*. Notice the spacing of the very soft sustaining chords and the three-part tremolos of the clarinets.

EX. 3. *TRIUMPHAL MARCH from Peter and the Wolf*

Serge Prokofiev, Op. 67
Arr. by Richard F. Goldman

Octave skips and broken chords here have a subdued accompaniment with outlining. Notice the piccolo sounding the top notes of the flute part.

The next excerpt illustrates a well-positioned flute *obbligato* which adds ornamental interest without obscuring the principal melodic line. (See Ex. 196a for another version in this category.)

EX. 4. *SUNDAY MORNING AT GLION*

from By the Lake of Geneva

Franz Bendel
Trans. by F. Campbell-Watson

EX. 4. (continued)

The next three examples show divided flutes as the solo instruments. The interval sequences, mostly in thirds, sound particularly good in this timbre. This interval pattern is also to be found quite frequently for the other soprano reeds.

EX. 5. *FUGAL FANTASIA*

James R. Gillette

This short unaccompanied cadenza for two flutes adds contrast to the more usual and thicker textures common in much band music. These parts have been cued so that they may be played by solo clarinets.

The following excerpt by Kechley has flute thirds in a more florid chromatic style over an A pedal point. The repeated bass notes are scored for baritone, cello, and bass—*pizzicato* for harp and timpani.

37

EX. 6. *II. LARGO ESPRESSIVO from Suite for Concert Band*

Copyright 1950 by Associated Music Publishers, Inc., New York.

The *staccato* thirds in the next example are placed well above the sustaining clarinets. This example demonstrates most felicitously that the absence of heavy bass parts now and then brings a welcome contrast by exposing thin textures.

EX. 7. *OVERTURE, First Movement from Symphony in B Flat*

Paul Fauchet
Revised by James R. Gillette

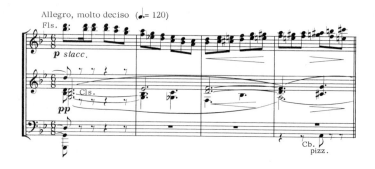

Copyright MCMXXVI by Evette and Schaeffer, Paris.
Copyright MCMXXXIV by M. Witmark and Sons, N.Y.

In the final example, the second flute maintains a steady rhythmic pattern without tonal weight. The first flute, in octaves with cornet, also adds brightness in a light timbre. Observe the spacing of the sustained chords in the bass clef.

EX. 8. *PAVANE*

Maurice Ravel
Arr. by Lawrence Fogelberg

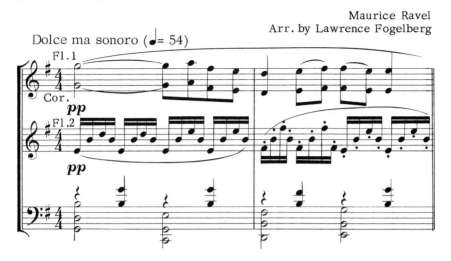

THE C AND D♭ PICCOLOS

The piccolo is actually a small flute, being half its size. Because it is the highest-pitched instrument in the band, it is important to examine its position in respect to tonal quality and adaptability. Although its written range is almost the same as that of the flute, the similarity does not apply equally well to the practicality of its full compass.

Range Divisions

The lowest octave is weak, not at all serviceable for important material louder than *mezzoforte*. Although this range has a unique dry quality, its use is restricted, as is the lowest octave of the flute. Its chief value here is in completing

(a)

figurations, and harmonic progressions. This octave is ordinarily more effective when played by the flute or the E♭ clarinet.

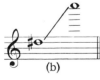

This register constitutes the piccolo's best playing range. Tones here can be heard in all *tuttis* and at all dynamic levels. Yet the tone, especially in the last few notes, is thin but piercing, lacking in depth or weight. The highest third

(b)

39

is difficult to control (and for this reason rarely played in tune) and all but impossible to control in the soft dynamics. These notes should, therefore, be studiously avoided except for the strongest dynamics.

Technically, the piccolo can be used effectively for all passages playable by the flute. Tonally, solo melodies which are slow and sustained are not very satisfactory unless doubled an octave lower by other wood-wind instruments. Bright, gay figurations, arabesques, and scale flourishes are among this instrument's best playing styles. The piccolo should not be used with the same frequency as the flute in concert music, as its high pitch and shrill tone soon pall. It is valuable, however, when combined with flutes and Eb clarinets for very high chords, either sustained or repeated.

Published scores are about evenly divided in the matter of including either the C or Db piccolo.[1] Regardless of which one is selected for inclusion in full scores, the parts should always contain music for both instruments. Their tone and playing characteristics are essentially the same.

Solo passages for the piccolo are very infrequent in concert music for the band. The piccolo is essentially a supporting instrument in that it increases range brilliance either melodically or harmonically. The following examples illustrate both of these facts.

EX. 9. *III. DANCE from Divertimento for Band*

Vincent Persichetti, Op. 42

[1] The present widespread use of the C piccolo would seem to indicate that the Db piccolo will be completely discarded in the near future.

This is one of the very few solo passages for piccolo. For it, the composer has indicated that the full flute unit is also to change over to piccolos. In this example, as well as in the following excerpts, the notation is the written and not the sounding one. Notice the broken chords in the clarinets, the muted horns on the middle chords, and the unison bass parts for baritone saxophone and a solo tuba.

EX. 10. *MILITARY MARCH No. 3 (trio)*

Schubert
Arr. by Felix Greissle

The Schubert excerpt, in full score, for divided piccolos is also a decided novelty in a humorous vein. Observe the alternating bassoons for the broken chords coupled with the repeated notes in the horns completing the chords. The glockenspiel (bells) outlines the tune. Both piccolos here are in the low range.

In the next example, the piccolo assumes its more common role of doubling the flute in the octave. The range span here is the most effective part of the instrument. Note the canonic imitation in the oboe and the light bass parts.

41

EX. 11. *ALLA MARCIA from Karelia Suite*

Jean Sibelius, Op. 11
Arr. by Richard F. Goldman

The following excerpt pairs the piccolo and flute again, but this time in their highest range. A passage of this kind could only be possible in the loudest dynamic, as given, and with first-class players.

EX. 12. *I. ALLEGRO SCHERZANDO from Suite for Concert Band*

Gerald R. Kechley

Piccolo parts are generally associated with music which is very loud and often noisy. The final two examples have been included here to show that this need not necessarily be a foregone conclusion. In the Thomson excerpt, the piccolo has a part in a soft melodic line, while the Haydn Wood music shows the piccolo in octaves with the Eb clarinet at a *mezzopiano* dynamic level. The piccolo is equally good in soft, chordal figurations and *arpeggios*, especially with the flutes and clarinets.

EX. 13. *A SOLEMN MUSIC*

Virgil Thomson

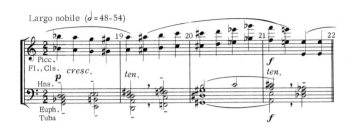

EX. 14. *THE SEAFARER: A Nautical Rhapsody*

Haydn Wood

〈〈〈〈〈

CHAPTER EIGHT

THE SINGLE REEDS

Clarinets - Saxophones

CLARINETS

Eb - Bb - Eb Alto - Bb Bass - Eb and Bb Contrabass

RANGES AND TRANSPOSITIONS

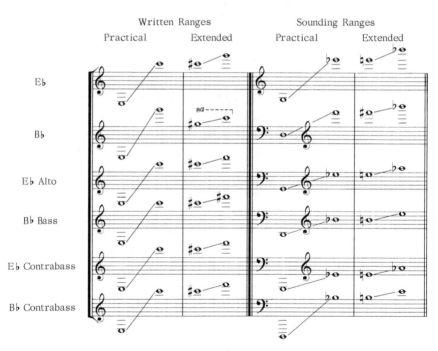

Fig. 17

THE E♭ CLARINET

The E♭ clarinet is of second importance in this family grouping. It greatest service is in reinforcing the weaker flute in the low and middle octaves. In the past, objections to its use have been made because of its shrill tone and insecure intonation. However, these criticisms do not always result from technical inadequacies of the instrument, but often from the scarcity of good players.

Range Divisions

The compass of the E♭ clarinet can, for all practical purposes, be divided into two parts.

(a)

The tone of this register is somewhat less vibrant than that of the B♭ instrument. Technical facility is the same.

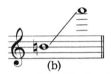

(b)

This register produces the highest tones of the clarinet family and may be regarded as excellent for the reinforcement of the piccolo, flute, oboe, and clarinet parts written in this high *tessitura*.

The E♭ clarinet has the same poor notes in the "break" register as notated (written—not sounding) for the B♭ instrument. The highest minor third can be unbearably shrill and out of tune when played by any but skilled players.

All playing characteristics and technicalities given for the B♭ clarinet apply equally well to the E♭ instrument, although the scope of its usefulness will naturally be more limited. The E♭ clarinet, like the piccolo, should not be overwritten in concert music for the band, as its effectiveness is definitely restricted.

Solos of any length or consequence for the E♭ clarinet appear to be practically nonexistent, except for some European, and principally Italian, publications. Nevertheless, its unique timbre can be exploited occasionally as a contrast by assigning the instrument to melodic passages in the high register. The following Copland excerpt, having the oboe answered by the E♭ clarinet, contains a nice but rare combination.

EX. 15. *AN OUTDOOR OVERTURE*

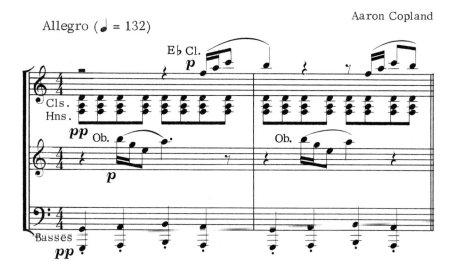

Allegro (♩ = 132)

Aaron Copland

The repeated thirds, as scored by Holst for divided E♭ clarinets,[1] are decidedly exceptional and problematical for the instrumentation of the great majority of bands and are cued, in this instance, for the flutes.

EX. 16. *II. INTERMEZZO from First Suite in E Flat*

Gustav Holst

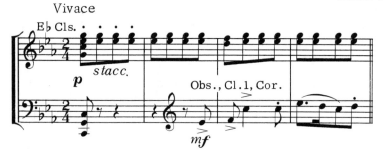

Vivace

[1] Divided parts for E♭ clarinets are found in European band publications, but rarely in those issued in America.

In Ex. 17, the melody is actually in three octaves: the piccolo an octave above the given part, the flute and E♭ clarinet as is, and the oboe an octave lower. The harmony for three-part B♭ clarinets and horn quartet furnishes a tranquil background.

EX. 17. *II. MY BONNY BOY, Intermezzo from Folk Song Suite*

R. Vaughan Williams

The solo lyric passage for the E♭ clarinet without doubling in Ex. 18 is indeed exceptional. It is well spaced to avoid conflict with the heavier harmony instruments. The solo cadenza in Ex. 19 may also be considered as unique among parts for this instrument.

EX. 18. *SHOONTHREE*

Henry Cowell

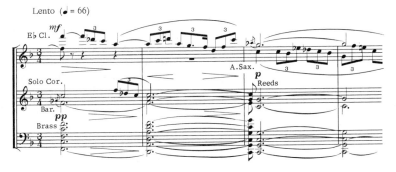

47

Lucien Cailliet

THE B♭ CLARINET

The B♭ clarinet[1] is the real prima donna of the wood winds. It has become the most useful and versatile instrument in the section, being adaptable to almost every kind of musical expression. The importance of this instrument in the band far exceeds its importance in the orchestra, since it takes the principal and leading part in the wood-wind section.

Although the entire range of the B♭ clarinet is used, there are marked variations in tonal strength and vibrancy. The complete compass divides into three distinct registers.

Range Divisions

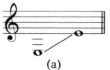

(a)

This lowest octave is known today as the *chalumeau* register since it represents the greater part of the compass for the clarinet's prototype, the *chalumeau*. The tone color in this register is unusually rich and round, although the instrument does not have the same carrying power here that it has in the middle or high registers and sounds unmusical if forced. The dynamic range, though applicable at all levels, *pianissimo* to *fortissimo*, needs to be balanced with textural factors if it is to be effective. Unison doubling, either with bassoons and/or saxophones, does help to reinforce these low tones when important thematic material must come through rather strong backgrounds.

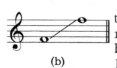

(b)

This middle octave is somewhat less distinctive tonally than other parts of the instrument's range and is also slightly troublesome technically because of the "break" register occurring here. It is, nonetheless, adaptable to playing styles identified with the clarinet. The tone is stronger, except for the "break," than in the lower octave and is good for all dynamic levels.

[1] The clarinet in A (written a minor third higher than it sounds) is not used in band scoring but will be encountered in making band transcriptions of orchestral music.

48

(c)

Most instrumental treatises call attention to the intonation and technical difficulties of the notes in this interval, which are known variously as the "throat," "bridge," or "break" register.

Actually, these difficulties are no longer feared as they were in the past, since the modern clarinet can be manipulated to minimize this "break" in the instrument's compass. While it remains true that the intonation of the notes in the interval, especially G–Bb–B♮, is not even or of good quality, the full octave is used regularly. Technical considerations are important here only when A and B♮ and Bb and B♮ are used rather continuously, for the reason that these note combinations cause awkward fingerings.

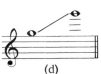
(d)

The penetrating, brilliant tone of this highest range is the band's chief source of tonal strength above the cornets and trumpets. The clarinet's tone has more depth here than that of the other wood winds. However, caution is advised in writing sounding notes above E as they are difficult to control, except for the experienced player; the tone becomes shrill, with unpredictable intonation, especially at the soft dynamic levels.

The Bb clarinet's great versatility makes it indispensable for all parts not idiomatic for the heavier tonal weights in the ranges of the cornet, trumpet, or horn. The division of the clarinets is rather flexible, although it is generally made in three parts in most band publications. In this form, the first part is primarily for the leading melodic instrument of the section. However, the first part is frequently divided for solo and first parts and occasionally simply divided in two parts when four parts for the unit are desirable.

The Bb clarinets have technical and tonal flexibility throughout the full compass, except in the "break" register. When combined with the other clarinets, Eb, Eb alto, and Bb bass, their homogeneous tonal qualities and range spread offer unique possibilities unmatched by any other section in the band's standard instrumentation. They are the band's best section for variety in playing styles—sustained notes, intervals or chords, broken or arpeggiated chords, scale flourishes, trills and tremolos, and detached or expressive melody passages.

EX. 20. *II. GLORIA VICTORIBUS from Two Marches*

Darius Milhaud

The *legato* scales here span the clarinet's lowest range. They are ingeniously placed, as their tone is apart from that of the melody and bass parts.

EX. 21. *AN OUTDOOR OVERTURE*

Aaron Copland

These detached octaves for clarinets cover the middle register. Note the contrast achieved by having the answering chords in a lower *tessitura.*

50

EX. 22. *ZANONI*

Paul Creston, Op. 40

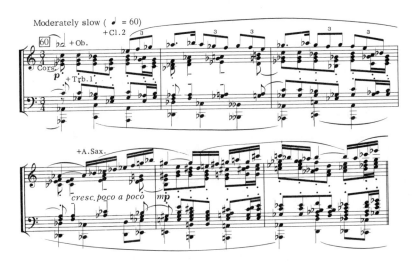

This is a good example of rather florid clarinet melody parts in the high register. In measure 64, the E♭ clarinet in unison and the E♭ alto saxophone are added to build up the gradual crescendo. The chords in the treble are for the oboe, cornets, and trumpets. Those in the bass are for the first horn and trombone. The *legato* bass part is scored for euphonium and tubas.

In Ex. 23, the *diminuendo* in the brass permits the arpeggiated solo clarinet to be heard clearly. Notice its entrance, supported by the baritone on the second beat of measure 1.

EX. 23. *EULOGY*

Joseph Wagner

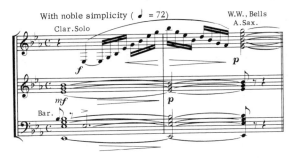

In Ex. 24a, the serene treble melody for the first clarinets is coupled with the repeated thirds in the second and third parts, supported by the alto saxophones. Example 24b gives the *staccato* triads to the clarinets in three parts.

EX. 24. *PAVANE*

Maurice Ravel
Arr. by Lawrence Fogelberg

The next Creston excerpt has an interesting juxtaposition of triads for clarinets above those for the cornets, as harmonic background for the melody in the euphonium. This arrangement gives the clarinets a feeling of timbre unity removed from the brass parts. It is a novel but nice scoring touch.

EX. 25. *ZANONI*

Paul Creston, Op. 40

Example 26 illustrates two rhythmic patterns derived from the chord structure for the second and third clarinets. The first clarinet is combined with the high wood winds and first cornet on the melody. The saxophones sustain the repeated brass chords.

The extent to which the arpeggiated chords may be heard will, of course, be dependent upon the proportionate numerical strength of the second and third clarinets. These *arpeggios* would be stronger if doubled by the alto saxophones. In this connection, it should be noted that there is no reason for excluding the alto and bass clarinets for arpeggiated chords. Actually, the two together can sound quite stunning, especially if the *arpeggios* are played quite rapidly.

EX. 26. *BEOWULF: A Symphonic Sketch for Band*

Bruce C. Beach

THE E♭ ALTO CLARINET

The E♭ alto clarinet is the least conspicuous and important member of the clarinet family. Its presence in the section is generally regarded as a concession to full family representation in each division of the wood winds. Its role as a secondary member of the group results from its somewhat unpredictable availability and partially from its range position. In this connection, it should be noted that the bass clarinet can play almost anything that might be given to the alto clarinet and, in most cases, can play it better.

53

Even the largest concert bands seldom have more than one alto clarinet as part of their instrumentation. This is no match for the tonally stronger clarinets in B♭. The range of the alto clarinet gives it a position in the clarinet family similar to that of the violas in the string section—between the violins and the cellos. But there the comparison ends, because of the superior tonal strengths and numbers of the other clarinets.

Range Divisions

The E♭ alto clarinet must, then, be assigned parts of secondary importance. The effectiveness of these parts can be best determined by consideration of its full compass.

(a)

This lower octave is particularly useful for reinforcing the bass clarinet, bassoon, and/or tenor saxophone parts. It is less satisfactory when the instrument is doubling brass parts only. The upper half of this range is good to support the second and third clarinets on parts of melodic or harmonic importance.

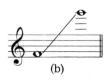
(b)

The upper register is used primarily for doubling wood-wind parts in the alto *tessitura*. These parts include all styles of chords or principal thematic material, whether for the full or partial section. Here too, doubling of brasses without other wood winds is of little value. The top octave of the high register is seldom used.

The E♭ alto clarinet has a sonorous tone which is slightly less vibrant than that of the B♭ instrument. No new technical problems are to be encountered in writing for it other than those previously mentioned. However, it would be unwise to assign important solo parts to the E♭ alto clarinet unless such parts are fully cued. The following excerpts show a few characteristic passages for this medium-low clarinet.

Solo passages, without doublings of some kind, are as uncommon for the E♭ alto clarinet as for the higher one in E♭. Example 27 is a rare instance of a brief use of the instrument for part writing which, in this case, places a single reed between the double-reed bassoon and oboe.

EX. 27. *E. F. G. OVERTURE*

Philip James

Allegro (♩ = 116)

The alto clarinet is useful in part writing when paired with the bass clarinet. The following example illustrates this point and demonstrates the potential of the alto clarinet for sustaining long notes.

EX. 28. *I. INTRODUCTION and ALLEGRO MODERATO*
from Concerto Grosso

Joseph Wagner

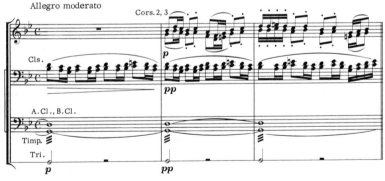

Similarities of range frequently suggest unison doublings. Example 29 shows this kind of association. Notice how the long, sustained F moves into an *obbligato* with the repetition of the phrase.

EX. 29. *II. ARMENIAN DANCES*

Aram Khachaturian
Arr. and edited by Ralph Satz

Another kind of doubling places the alto clarinet in its low register for bass parts with figuration. In Ex. 30, it doubles the bassoon in unison, as given, while the bass clarinet sounds an octave lower.

EX. 30. *FUGUE No. IV from The Well-tempered Clavier, Book 1*

J. S. Bach
Arr. by C. K. Wellington

THE Bb BASS CLARINET

The position of the Bb bass clarinet in the band is, in one respect, analogous to that of the Eb alto clarinet; it is outnumbered by the higher Bb instruments. This highly desirable bass voice of the clarinet family has become an increasingly popular addition to the school and dance bands of America, where its usage threatens the eventual displacement of the equally important bassoon.

Undoubled bass clarinet parts require considerable finesse in scoring, since the smooth, mellow tone of the instrument cannot survive heavier surrounding timbres. This can be done by selecting accompanying timbres and textures which complement the attractive, but rather subdued, tone qualities of this clarinet. There remain several interesting playing styles yet to be imaginatively exploited for this single-reed bass instrument in concert music for the band.

Range Divisions

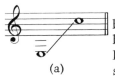

(a)

This is a fine register of the instrument for bass parts, either alone or with other reeds doubling. The tone quality is full and round, but with less spread than those of the tenor or baritone saxophones and not as pungent as that of the bassoon. Tone here would not be heavy enough to support brass instruments by itself but could be adequate to carry bass parts, without doubling, for light wood-wind combinations. Extremely rapid *legato* passages are technically possible and can convey unusual and grotesque ideas, since they sound smeared and unclear. Detached figurations have greater clarity, especially in moderately fast tempos, but lack the bite of the bassoon (see Ex. 32).

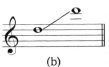

(b)

The tone in this high octave tends to thin out toward the top, with a resulting loss of richness and vibrancy. This range is, therefore, used less frequently than the lower tones. Actually, parts in the high *tessitura* are more effective when played by Bb clarinets, with or without the alto clarinet. The highest fourth of this range is of no practical value.

All idiomatic playing styles are possible on this bass instrument: short swirling scales, broken or arpeggiated chords, and figurations. Solo melody passages appear rather infrequently in music for the band. When used, they should be well exposed and, if accompanied, combined with light timbres. Important bass clarinet parts should always be cued to ensure that the part will be played. *Note*: The nineteenth-century practice of writing orchestral parts for it[1] in the bass clef[2] is not practiced in its notation for band music. Some representative passages for the bass clarinet are given here.

EX. 31. *III. HORNPIPE from Celtic Set*

Henry Cowell

The above passage is decidedly unique in music for the band. The drone of the sustained E sets the mood for the tune. Two-voice passages, in any style and register, are welcome interludes of contrast, since they give temporary relief from the more frequent band textures and sonorities.

EX. 32. *CELEBRATION OVERTURE*

Paul Creston, Op. 61

The bass clarinet is surprisingly effective when playing *arpeggios*, either *staccato* or *legato*, at all but the fastest tempos. Its tone, less reedy than that of the bassoon, has a richer sonority and a broader tonal weight.

[1] The bass clarinet in A is now extinct.

[2] Parts for the B♭ bass clarinet in the bass clef are written a major second higher than they sound.

EX. 33. *II. PASSACAGLIA from Concerto Grosso*

Joseph Wagner

In the excerpt above, the bass clarinet is used melodically with the Bb instruments. At the fifth measure, the three parts become the harmonic background for the oboe melody.

EX. 34. *I. ALLEGRO SCHERZANDO from Suite for Concert Band*

Allegro scherzando

Gerald R. Kechley

The bass clarinet is scored rather freely with other winds, mostly for chord progressions. In the version above, the alto and bass clarinets have the top notes. The lower three notes are for the second horn and divided bassoons. It should be noted here that this latter grouping is a very good one, as the horn-bassoon combination gives the impression of a single-timbre unit. Also, observe the trombones on the afterbeats—usual in much band scoring.

EX. 35. *I. OVERTURE from Symphony in B Flat*

Paul Fauchet
Revised by James R. Gillette

Pairing the bass clarinet and the timpani in octaves is an original touch of unusual interest. Also, notice the part writing for the cornets and horns which, in the full score, shows divided bassoons doubling the two inner voices, starting in the second measure.

THE E♭ OR B♭ CONTRABASS CLARINET

This deepest-toned member of the clarinet family has not as yet been recognized as a standard instrument in the wood-wind section. Although a few scores include specific parts for it, some directors of college bands are using it increasingly as a substituting instrument. From the ranges shown in Fig. 17, it will be observed that both models in B♭ and E♭ have the same *written* ranges as do the other clarinets and that their compasses *sound* one octave lower than the B♭ bass and E♭ alto clarinets, respectively.

The availability of these instruments as standard members of the wood-wind section would greatly extend the very lowest range for the reeds, making this section comparable to the brass in this respect. The following full scores list parts as being available for both models. However, most of the full scores show the part for the E♭ model.

Bach–Frackenpohl, Five Chorals (Shawnee Press)
Hallberg, *Erik the Red* (Shawnee Press)
Strauss–Harding, *A Hero's Courtship* (Kjos)

Tscheskoff–Houseknecht, *Salvation Is Created* and *Choral* from
    Act 3 from *Die Meistersinger* (Kjos)
Williams, *Arioso* (Summy-Birchard)
Williams, *Fanfare and Allegro* (Summy-Birchard)
Williams, *Pastoral* (Summy-Birchard)
Williams, Symphonic Suite (Summy-Birchard)
Work, *Portraits from the Bible* (Shawnee Press)

THE CLARINETS AS A UNIT

Concert music for the band contains occasional passages with
the full clarinet section, either as an independent unit or treated
as such with other combinations. This scoring style is to be found
in original band scores as well as in orchestral or piano transcriptions. When so used, the scoring style has a unified timbre
quality which approaches the smooth evenness of the full strings.

In the following examples, and in those that will be given later
for the complete wood-wind section, further application of the
salient points discussed for each instrument will be illustrated.
These examples should be regarded as an additional applied sum-
marization for the scoring of the clarinets.

EX. 36. *A TRIBUTE TO SOUSA*

Maurice C. Whitney

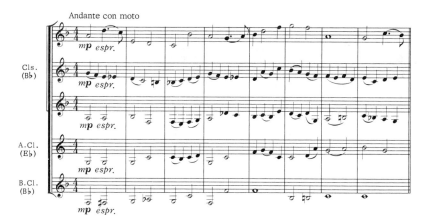

EX. 37. *PRAYER AND DREAM PANTOMIME*

from Hansel and Gretel

Engelbert Humperdinck
Trans. by Joseph C. Maddy

AN EVENING IN THE VILLAGE

Béla Bartók
Arr. by Erik Leidzen

SAXOPHONES

Bb Soprano - Eb Alto - Bb Tenor - Eb Baritone - Bb Bass

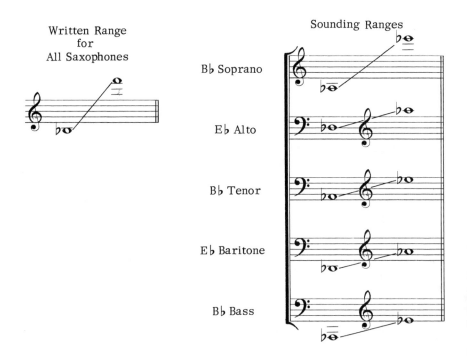

Fig. 18

The saxophones are composite instruments, as their tonal qualities resemble those of both the wood winds and the brasses. They function as a tonal link between the two sections, but with less strength than the horns, which are similarly used. Their tonal depth is greater than that of the other reeds, which enhances their sustaining potential. This fact is important in the scoring of the saxophones, as these tonal characteristics lose some of their edge if overscored in concert music.

Saxophones are not customarily treated as leading melodic or rhythmic instruments in band scoring, except for short passages where their timbre can be profitably employed as an element of contrast. Ordinarily, musical ideas in this category, designed for the wood winds, are given to the clarinets or double reeds. The saxophones are used often to reinforce these parts and can, in this respect, be considered as supporting instruments.

However, the saxophones are frequently treated and scored as "lead" instruments in band arrangements of "musicals," popular songs, and "novelty numbers," since the dance-band style of scoring can be effectively integrated with the standard scoring technique for this style of music.

Range Divisions

The tonal variations in the range divisions of all saxophones are quite uniform and can, therefore, be examined from the single written compass used for the whole unit.

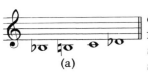

(a)

The lowest four notes (B♭, B, C, and D♭) on each instrument are somewhat difficult for the average player, especially in the softer dynamics. These notes tend to speak slowly but, when well played above *mezzo-forte*, have a full, sonorous tone of considerable strength.

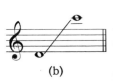

(b)

The middle register is easy to play and adaptable to all playing styles previously noted for the clarinets. Sustained melodic lines and chord tones, in combination with other reeds, are idiomatically effective and reliable. Strictly speaking, double and triple tonguing are not possible for the saxophones. However, a very rapid single-tonguing style serves as a good substitute and achieves about the same effect.

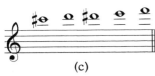

(c)

The high register of the saxophone is one which varies in quality with each player. These tones, comparatively difficult to produce and control, have some value in massing tonal climaxes but the top three semitones are hazardous for the average player in any dynamic softer than *mezzoforte*.

In this connection, it should be remembered that the high extremes of all wind instruments may be used in loud passages without undue difficulty for the player when these passages weave in and out of high melodic *tessituras*. Intonation dangers lie in writing parts which remain in this register too long to permit adequate control of the player's embouchure and fingerings. It is likewise true that quick, splashy, detached jabs of very high notes, though effective if used sparingly, are tonally insecure in direct relation to their range position. The higher the tone, the more difficult will be the intonation, unless these tones are prepared for or led into.

The saxophones blend equally well with reeds or brasses. Yet their tone absorbs that of any instrument they double. Tonal qualities, contrary to some observations, do not always remain unchanged throughout the full compass of each instrument. Actually, the highest tones can be shrill and unmusical. The large middle range does have an even scale and good sonority. The lowest tones have greater tonal spreading than corresponding ranges in the clarinets. These factors should be considered when saxophones are to be used as doubling instruments.

Saxophones are the least difficult of the reeds to play and all may be played with equal facility. Because of their listed assets and greater availability, they have become second in importance only to the clarinets in the wood-wind section of American bands. In bands of minimum size, they are practically indispensable, not only for the performance of their own parts, but for the playing of cues of the scarcer single and double reeds.

THE B♭ SOPRANO SAXOPHONE

The B♭ soprano saxophone seems to have become an unfortunate casualty in the standardization of the American band's instrumentation. This has been more or less coincidental to the disuse of the instrument in dance bands since the first decades of the twentieth century. Charges similar to those leveled at the E♭ clarinet—that its highest-register tones tend to sound shrill and unmusical—have also been directed at the soprano saxophone. The prevailing practice of substituting a second, smoother-toned alto model does not compensate for the loss of a fifth in the high ranges of these two instruments. This substitution also prevents the saxophone unit from approximating the tonal spread of the clarinets.

The almost total elimination of the B♭ soprano saxophone from band scoring in America is attested to by the fact that mid-twentieth-century publications contain few parts for it. The two following excerpts have been selected from the less than a dozen examples available in full-score publications. The Milhaud scoring, in its employment of the soprano saxophone, seems to be something of a revival, as the instrument seems to have been neglected since its earlier usage by Percy Grainger. Example 42 illustrates more conventional doublings for this highest-voiced saxophone.

66

Its uncertain availability would seem to indicate that all undoubled important parts of the soprano saxophone should be cued.

EX. 39. *II. RECITATIVE from West Point Suite*

Darius Milhaud

EX. 40. *III. HORNPIPE from Celtic Set*

Henry Cowell

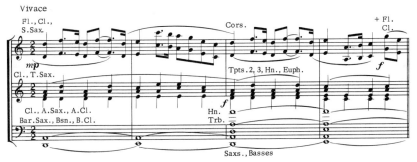

THE E♭ ALTO SAXOPHONE

Of the saxophones listed in Fig. 6, only two—the E♭ alto and the B♭ tenor—have become standardized in the instrumentation of American bands. Of these two, the E♭ alto seems to have emerged as the most versatile, being the only one to be divided regularly

67

into two parts. This practice has enlarged the scope and usefulness of the instrument, as parts in both the soprano and alto registers are now included and are used interchangeably.

One difficulty in planning solos for saxophones concerns the
problem of achieving balance without resorting to doublings. This
is, of course, the result of the instrument's individual tonal quality.
For example, the alto saxophone does not have the decisive attack
or tonal vibrancy that the clarinets and oboes have in the same
registers. Quite naturally, these tonal variants make it difficult
to plan imperceptible saxophone entrances. Conversely, when saxophones are dropped out of the ensemble, their unique tonal qualities are missed considerably, especially if a comparatively small
reed section is employed.

Divided alto saxophones are used almost entirely in close position (chord tones within the compass of an octave) with the tenor
model. The increasing use of the E♭ baritone saxophone shows
that its parts are quite similar in range and scope to those for
the bass clarinet and bassoons in the bass register.

Concert music for the band has surprisingly few strictly solo
passages—without doublings—for the saxophones, either alone or
collectively. The first three of the following excerpts illustrate a
few of the exceptional instances of solo saxophone parts; the remaining ones show the more common parts with doublings.

EX. 41. *ANDANTE*

Albert M. Ingalls

The quiet, melodic style of the solo alto saxophone and the
later duet contrast well with the lower harmonic progressions
for bassoons and horns. Notice the spacings of the chords in the
bass part, all in open position.

EX. 42. *SUMMER DAY*

Elie Siegmeister

A slightly more elaborate version in this style is used in the melodic setting for Ex. 42. Note the all-brass bass parts and the reeds for the last two measures.

EX. 43. *WALTZES from Der Rosenkavalier*

R. Strauss
Arr. by Lucien Cailliet

In this waltz movement, the alto saxophone extends the previous short phrases in a contrasting timbre. The *staccato* second-beat chords, starting in the third measure, are for divided clarinets. The third-beat bass part is for the bass instruments without trombones.

EX. 44.   *3. CAKEWALK from Carnival Suite*

Alexander Tansman

Molto vivace (♩ = 160)

A.Sax., solo

This is a good example of a more rapid style of figuration for solo alto saxophone. It is a style which can easily stand expansion, as all saxophones are available for a great variety of rhythmic patterns in very fast tempos.

The next examples illustrate two kinds of doubling, melodic and harmonic. That in Ex. 45 increases the sonority of the sextolets in single-reed timbres. In Ex. 46, the alto saxophones are divided in the tenor register, doubling the bassoons and alto clarinet.

EX. 45. *GARDENS OF GRANADA*

F. M. Torroba
Arr. by Walter Beeler

Allegro vivace

Cls., Saxs. in E♭

70

EX. 46. *WAKE ME UP FOR THE GREAT JUBILEE:*
　　　　　Variations on an Old American Song

George Frederick McKay

THE B♭ TENOR SAXOPHONE

The playing styles of the tenor saxophone are essentially the same as those given for the alto. The tenor's different range does, of course, alter the scope of its potential. When properly played, its rich, low tones add immeasurably to the sonority and carrying power of the other bass wood winds. It is in the same relative position in the section as the bass clarinet and bassoon are in their respective groupings.

Solo passages for the tenor saxophone—without doubling—are rare indeed. The following excerpts contain characteristic passages in different ranges.

EX. 47. *III. SCHERZO from Symphony in B Flat*

Paul Fauchet
Rescored by F. Campbell-Watson

The tenor saxophone solo here, mostly in the low register, is a distinct novelty and one rarely duplicated. However, if other accompaniments could be so adroitly managed, there seems to be no reason why there should not be further experiments along the same line.

EX. 48. *TRIUMPHAL MARCH from Peter and the Wolf*

Serge Prokofiev
Arr. by Richard F. Goldman

The doubling in this arrangement is most effective, as this higher octave of the tenor saxophone enriches the *chalumeau* register of the clarinets and gives the melody greater body. Note the absence of sustained harmonies in any middle parts, which clears the way for the tenor register.

Further excerpts with doublings are shown in the next two examples. In Ex. 49, the composer announces the main theme of the *Fantasia* , scored for the alto clarinet, and the alto and tenor saxophones in unison, without harmonization. This unusual procedure achieves a subdued voicing of the tune but without the incisiveness it would have if scored for either an all-clarinet or double-reed combination. This scoring places the tenor saxophone in its medium-to-high registers and the other two instruments in their medium-to-low registers.

EX. 49. *IV. FANTASIA ON THE DARGASON*
from the Second Suite in F

Gustave Holst, Op. 28, No. 2

Allegro moderato

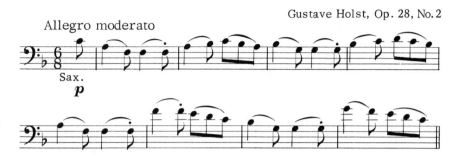

Sax.
p

Example 50, the final excerpt for the tenor saxophone, has it doubling the brass instruments on a melodic bass part. The lead-in notes at the beginning and end of the phrase are, because of range limitations, placed an octave higher than given at Tempo I. The remaining parts of the phrase have the tenor saxophone and euphonium playing in unison on the top of the octaves.

EX. 50. *II. MY BONNY BOY, Intermezzo from Folk Song Suite*

R. Vaughan Williams

Poco allegro (scherzando)
Tempo I

Cl.1., Cor.1

Cl.2., Cor.2
Cl.3, Tpt.

Trb.

pp

Basses
Euph.
T.Sax.

73

THE E♭ BARITONE SAXOPHONE

The E♭ baritone saxophone completes the four-part family grouping of the saxophones. Although many band scores now have parts for this instrument, its usage in the past has been somewhat irregular. This has been due, no doubt, to its absence from standardized listings of instrumentation and its unpredictable availability rather than to its value to the unit. It is usually represented in the large bands but sometimes absent from the smaller ones.

This saxophone is also of considerable value in supporting a second weak register (the bass) in the wood winds, which is otherwise covered by the bass clarinet and bassoon. Its ease of performance and full sonority make it highly desirable for both melodic and harmonic bass parts for full wood-wind groupings with the brass.

This point refers to the ever-present problem of balance resulting from superior numbers of B♭ clarinets and the preponderance of instruments for the alto and tenor registers. The scoring of mixed reed and brass timbres, with their unequal tonal strengths, has a direct effect upon the scoring of this saxophone. So too, does the relative importance of melodic bass lines in each piece. This can be observed in practice when this saxophone doubles the bass brass instruments.

The baritone saxophone has the advantage of a full tonal strength and depth not found among the other bass reeds. Its most useful low register precludes very much unit writing in close position with the alto and tenor saxophones, except when it is required to complete the quartet in straight four-part settings.

The first two quotations for solo baritone saxophone are decided novelties, as this instrument is almost never used without doubling of some kind. Compare the Cowell excerpt with the earlier one (Ex. 31) for solo bass clarinet and the later one by Copland (Ex. 80) for solo bassoon.

EX. 51. *III. HORNPIPE from Celtic Set*

Henry Cowell

EX. 52. *AN OUTDOOR OVERTURE*

Aaron Copland

Mention was made previously of the baritone saxophone completing the saxophone quartet. The next example shows this usage most felicitously with the sustained chords arranged for two altos, a tenor, and baritone saxophones.

EX. 53. *ZANONI*

Paul Creston, Op. 40

Moderately fast (♩ = 104)

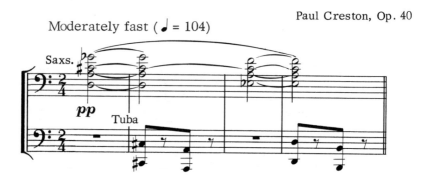

The following excerpt illustrates the baritone saxophone's more ordinary assignment, namely, that of playing melodic or harmonic bass parts. In Ex. 54, the top notes of the octaves are scored for the bass clarinet, bassoon, and baritone saxophone in unison with the tuba and string bass on the lower notes.

EX. 54. *I. OVERTURE from Symphony in B Flat*

Paul Fauchet
Revised by James R. Gillette

Tranquillo ed espressivo

The two final illustrations shown here utilize the higher range of the instrument. In Ex. 55, the duet for tenor and baritone saxophones shows the importance of selecting instruments which can carry through a phrase in its entirety. Note the subdued accompaniment for this duet. The final excerpt has a rich-sounding tenor melody with well-placed sustaining chords for the horns and embellishing phrases for the higher reeds.

EX. 55. *SHOONTHREE*

Henry Cowell

EX. 56. *SUNDAY MORNING AT GLION*

from By the Lake at Geneva

Franz Bendel
Trans. by F. Campbell-Watson

THE B♭ BASS SAXOPHONE

The chance for the availability of this saxophone in American bands is only slightly better than that for the even scarcer contrabassoon. In playing styles, these two instruments have much in common, since their low tones speak quite slowly and require more breath than the other reeds. However, the bass saxophone has the heaviest tonal weight, or depth, in the wood-wind section.

77

Its tone quality could be profitably employed to offset and frequently supplant the much heavier and overworked tubas. For example, many all-reed scorings frequently have tubas on the lowest bass notes because these notes are not in the ranges of the low reeds. And this difficulty is further emphasized by the possible absence of one or more of these bass wood winds from the instrumentation of both large and small bands.

The scoring for the bass saxophone follows the same general patterns as those which are regularly assigned to the tubas. Its tone is firm, with considerable dynamic flexibility. In scoring it, due consideration should be given to its tonal strength and depth, along with the demands it makes upon the player.

Although the bass saxophone is an extremely scarce instrument, it has been included in a surprisingly large number of scores for the concert band since 1925. Nevertheless, its inclusion should be regarded as optional and therefore it should be treated as a supplementary instrument. A few sample passages are given here.

EX. 57. *TRAUER-MARSCH*

Mendelssohn, Op. 103
Revised by Erik Leidzen

The bass saxophone is in unison with the string bass and tuba on the lower octave notes in the following excerpt, with the top notes solely for the bass clarinet. Notice the continuation of the reed timbre for the eighth notes in the third measure.

EX. 58. *I. FINALE from Symphony in B Flat*

Paul Fauchet
Revised by James R. Gillette

Allegro vivace (♩ = 152)

In this scoring, the bass saxophone is again on the lower notes of the octaves which stop on the first beat of the third measure.

EX. 59. *I. HORSE-RACE from Newsreel in Five Shots*

William Schuman

Fast (♩ = 160)

The octaves here are for bassoons, baritone, bass saxophones, and string bass (*pizzicato*), with the two latter on the lowest notes. These octaves are cued for divided tubas.

79

THE SAXOPHONES AS A UNIT

Scored examples for the saxophones as a solo choir are far less numerous than those for the clarinets, but more frequent than those for the double reeds. One can only speculate why this is so, since this choir is an excellent means of securing contrast through juxtapositions of its timbre with that of the other reeds or brasses. No doubt the broader and mellower tonal spread of the saxophones, as compared to the more incisive and brighter tone of the other reeds, has prompted band scorers to consider the saxophones primarily as supporting instruments and only secondarily as an independent, satisfactory choir.

The next three excerpts are good illustrations of scoring devised to secure contrast by means of timbre opposition. In Ex. 60, the four parts have been cued for solo brass quartet: cornet, horn, euphonium, and tuba. Certainly the saxophone grouping, in this case, is preferable.

EX. 60. *RIVER JORDAN: Fantasy on Negro Spirituals*

Maurice C. Whitney

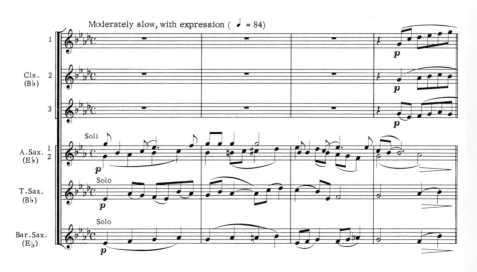

The second illustration in this category shows the effective use of the smooth, mellow timbre of the saxophones as one way of securing sudden contrast. This is a scoring device which can occasionally be advantageously employed when sustained tones, without the depth of the brass, would be adequate.

EX. 61. *IN THE CATHEDRAL*

Gabriel Pierné
Trans. by Irving Cheyette

The saxophones are frequently used as a four-part unit to establish and maintain harmonic and/or rhythmic backgrounds upon which melodic material is superimposed. This is the device used to good effect in the following example. (Also review Exs. 53, 61, 63, 68, 69, and 72.)

’ EX. 62. *SPIRITUAL*

H. Owen Reed

Copyright 1948 Associated Music Publishers, Inc., New York, N.Y.

Scoring saxophones as a trio, with two altos and a tenor, is quite frequent for melodic and harmonic parts, as shown in the three following excerpts. Example 63 demonstrates good melodic writing with horizontal freedom above the drone of the fifths in the bass part.

82

EX. 63. *4. ALSACE-LORRAINE from Suite Française*

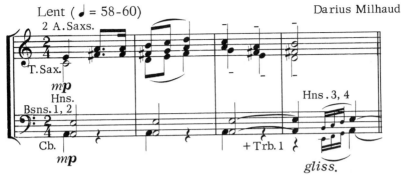

Lent (♩ = 58-60)   Darius Milhaud

A second and different style of trio writing is illustrated in Ex. 64. Here the undoubled saxophones have the same detachment from the bass octaves. Also observe the saxophone-horn doubling at measure 55 and the last chord. The swirling scale in the bass clarinet is finished off with the high treble parts in a humorous touch which is deftly executed.

EX. 64. *III. DANCE from Divertimento*

Vincent Persichetti, Op. 42

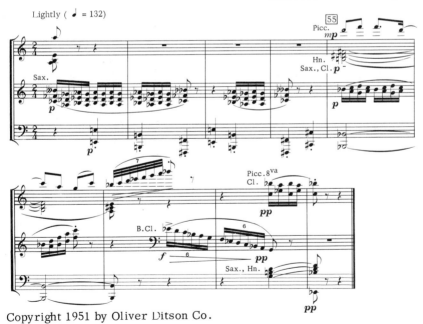

Lightly (♩ = 132)

83

Saxophones are idiomatic for giving rhythmic representation (intervals or chords) to harmonic parts sustained in other instruments (see Exs. 65 and 66). They sound less reedy in this style of scoring than do the other wood winds.

EX. 65. *PRELUDE FOR BAND*

Donald O. Johnston

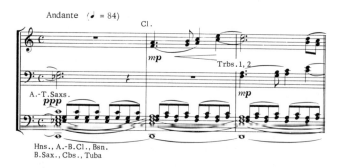

EX. 66. *SYMPHONIC TRANSITIONS*

Joseph Wagner

✧✧✧✧

CHAPTER NINE

THE DOUBLE REEDS

Oboe - English Horn - Bassoon - Contrabassoon - Sarrusophone

RANGES, CLEFS, AND TRANSPOSITIONS

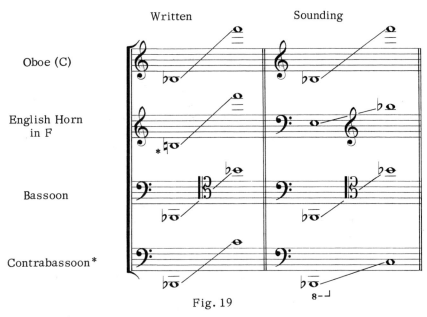

Fig. 19

*The B♭ is possible on some instruments.

Double-reed instruments, included in the band much earlier than the single reeds, still remain the chief source for timbre contrast in the wood-wind section. One has only to hear a concert band—minus double reeds—to fully appreciate their tonal value and importance to the ensemble.

The tone qualities of these instruments are different from the tone qualities previously noted for the non-reeds and the single reeds. In fact, the double reeds constitute a unique tonal paradox. Their tone has far greater vibrancy in a fixed, penetrating timbre than that of the other reeds. Yet this tone is fragile and cannot withstand *constant* playing or overelaboration. Its very reediness demands the band scorer's careful attention to timbre juxtapositions if its full contrast value is to be realized.

Double-reed timbres, which result from greater accumulation of overtones, speak with a more pronounced definition than the other reeds. The tone is thicker because it is reedier. The player is responsible for its degree of quality.

These timbre differences are to be noted in both *legato* and *staccato* styles of playing. In the former, melodic lines have clear profile, while detached passages sound with more bite or incisiveness. These characteristics are important factors in achieving balance when single and mixed timbres are involved. Double reeds are best for voice parts which can benefit from mild emphasis and extra tints of *espressivo*.

THE OBOE

The oboe is, without doubt, the most distinctive instrument in the wood-wind group. Its plaintive, yet clear, timbre carries quite well in most combinations unburdened with heavy brasses. Its tone qualities enhance melodies that are expressive but restrained. It is superior for music with pastoral connotations; short, *staccato* phrases have a delightful lilt and crispness quite apart from the remainder of the section.

Range Divisions

The practical playing registers of this most difficult of all reeds require detailed study.

(a)

These lowest tones are somewhat thick, difficult to produce, and equally difficult to control softer than *mezzoforte*. These four notes are easiest if approached scalewise rather than by skips. The tone here, when well played, is sonorous, but reedy.

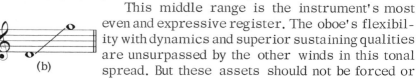
(b)

This middle range is the instrument's most even and expressive register. The oboe's flexibility with dynamics and superior sustaining qualities are unsurpassed by the other winds in this tonal spread. But these assets should not be forced or

86

crowded by heavier timbres. Oboe tone becomes rough if pushed.

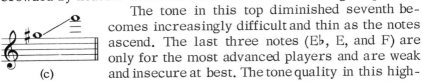

The tone in this top diminished seventh becomes increasingly difficult and thin as the notes ascend. The last three notes (E♭, E, and F) are only for the most advanced players and are weak and insecure at best. The tone quality in this highest register lacks the warmth it has in the middle register. Notes up to the high E♭ are serviceable, mainly for well-doubled woodwind passages at loud dynamic levels.

(c)

The oboe is essentially a lyric instrument. Although most scale passages and figurations are technically possible on this instrument, large and/or chromatic intervals in fast tempos carry intonation risks. Rapidly broken or arpeggiated chords are not basically idiomatic; they belong to the single reeds. However, rapidly repeated notes in all tonguing styles are very good in chord formations with mixed timbres.

Timbre juxtapositions, so important in orchestration (see Chap. 14 in the author's *Orchestration: A Practical Handbook*), do not seem to have quite the same significance in band music, where instrumental color is less subtle and more broadly employed. Nonetheless, double reeds in unison or octaves with the other winds produce interesting blends of mixed sonorities with definite contrast values. Massed doublings of single and double reeds in the strong dynamics are sound standard practice.

The oboes in the band are frequently divided into two parts whenever the voice structure is adaptable to highly individualized tone quality. The following excerpts are to be considered as solo passages, with one exception.

EX. 67. *III. MINUET from Water Music Suite*

Handel
Arr. by Hershy Kay

The Handel excerpt above is a representative passage covering both the low and medium ranges of the oboe. Notice the lightly scored alto and tenor parts and the slightly more substantial bass part.

The following excertp for unaccompanied oboe expands the melodic spread to the maximum safe compass. Here is a most effective recitative with well-subdued chordal responses.

EX. 68. *II. RECITATIVE from West Point Suite*

Darius Milhaud

In the Creston excerpt below, the solo oboe is in its most expressive *tessitura* and is nicely separated from the sustained harmony. The quartet of accompanying saxophones is well placed.

EX. 69. *LEGEND*

Paul Creston

88

Florid passages for the oboe are technically possible and practical if they are kept within the idiomatic styles of the instrument. As used below, the intended effect of the bagpipe is effective and playable without difficulty.

EX. 70. *AFTERNOON IN THE VILLAGE*

Jaromir Weinberger
Edited and scored by F. Campbell-Watson

The oboe's natural reedy timbre is particularly felicitous for folk tunes in dance rhythms with moderately fast tempos and for pastoral-style melodies with lyric expressiveness, as shown in Ex. 71. The tone quality of the solo instrument blends nicely here with the horn-bassoon chords. (The full score has been condensed by the author.)

EX. 71. *MOSES from Portraits from the Bible*

Julian Work

The final quotation here is for divided oboes used melodically with the Bb clarinets. This doubling gives an extra vibrancy and profile to these thirds available only with the single-reed combination. The passage is a continuation of Ex. 53.

89

EX. 72. *ZANONI*

Paul Creston, Op. 40

THE ENGLISH HORN

The name English horn (in French *cor Anglais*) is a misnomer, since this instrument is neither English nor a horn. It is actually an alto oboe pitched in F. Baroque and Classic composers wrote for its earlier prototype, known as both *oboe d'amore* and *oboe da caccia*. The English horn, said to have been invented about 1760, superseded its earlier prototype in about 1830 with its acceptance in *William Tell* by Rossini and in *Robert le Diable* by Meyerbeer.

Much early orchestral scoring of the English horn during the Romantic period had it typed almost exclusively for solo passages of a distinctly melancholy and nostalgic nature, with an almost total absence of harmonic figurations. This tonal casting of the English horn continued well into the twentieth century, when composers enlarged its scope to include playing styles idiomatic for an alto oboe—short, rhythmic motives and figurations, pastoral arabesques, and *ostinatos*. In addition, composers began to make use of its natural potential for lyric expressiveness. The English horn is now treated in ensemble scoring as an alto and high tenor oboe.

Unfortunately, comparatively few American bands have an English horn available at all times. When scored, its part can be written in one of two ways: first, as a straight part for one player; second, as an alternating instrument, generally for the second oboe part and written into it. If the latter procedure is followed, sufficient time must be allowed for the change-over of instruments.

90

Range Divisions

The tonal registers of the English horn differ from those given for the oboe, notwithstanding their similar written ranges.

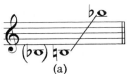
(a)

This two-octave spread contains the best notes for all playing styles. The first three notes (Bb, B, and C) are only slightly less difficult for the English horn than they are for the oboe. The tone in the lowest octave has a rich, sonorous quality of exceptional beauty that should not be forced beyond a moderate *forte*. The notes in this octave are best for only moderately fast melodic lines. The higher octave is slightly more adaptable to harmonic figurations which do not exceed a strong *forte*.

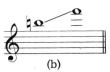
(b)

This top fourth of the range is rarely used, as the tone is thin and unsatisfactory. Actually, the oboe is far superior to the English horn for the notes in the highest octave. The tonal disparity between these two instruments is most evident at loud dynamic levels. English horn tone is not completely successful louder than *forte*. For this reason, very few *fortissimos* find their way into parts for it. Instead, the oboe is substituted for the full wood-wind ensemble when loud passages are called for.

Inclusion of English horn parts in American band scores is a twentieth-century innovation. A few excerpts indicate the extent of its use thus far.

As solos for the English horn are often anticipated by a diminution of texture and sonority, the following excerpts will serve to show the technique used by three composers. Partial tonal fadeouts are arranged so that the entrance of the solo instrument becomes easily distinguishable. In each scoring, note the dynamic markings for both the solo and the accompanying instruments along with the disposition of contrasting timbres. Also, observe how the melodic spread of the solo part is confined to the instrument's best playing range. Example 75 has been included so that a comparison can be made for the band scoring of this familiar orchestral passage.

EX. 73. *OVERTURE from Symphony in B Flat*

Paul Fauchet
Revised by James R. Gillette

EX. 74. *WAKE ME UP FOR THE GREAT JUBILEE:*
Variations on an Old American Song

George Frederick McKay

92

EX. 75. *FINALE from Symphony in D Minor*

Franck
Trans. by James R. Gillette

In the next example, the four winds are scored in chamber music style, thus retaining the spirit and texture of the Classic minuet. The sustained horn deserves special attention, as this instrument, more than any other, can bind a passage together whenever mixed timbres are used.

EX. 76. *II. MENUET from Royce Hall Suite*

Healey Willan
Edited and scored by William Teague

93

The following example introduces a subject of considerable importance. In the first place, this example serves to illustrate the fact that two instruments with the same timbre, playing in octaves with soft dynamics, run the risk of exposing possible faulty intonation. Octaves played with mixed timbres are much less conspicuous in this regard. The second point concerns the fact that the bass clarinet takes over the phrase from the English horn two measures before (1). Although this scoring is entirely feasible, the timbre line is broken off at that point, and this fact should be recognized.

EX. 77. *LOHENGRIN, excerpts from Act I*

Wagner
Arr. by Lucien Cailliet

The final excerpt has the English horn—without doubling—on the bottom notes of the lead octaves in the high treble part. As shown in the full score (Ex. 78), the top notes of these octaves have the superior strength for the passage, thereby ensuring its proper tonal profile. The English horn part, falling between the alto and tenor parts, does not conflict with their independent movement and will carry out the octave pattern, though rather weakly.

EX. 78. *CHORAL PRELUDE: We All Believe in One God*

J. S. Bach
Trans. by James R. Gillette

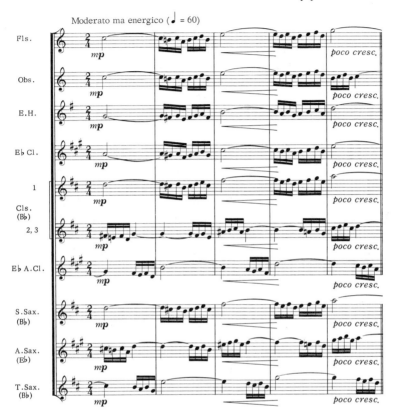

Additional parts for the English horn may be examined in the full scores of the following:

Hallberg, *Erik the Red* (Shawnee Press)
Rimski–Korsakov–Harding, *The Tsar's Bride*, Overture, (Kjos)
Strauss–Harding, *A Hero's Courtship* (Kjos)
Work, *Portraits from the Bible*, (Shawnee Press)
Williams, *Arioso* (Summy-Birchard)
Williams, *Pastoral* (Summy-Birchard)
Williams, *Symphonic Suite* (Summy-Birchard)

THE BASSOON

The bassoon, in timbre and usage, can be considered as a bass oboe, although its compass spans the tenor, baritone, and bass registers. It is ordinarily written in the bass clef, except for passages in the high register when the tenor clef is necessary to eliminate excessive ledger lines. *Note:* Student players of this instrument are rarely familiar with this clef, but should be !

Range Divisions

This instrument's large range has three rather distinctive tonal divisions.

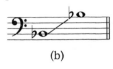

(a)

This lowest octave has full, sonorous tone that is quite reedy. It makes an excellent bass for the wood-wind choir and for doubling melodic bass parts with strong dynamics. Lyric solos here can be quite expressive, if a suitable balance between the solo and accompanying parts can be arranged. Such a tonal relationship between these parts is secured through contrast of timbres and dynamics. This octave also has unusually attractive potentialities for conveying musical humor if a crisp *staccato* is employed. *Note:* The four lowest semitones are difficult to control *pianissimo*.

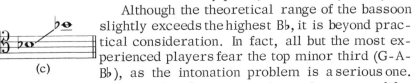

(b)

The strong, reedy quality of the lowest octave is less pronounced in this middle octave. The scale tones here are even and they have fair tonal strength. It is a good register for broken chords, sustained harmony parts, and some lyric styles.

(c)

Although the theoretical range of the bassoon slightly exceeds the highest Bb, it is beyond practical consideration. In fact, all but the most experienced players fear the top minor third (G-A-Bb), as the intonation problem is a serious one. This high octave, constituting the tenor register, is very good for slow melodies that are poignantly expressive. The instrument's tone is thinner here and will not carry except above the softest accompaniments. These conditions limit the opportunities for solo parts in this register in the band.

Parts for bassoons are written in pairs, but there is usually a preponderance of unison writing here. Successions of broken intervals and chords, up to and including an octave, are comparatively easy to play if confined within an octave. Slurred skips in rapid tempos are more difficult. Double and triple tonguing is not technically possible. However, adaptations of single tonguing can be substituted quite satisfactorily. *Staccato*, at rapid tempos, is clear and bright.

EX. 79. *II.PASSACAGLIA from Concerto Grosso*

Joseph Wagner

The bassoons announce the theme of the *Passacaglia* in a *tessitura* which carries very well. Single voices of this kind are an effective means of supplying contrast when they are placed between passages with several voice parts.

EX. 80. *AN OUTDOOR OVERTURE*

Aaron Copland

This excerpt balances three-part B♭ clarinets nicely with *staccato* bassoons. Another example of a thin texture, which can be so effective in concert music for the band, follows.

EX. 81. *I.ALLEGRO SCHERZANDO from Suite for Concert Band*

Gerald R. Kechley

Example 81 is a very good illustration of the occasional necessity for adjusting dynamics so that they compensate for unequal tonal strengths. Notice that the solo bassoon is marked *forte*, while the other parts are to play *pianissimo*. The full score indicates that the accompanying parts are reduced further in this way: only the first desks of the B♭ clarinets and muted solo cornets are desired. The harp, which doubles the harmony, is marked *forte*.

EX. 82. *III. DANCE from Divertimento*

Vincent Persichetti, Op. 42

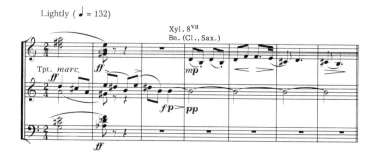

This unusual bassoon solo in the tenor register is accentuated by the xylophone doubling, actually sounding two octaves higher. The absence of any sustaining harmony is no oversight, for the composer achieves both clarity for the part and contrast of sonorities with this scoring.

EX. 83. *POLKA and FUGUE*
from the Opera, Schwanda, the Bagpiper

Jaromir Weinberger
Trans. and adapted by Glenn C. Bainum

This is the kind of rapid *staccato* passage which the bassoons can manage most effectively. It has a dry humor which sounds with pointed clarity.

Many of the previous examples, shown to highlight the various instruments separately, have shown the bassoon in bass parts in a variety of scoring combinations. These examples should now be reviewed so that they can be correlated with those in this section which have similar scoring intent.

THE CONTRABASSOON

This tonally heavy, slow-speaking double reed occupies a position in the wood-wind section similar to that of the contrabass in the string choir. The contrabassoon is the least versatile of the reeds and has been included in only a very few American publications of band music, as yet. This instrument is essentially one for supporting bass parts, particularly when scored for the wood winds. It is written an octave higher than it sounds, as is the case with the string bass. The following scores list parts for the contrabassoon:

Franck–Gillette, Symphony in D Minor, Finale (Witmark)
Gillette, *Fugal Fantasia* (Witmark)
Kechley, Suite for Concert Band (Associated)

Reed, *La fiesta mexicana* (Mills)
Rogers, Three Japanese Dances (Presser)
R. Wagner–Cailliet, Excerpts from Act 1, *Lohengrin* (Remick)
R. Wagner–Cailliet, *Siegfried's Rhine Journey, Die Götterdämer-
ung* (Remick)

THE SARRUSOPHONE

The sarrusophone family grouping represents an attempt of a
French bandmaster, Sarrus, to provide the wood-wind section
with another variety of double-reed instrument with a key system
similar to those devised for the saxophones. Originally made in
six sizes, only the lowest ones, E♭ and C contrabass, continue to
be available; the former mostly in America and the latter in Europe, notably in France. The sarrusophone's tone color is heavier
and thicker than that of the contrabassoon, which it resembles in
range and for which it is sometimes substituted. The one in E♭
has the same written and sounding notation as the E♭ baritone saxophone. However, another model in C, written in the bass clef and
sounding an octave lower than written, has the same written and
sounding ranges as those of the contrabassoon. This sonorous instrument has good potentials for blending with either the reeds or
the brasses, but it should be considered as a substituting instrument, since no parts appear to have been written specifically for
it in American band publications.

THE DOUBLE REEDS AS A UNIT

The advisability of scoring the double reeds as a unit—without
doubling unless cross-cued—for concert music for the band is
questionable from a practical but not from an artistic viewpoint.
As previously stated, their availability is quite uncertain and the
section is not always at full strength. Consequently, in most general scoring plans the double reeds may be considered as an auxiliary unit to the basic clarinet choir. Brief melodic phrases and
rhythmic passages in the double reeds do have fine contrast value
but, unfortunately, they should be employed sparingly.

The following excerpt is the one illustration available from the
numerous scores considered. This passage for two oboes and a
bassoon has an antique charm characteristic of the period before
single reeds were available.

EX. 84. *GAVOTTE from Le Journal du printemps, Suite No. III*

J. C. F. Fischer
Arr. by Keith Wilson

CHAPTER TEN

∞∞∞

THE WOOD-WIND SECTION AS
A COMPLETE UNIT

Scoring the wood winds as a complete unit, without brass doublings, is somewhat frequent—more frequent than it is for the smaller groupings of a single family unit. Such passages represent this section's maximum tonal strength used to balance that of the heavier brass choir. The following excerpts have been selected to illustrate some of the practical ways in which the full section functions in concert music for the band.

Example 85 is a *tutti* passage for wood winds, minus the piccolo. In analyzing full scores, it will be helpful to know that parts which have the same rhythmical patterns usually double each other either in unison or octaves, often as voices in a melodic or harmonic unit.

EX. 85. *GAVOTTE from Le Journal du printemps, Suite No. III*

J. C. F. Fischer
Arr. by Keith Wilson

103

The next excerpt has a thinner scoring of a simple melody-harmony combination. Notice the absence of needless padding (fillers) which preserves the spirit of the piano original.

EX. 86. *TWO GERMAN DANCES, No. I*

Beethoven
Arr. by Howard Kilbert

In the following excerpt, the wood-wind section is used as an answering choir with the brass section, which precedes and follows it.

EX. 87. *ALLEGRO VIVACE from Organ Sonata in D major*

Alexandre Guilmant, Op. 50
Arr. by Albert D. Schmutz

Another example of chordal progressions is given in the next quotation. Here the wood winds precede the answering phrase in the brass. Notice how the *staccato* bite in this passage accentuates the rhythmic pattern.

EX. 88. *GEORGE WASHINGTON BRIDGE*

William Schuman

106

The next two excerpts show two scorings of contrapuntal style. Example 89 is a short fugal exposition. In Ex. 90, the brass is used only on the first two beats at J and four measures after J. This scoring provides great contrast for the soft contrapuntal entrances of the reeds. The string bass doubles the lowest bass part, starting two measures after J.

EX. 89. *OVERTURE from Le Journal du Printemps: Suite III*

J. C. F. Fischer
Arr. by Keith Wilson

107

Mendelssohn, Op. 24
Adapted by Felix Greissle

Allegro vivace (♩ = 152)

Florid scale passages in fast tempos are regularly allotted to the wood winds rather than to the heavier brasses. Sometimes scales take the form of single-note embellishments, which is the case in Ex. 91. Note here that the final note in each sequence coincides with the starting note of another part. This device promotes the illusion of continuous movement within the range of the participating instruments. Failure to create this illusion often gives the impression of blocked scales rather than a continuous flow.

EX. 91. *BEOWULF: A Symphonic Sketch*

Bruce C. Beach

Another form of scale sequences ascending or descending, spanning more than one register, is best carried out by the woodwind section. The following excerpt is a good model, showing the ascending scale and the gradual entrance of each instrument, arranged to increase the tonal strength for the *crescendo*. The brass and percussion are also included with these reeds.

109

EX. 92. *2. INTERMEZZO from First Suite in E Flat*

Gustav Holst

The final quotation represents the maximum tonal strength and brilliance obtainable from the wood winds in swirling scale passages played *legato*. Notice how the rolls on the snare and bass drums increase the tension and drive of the last few measures of this masterful work for the band.

EX. 93. *TOCCATA MARZIALE* R. Vaughan Williams

111

∞∞∞

CHAPTER ELEVEN

SCORING THE WOOD WINDS AS
AN INDEPENDENT SECTION

The previous chapters have established general voice distributions for the winds by range (see Table 5) and have given basic technical data necessary for the scoring of chorals by the wood-wind instruments. The interval pattern found in the harmonic series (Fig. 1) provides additional background for dealing with spacings in limited scoring exercises. From the harmonic series it will be observed that no tones form close-position chords in the bass register and that the chord tones become closer together as the scale ascends.[1] This information can now be applied to the scoring of chorals and short pieces essentially written in four voices. Close-position chords in the bass, not tenor, register are to be avoided, since they sound thick and unclear. However, these chord positions are often necessary and desirable in the higher registers.

The "mixedness" tone quality of band music may seem to restrict the timbre distinctions which are possible in orchestral music. However, instrumental combinations in the band can be balanced with singular effectiveness and clarity when timbre strengths and weaknesses are properly evaluated, considered, and understood. Scoring *America*[2] for various wood-wind ensembles provides some pertinent observations which are applicable to more complex scoring plans.

An example of the nonrecognition of timbre differentials may be found in Ex. 94, which gives the highest voice part to the flute with the other parts assigned to double and single reeds in the order of their appearance on the score page. This scoring produces the result shown here.

---

[1] For further application of the harmonic series to band scoring, see Chap. 24.

[2] America has been used throughout this text as a representative four-part choral so that the student can compare sectional and full-band scorings of it with those given in the author's Orchestration: A Practical Handbook.

The weakness of this literal setting with parts transferred without change from one medium to another, lies in the poor balance between the soprano and alto parts. If this setting is played by the full wood-wind section of a band, the discrepancy is further emphasized by the superior numbers of the Bb clarinets. Whenever unequal mixed timbres occur, extra care must be taken to ensure clear definition of the melodic line. The low flute and the lower oboe do not give this kind of clarity in Ex. 94. The reedier oboe tone dominates the flute in this register. Replacing the flute with a Bb clarinet or Eb alto saxophone would improve the balance, but would not correct it. Furthermore, the close-position chords, though good for voices, have little resonance potential for many mixed-timbre instrumental combinations.

There are two possible ways to improve this poor tonal balance. The first and most obvious way is to invert the flute and oboe parts so that the latter would play the soprano. This inversion would be even more effective if a clarinet or saxophone were substituted for the flute, as mentioned above. However, a second and more effective method calls for the rearrangement of the voice parts from close to open position, without altering the *tessitura* of the bass part. This can be accomplished by raising the melodic soprano an octave, lowering the alto an octave (to become the tenor part), and

113

raising the tenor an octave (to become the alto part). *Note:* Many problems of balance caused by poor positioning of inside parts frequently can be improved or corrected by repositioning one or more of these parts, as shown in Ex. 95.

EX. 95. *AMERICA*

A setting of this anthem for four saxophones illustrates close-position chord progressions for instruments with equal timbre. With this and similar combinations, disparities of tonal balance are less likely. As mentioned earlier, two alto and a tenor saxophones, playing as a unit, rarely move into open position when used for chord progressions.

EX. 96. *AMERICA*

These two settings (Exs. 95 and 96) should be used by the student as models for further quartet settings. Instruments with one timbre (two oboes, English horn, and bassoon, for example) can remain in close position. Combinations with mixed timbres (oboe, B♭ clarinet, alto saxophone, bassoon, etc.,) should be tried in both open and close positions and the results appraised in rehearsal, if possible.

Scoring this anthem for the wood winds of the basic band requires some voice extensions and a minimum of doubling.

EX. 97. *AMERICA*

Several pertinent observations may be made here:

1. The ensemble is top-heavy with melody.

2. The bass in the tenor saxophone is hardly sufficient to support the seven higher parts.

3. This setting, unbalanced as it is, would be satisfactory if combined with an adequate scoring for the brass of the basic band. However, this combination could be still further improved by changing the tenor saxophone from the bass to the tenor part.

Still another arrangement follows. Here there are eight parts, including saxophones. There is some intentional interlocking or overlapping of parts, which is a useful device for blending mixed timbres and relieving the effect of blocked sonorities (chord progressions with few or no interval changes). The student should continue these voice patterns for settings with different instrumental combinations.

115

The final setting is composed of twelve parts with some unison doubling, principally in the middle register. This example represents the maximum tonal spread possible with this section. The Db piccolo has been used so that signature differences can become familiar in practice. The writing of the saxophone parts illustrates their sustaining potential, which is a great asset in securing tonal cohesiveness.

EX. 99. *AMERICA*

117

The following conclusions may be drawn from experience with voice extensions and developments in scoring chorals.

1. Limited tonal spreads produce limited resonance and massed volume.

2. Most harmony parts should be regarded as independent voices to be moved with horizontal freedom and not viewed simply as chord tones with rigid vertical movement.

3. Thick part writing in the bass register is to be avoided.

4. Models discussed thus far can be adapted for the full band (see Chap. 25).

5. Overpadding with doublings and/or fillers may increase volume, but it thickens the sonority.

6. Melodic soprano parts should not be moved arbitrarily to inside alto or tenor parts. They should remain in essentially the same register as in the original. (Use the examples in the author's *Workbook* for scoring in this category.

All of the settings given thus far are essentially utilitarian rather than artistic. This kind of scoring is useful when full band sonorities are needed.

Learning based on the scoring of chorals may be further applied to scoring wind settings of four-part music originally written for a keyboard instrument. This includes wind transcriptions of orchestral music, with a few reservations (see Chap. 28).

Source material in this form (instrumental, not vocal music) is concerned primarily with artistic rather than utilitarian representation. It is usually homophonic in style, having one main theme or melodic line, with harmonization. It is usually simple in structure or arrangement of the voice parts. In its most elementary form the harmony has very little movement, which has the effect of highlighting the melody. More elaborate pieces may have one or more parts with broken chords.

When scoring for the separate wind sections, allow the music itself to be the guide in determining the scoring plan. The following questions should be answered before actual scoring is begun. How are the parts allocated—are they in high, medium, or low registers? What is the tempo? Is the dynamic level rather even, or does it change considerably? What are the style and character of the music—placid or tense, light or heavy? The answers to these and similar questions can help to determine the scoring of wind settings. The band scorer should concern himself especially with color, resonance, and balance. The illustrative examples have shown how sectional scoring for the wood-wind section promotes contrast. In scoring of any kind, it is also most important to establish the variability of timbre combinations. There may be, and frequently are, several ways to score a given passage—each quite different, yet each quite appropriate. Musical intuition and experience are invaluable, since there is no complete set of rules governing the creative process. The transcriber's task is to represent faithfully the composer's musical intentions without distortion. In the case of an original work for band, the composer is his own judge and master. In transcriptions, the transcriber must be guided by many external factors, but the music itself should furnish most of the clues and inspiration.

The following settings illustrate wood-wind transcriptions of piano music in four parts. The student should make many similar settings from the source material given in the author's *Workbook for Band Scoring*, in addition to the work with chorals suggested earlier.

EX. 100. *MORNING PRAYER*

Tchaikovsky, Op. 39, No. 1

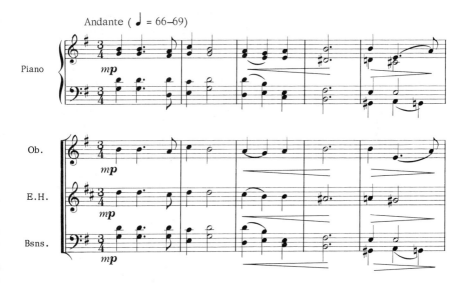

EX. 101. *ELEGIE*

Grieg, Op. 38, No. 6

120

The literal double-reed scoring in Ex. 100 is, of course, unusual, as discussed earlier. However, it would have a nice sound in one timbre. Scoring projects should include the unusual as well as the usual.

The setting given in Ex. 101 has several points of interest. The four-part texture is carried out entirely with single reeds. The saxophone parts add a sustained dimension to the clarinets, which is worth investigating. Their release in the last measure leaves the clarinets, with their lighter tone, sustaining the *fermata*.

CHAPTER TWELVE

THE BRASS INSTRUMENTS

Composition of the Brass Section · Common Characteristics

Tone Production · Playing Styles

The brass section of the band has passed through many stages of experimentation and development in Europe and America. The result has been, as of the mid-twentieth century, a general acceptance and uniformity of a brass instrumentation for all types of band (other than the brass band), namely, cornets, trumpets, horns, trombones, baritones and/or euphoniums, and tubas. The inclusion of the Bb fluegelhorn in American band publications varies with individual scorers, and parts for the alto and tenor horns, indicated in some scores, are considered essentially as duplicating parts. *Note:* Brass bands, notably those in England, add an Eb cornet and a Bb fluegelhorn to the standard instrumentation. Also, the notation for all brass parts is given in the treble clef in some English publications. Consult full scores (Besson) for arrangements and original works for this medium.

Individual brass parts are generally played by more than one player. The exact number of players is determined by each director, who bases his decision on both musical and personnel considerations. Some idea of the structural textures required for the full-brass choir can be gained from perusing a full-band score (see page 16), which reveals a minimum of fifteen real playing parts. Obviously, *tutti* passages for the complete brass choir necessitate considerable doubling of the two middle registers, alto and tenor.

A generally high level of performance can now be found almost universally among brass player's, with the exception of horn players. This has given the band scorer working with these instruments a new approach—fresher than that of scorers in the early 1900s and before. The tonal and technical flexibility of the section and the introduction of many new effects[1] have been shown in its scoring as the basic choir of marching and "show" bands. The constantly developing potential of the section has also been seized by many band scorers in their bolder approach to music for the concert band, where the section frequently becomes less dominant than the wood-wind choir. Yet the writers for both concert and marching bands, having recognized the idiomatic assets and liabilities of the brass instruments, continue to explore still newer ways of scoring them, both separately and in combination. Since the brass instruments have many common characteristics and technical peculiarities, they can be considered as a unit for certain aspects affecting tone production.

The section is not a completely homogeneous grouping, as its instruments vary in construction and means of tone production.

The horns form one complete tonal unit. The cornets, alto horns, mellophones, euphoniums, baritones, and tubas belong to another grouping, being members of the saxhorn family, and have similarities of construction and tone qualities. The trumpets and trombones are considered the third unit because of their tonal similarity. These divisions of the brass instruments result from differences in construction which affect the bore or tube shape and variations in size and shape of the mouthpiece.

It will have been noted from Tables 1 and 2 that brass instruments are designed according to their pitch fundamentals (Bb, F, Eb, and BBb) in addition to their ranges (soprano, alto, tenor, baritone, and bass). These keyed pitches refer to the fundamentals of each instrument which, in turn, become a determining factor in range positioning.

Each instrument is constructed so that the player can produce most of the tones in the harmonic series from a given fundamental without valve or piston fingerings (see Fig. 1). Then, by using various combinations of valves, pistons, or slide positions, the fundamentals are altered until all the chromatic tones within an octave have been accounted for. This method converts each brass instrument from its closed position (semidiatonic) to one with a full chromatic scale. All brass instruments, with the exception of the trombone, accomplish these pitch changes by means of valves or pistons. In the case of the trombone, slide positions are used to accomplish the same thing.

The variations of tonal strengths in the brass section are enormous, covering a dynamic range from an organ-like *pianissimo* to an ear-shattering *fortissimo*. No other section of the band, with

---

[1] See Chaps. 24 and 26.

the exception of some percussion instruments, is so capable of making quick changes in dynamics heard and felt. Separately and collectively, the brass instruments have the strongest tonal strengths and weights in the band and, for this reason, are a constant factor to be considered in estimating tonal balance. In concert music, overscoring of the brass can be as detrimental as overusage of the percussion instruments.

The method of tone production for the brass instruments is familiar to most students of music. Held against a cup-shaped mouthpiece, the player's lips function as do the vibrating reeds of the wood winds. As the player forces an air stream through the lips, the air column within the tube is set in motion. Various kinds of articulation are brought about by controlled, skilled movements of the player's tongue, called tongue attacks.

The tonal intensity of each brass instrument varies in much the same manner as that of the wood winds. The player's embouchure (position of the lips against the mouthpiece) and tongue attack (single, double, or triple) are combined to produce tone, including intensity, and to determine pitch and tonal quality. These technicalities account for the negative as well as the positive aspects of brass playing. They help to explain why some players crack on extremely high notes, why very low tones sometimes sound fuzzy, and why attacks are either strong and clear, or weak and insecure.

Although the brass instruments now are technically excellent, there remain certain areas of idiomatic peculiarities, both technical and tonal, which constantly require consideration and evaluation in scoring. Here, as with the wood winds, it is not always a matter of whether or not a given passage or figure can be played by the brass. Rather, the question is whether the timbre and sonority will be appropriate from the standpoint of tonal quality and balance and artistic appropriateness. In addition, it is desirable to maintain a consistent level of technical difficulty for the player, as was recommended in the case of the wood winds.

In Chap. 6 there was a discussion of phrasing styles and their notation (see Figs. 7-15), together with optional ways of indicating divided parts for the wood winds. This material applies equally well to the writing of parts for the brass instruments. One basic difference in writing for the two sections concerns the use of non-*legato* passages, since double and triple tonguing are essential parts of a brass player's technique.

Single tongue strokes are used for all non-*legato* passages and types of accents. This tonguing is used for repeated notes at all dynamic levels. Insecurity of intonation and lack of incisiveness may occur at range extremes. Double or triple tonguing is used for very rapid note sequences to be played in small clusters. Both styles are most satisfactory for cornets, trumpets, fluegelhorns, and trombones and only slightly less satisfactory for baritones and euphoniums. Horns and tubas speak more clearly if only single tonguing and adaptations thereof are required. It is useful to know that in the lowest tones, each instrument speaks more slowly and responds less clearly than it does in the medium and high registers.

The observations previously made concerning the use of long slurs for the wood winds are perhaps even more pertinent to brass instruments. Short slurs are preferable to longer ones, although the latter can be found in some *cantabile* passages for horns, trombones, and baritones. Phrasing provides the means for securing tonal articulation and inflection and requires the same attention to detail as that urged for the wood winds.

Proper breath control is a major factor in the tone production of all brass instruments. The relative importance of this problem can be better understood when it is known that the air column of a horn must travel a distance that is more than double that of an oboe or a clarinet. From this comparison, it is obvious that the writer of band music must remain alert to this breath factor, especially when writing for the heavier, deeper brass instruments. Suitable breaks for changes of breath should be provided where they will not interfere with the natural flow of the parts or disrupt their rhythmic significance.

The pre-twentieth-century custom of using accidentals in place of key signatures for horn and trumpet parts in orchestration has not been followed in band scoring, except for one deviation. An occasional full-band score can be found showing horns in F without key signatures. This type of notation, resulting from the use of valveless instruments, is no longer valid and should be discouraged in band scoring.

~~~~

CHAPTER THIRTEEN

HIGH-RANGE BRASS INSTRUMENTS

Bb Cornet · Bb Trumpet · Bb Fluegelhorn

RANGES AND TRANSPOSITIONS

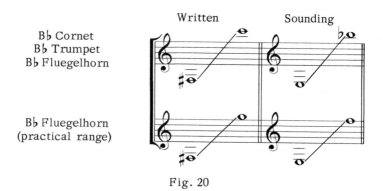

Fig. 20

THE Bb CORNET

The Bb cornet has a conical tubing (bore), is played with a deep cup mouthpiece, and is a member of the saxhorn family. It was constructed originally along the lines of the post horn. Prior to the 1920s, cornets were short and stubby, with a tone quality that was between those of the horn and the trumpet. Since then, trumpet-model cornets have been introduced and improved to the point where many authorities believe that the tone of the cornet is almost identical with that of the trumpet. It should be noted that some band directors do mix cornet and trumpet parts and that some composers do the same. However, although trumpets can be substituted for cornets, the reverse arrangement is not desirable. *Note*: There is a mid-twentieth century trend toward replacing cornets with trumpets in American bands.

The cornet has certain tonal and technical advantages which warrant its position as the band's principal melodic brass instrument. In this respect, the first cornet acts as a leader of the brass section. This instrument excels in flexibility, agility, and lyric expressiveness—qualities which make it the best high-range brass instrument for both *cantabile* melody and rapid, intricate passages of great variety. Cornet tone does lack the brilliance, power, and incisiveness associated with the trumpet. However, the cornet has an advantage in blending potential and is more adaptable to the great variety of parts found in band scores.

Range Divisions

The practical, safe-sounding range of the cornet is the same as that of the combined ranges of women's voices (G below middle C to G above the staff). Part writing for the cornets, in each respective division is similar to that for a three-part women's chorus.

The cornet has an unusually even tone throughout its full compass, with the exception of a few notes in the lowest and highest registers. Its tone at these extremes, of course, varies with the technical capacity of each player.

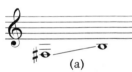

(a)

The lowest tones in this register (F♯, G, and G♯) are likely to be insecure and played with poor intonation. The sounding note G is the best low tone at which to start the cornet's full compass. The notes in this low register are rarely used for solo passages and only occasionally for chord tones. They have better quality when played either by a trombone or euphonium.

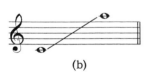

(b)

All of the notes in this range are even, easily produced, and carry well. It is the instrument's best register for all melodic styles, figurations, and chord tones, and can be controlled at all dynamic levels.

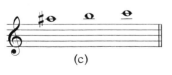

(c)

These few top notes are brilliantly effective but they are comparatively difficult to produce, especially at soft dynamic levels. And, of course, the quality of these extremely high notes is variable, depending on the technical capacities of each player.

As new techniques have been developed and exploited, the band repertory has been enriched with an almost totally new style of writing. Parts for the cornet are no exception. Cornet solo parts for the concert band are now varied in style, unlike those of an earlier period when long-drawn-out, sentimental ballads were the vogue.

The cornets are ordinarily divided into three distinct parts with the first part often subdivided into solo and first parts, as is the case with the first clarinets. Both solo parts assume leading positions in the band. Dividing the first parts in this manner permits virtuoso solo passages for a single player that ordinarily might be beyond the technical capacities of the average player.

A few scores show divisions for four parts, and one piece, *Circus Polka*, by Igor Stravinsky, is written with the cornets in five parts. But these two latter divisions are the exception and not the rule.

EX. 102. *ATHLETIC FESTIVAL MARCH*

Serge Prokofiev, Op. 69, No. 1
Arr. and edited by Richard F. Goldman

This simple, melodic passage for the cornets is in the instrument's best playing range. Notice the third cornet leaving the melody for a sustained part in the fifth measure.

EX. 103. *CHACONNE from LeJournal du printemps, Suite III*

J. C. F. Fischer
Arr. by Keith Wilson

In the passage for the cornet in this excerpt, there is more rhythmic interest than there is in the preceding one. The middle harmonies in the saxophones have contrast value because of their lighter timbre. The trombones give the bass part a tonal solidness comparable to that of the cornets, thus emphasizing the two-part writing characteristic of much music of the Baroque period.

Paul Creston, Op. 40

This is a good illustration of a newer style of florid *cantabile* for solo cornets. Notice that the tonal spread is confined to a minor seventh. The three introductory measures contain interesting scoring for the reeds. Also, the writing for the horns, tubas, and string bass at (20) should not be overlooked.

The next example illustrates leading melodic content for cornets in two parts. The tonal strength of the lower part is sufficient to carry above the countermelody in the reeds and the afterbeats in the horns. Notice how the figuration in the high treble (reeds) alternates in units; observe the similarity of this excerpt to Ex. 91

EX. 105. *ARMENIAN DANCES, No. 1*

Aram Khachaturian
Arr. and edited by Ralph Satz

Divided cornet parts are used rather frequently, with or without doubling, to give tonal solidity to chords in the middle register. These harmonic parts often appear as extensions of chords in the trombones and/or horns and sometimes are used as an independent unit. They are scored either as sustained progressions or as percussive chords, as shown in Ex. 106. Example 107 illustrates the same function, but in a sustained style.

EX. 106. *SYMPHONIC TRANSITIONS*

Joseph Wagner

131

EX. 107. *GARDENS OF GRANADA*

F. M. Torroba
Arr. by Walter Beeler

Andante molto tranquillo

Cornets in three parts are frequently chordal and occasionally contrapuntal. When the former style is used, a melodic line will carry in most textures and at most dynamic levels, providing it is placed in the cornet's high range. The following excerpt illustrates this particular scoring plan. The arpeggiated chords in the wood winds here will not seriously interfere with the clarity of the melody in the first cornets.

EX. 108. *POP! GOES THE WEASEL:*
Variations on the Theme, Var. 7, In Jazz

Allegro (♩ = 130)

Lucien Cailliet

Writing for three cornets, as in Ex. 109, has part interest not to be found in strictly chordal progressions. It is playable at all dynamic levels but, because the combined parts are not played as blocked chords, the results are best with the soft nuances.

EX. 109. *II. AIR from Water Music Suite*

Handel
Arr. by Hershy Kay

The following chordal parts for muted cornets are coupled effectively with a wood-wind tremolo, which provides a good background for the melodic instruments in the tenor register. Although the dynamic of *forte* is the same here for all parts, the cornets

133

should not cover up the wood winds or the melodic parts in the tenor brass. Actually, the added, duplicated, high wood-wind parts and the muted timbre of the cornets minimize the possibility.

EX. 110. *AMERICAN FOLK RHAPSODY:*

Four American Folk Songs

Clare E. Grundman

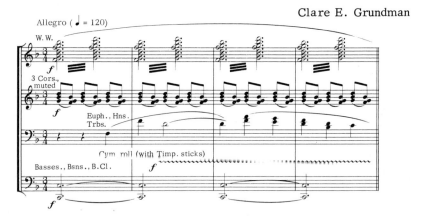

Cornets are also useful as supporting instruments. They lend tonal depth and/or strength to melodic ideas when doubled in unison or octaves with solo wood winds. The following excerpt places the cornet in its low range in unison with the alto saxophones.

Ex. 111. *EULOGY*

Joseph Wagner

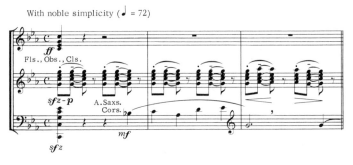

134

Another scoring plan finds the cornets in two or three parts in the regular treble register, with duplicating parts an octave higher in the wood winds. Sometimes, when possible, these chord extensions start with unison doubling of the cornets by the wood winds, the chords building upward from this lower range.

EX. 112. *BEAR DANCE*

Béla Bartók
Arr. by Erik Leidzen

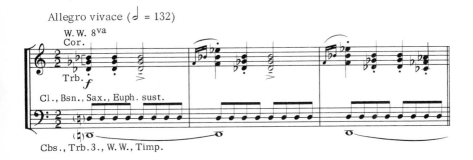

THE Bb TRUMPET

The trumpets[1] in the concert band have assumed a position somewhat similar to that of the cornets in the symphony orchestra; they function as supplementary instruments rather than as leading parts in the brass section. They are treated, for the most part, as an extra source of brilliance and tonal power. They figure prominently in fanfares, melodic lines, and figurations, where their incisiveness, power, and sharp attacks make them superior to the more lyric cornets.

The trumpet has a narrower bore than the cornet, which is semicylindrical. The mouthpiece used lies between the V-shaped one used for the horn and the cup-shaped one employed for the cornets. To a large degree these two factors account for whatever

---

[1] Other trumpets, particularly those in Eb, D, and F, and the bass trumpet in C or Bb, though scored by some European writers of band music, have not met with favor in America.

135

tonal difference exists between the cornet and the trumpet. Actually, these two instruments are more alike now than at any previous time in their development.

Only two trumpet parts are scored regularly for the modern concert band. Inasmuch as the principal high-brass parts are scored for the cornets in the soprano and alto ranges, it follows that the trumpets in the same registers must do considerable doubling, especially in *tuttis* for the full band. These doublings occur rather frequently as unisons or octaves for a forceful statement of important thematic material. Trumpets are also used as supporting instruments with the wood winds. The range analysis and playing characteristics mentioned for the cornet apply equally well to the trumpet.

The band repertory at mid-century includes a surprising number of interesting parts specifically for the trumpet, in addition to the conventional fanfare. In this connection, it is worth noting that a few composers[1] have written for trumpets, to the exclusion of the cornets, in some of their original works for the concert band.

This preference is reflected in the first excerpt for solo trumpet in a lyric style. It is a passage of infrequent occurrence in the band repertory. Notice the texture of the parts preceding and following the solo part. An impression of continuous flow is achieved by having the trumpet start on the last wood-wind notes. The soft entering chords in the last measure pick up the resumption of harmonic ideas effectively. (See Exs. 39, 68, and 131 for other excerpts of this movement.)

EX. 113. *II. RECITATIVE from West Point Suite*

Darius Milhaud

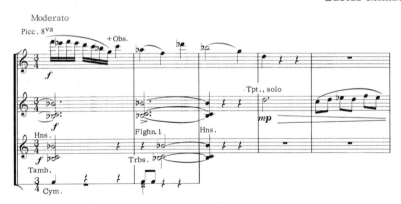

[1] George F. McKay, Darius Milhaud, and Walter Piston.

EX. 113 (continued)

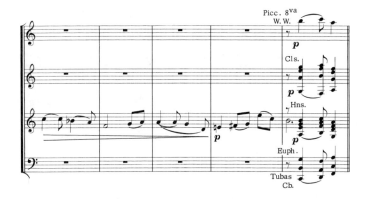

The next excerpt is the second entrance of a two-voice canon for tuba and trumpet. (See Ex. 164 for the first part of this *fugato*.)

EX. 114. *IV. BURLESQUE from Divertimento for Band*

Vincent Persichetti, Op. 42

In the last movement of the same work, the composer has given the leading melodic parts to two trumpets, without doubling. A polytonal effect is produced by combining the trumpets with a wood-wind tremolo.

EX. 115. *VI. MARCH from Divertimento for Band*

Vincent Persichetti, Op. 42

Detailed comparison of the next example with a similar one, Ex. 105, shows two basic changes to be considered. First, the figuration in Ex. 116 is in a higher *tessitura* and will, therefore, have greater brilliance. Second, the countermelody has been strengthened by the addition of the euphonium in a lower octave, and the afterbeats now include the second and third cornets. Thus, the change to trumpets here will ensure a more incisive melodic line.

EX. 116. *ARMENIAN DANCES, No. 1*

Aram Khachaturian
Arr. and edited by Ralph Satz

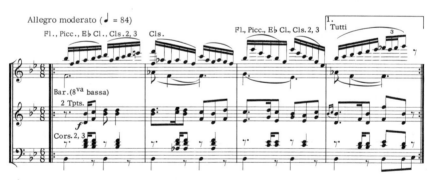

Occasionally the trumpet takes the leading part, to which wood winds are added to increase sonority and brilliance. This scoring plan has been used in Ex. 117 with good results.

138

EX. 117. *VIENNA 1913*

Bainbridge Crist

The trumpets are useful as supporting instruments when the cornets have other parts with the brass ensemble. In the following example, the trumpets double the reeds on the middle part of the three-octave melodic spread.

EX. 118. *AMERICAN JUBILEE, Overture*

Joseph Wagner

139

The trumpets are muted as frequently as are the cornets. Example 119 is a rare instance of a muted solo trumpet with no accompaniment other than the piccolo, which will sound an octave higher than written. This passage represents a symphonic composer's way of securing contrast.

EX. 119. *3 CAKEWALK from Carnival Suite*

Molto vivace (♩ = 160)   Alexander Tansman

Muted trumpets are likewise effective for sustained harmony parts. In this connection, it is significant to note that muted cornets, trumpets, horns, and/or trombones blend especially well with double reeds. When so combined, they form a homogeneous tonal grouping as distinctive as the two single-reed divisions. This kind of grouping, with three trumpets replacing the usual cornets, has been used by the composer of the next excerpt.

EX. 120. *II. MIDNIGHT SPECIAL from Railroaders Suite*

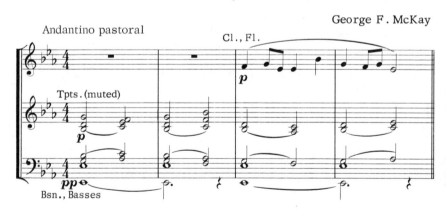

Andantino pastoral   George F. McKay

THE Bb FLUEGELHORN

The fluegelhorn represents the effort of the inventor Sax to provide a bugle-type instrument for the band. Its round, mellow tone is between that of the cornet and the baritone and is somewhat heavier and more sonorous than the standard cornet. Although its written and sounding compasses are the same as those of the cornet and trumpet, the highest-sounding fourth (F—Bb) is considered not to be in a practical playing range. For this reason, the fluegelhorn is generally scored as the mezzo-soprano voice of the brass choir.

Ordinarily, fluegelhorns are written in two parts, in the lower soprano and alto registers. With or without doubling, they bring a tonal warmth to lyric passages. All technical data given for the cornet is applicable to the fluegelhorn. *Note:* Mutes are not generally regarded as being practical for this instrument.

Very few American publications of band music have parts for the fluegelhorn. However, music for European, notably Italian, bands includes this instrument as an important solo voice in the soprano and mezzo-soprano ranges.

The three following excerpts have been selected to show the instrument in melodic and harmonic settings. Example 121 amply illustrates its *cantabile* potential in the alto *tessitura*. The fluegelhorn here has a rich, sonorous quality not associated with the cornet or trumpet. And this tone is just different enough from the accompanying horns to give character to the melody.

EX. 121. *V. TOLD AT SUNSET, Excerpts from Woodland Sketches*

Edward MacDowell
Arr. by Lucien Cailliet

Andante with pathos (♩ = 48)

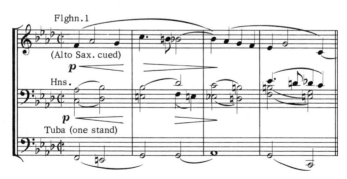

Examples 122a and 122b show how the fluegelhorns can be used for chords with other winds. Additional parts for the fluegelhorns are found in Exs. 113, 138, 166, and 172.

EX. 122. *III. FROM UNCLE REMUS,*

Excerpts from Woodland Sketches

Edward MacDowell
Arr. by Lucien Cailliet

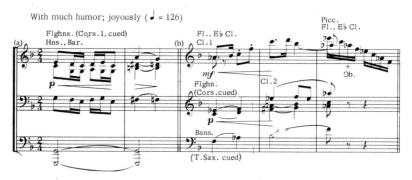

THE CORNETS AND TRUMPETS IN COMBINATION

Concert music for the band can have considerable part interest in the treble register, resulting from a skillful scoring of the cornets and trumpets. Quite a variety of settings for this combination are possible and at all dynamic levels. Many of the previous examples have included this combination but it has been a secondary consideration. The remaining excerpts in this chapter are devoted to this phase of scoring.

The analysis of the cornet stressed its lyric superiority; that for the trumpet focused on its incisiveness and power. These two characteristics are to be noted in the scoring of the next excerpt. In fact, the cornet-trumpet setting here constitutes a simple, but effective, model for the idiomatic usage of these two instruments. It can be expanded to include ways of combining them in future scoring plans.

142

EX. 123. *TRIUMPHAL MARCH*

Fast (♩ = 120)
Nicolas Miaskovsky

Example 124 shows a method of securing cumulative tonal strength. It is a device which can be applied successfully to the other sections of the band when a mounting power is desirable.

EX. 124. *1. MARDI GRAS from Carnival Suite*

Alexander Tansman

Cornets and trumpets are effective when used antiphonally. The echo effect, as in Ex. 125, has contrast value, especially when it is used to relieve heavy, thick textures and sonorities.

EX. 125. *BEOWULF, A Symphonic Sketch*

Bruce C. Beach

Cornets and trumpets are often combined for repeated chords in fast tempos. This grouping gives crisp, rhythmic vitality without a loss of controlled dynamics.

EX. 126. *3. ILE DE FRANCE from Suite Française*

Darius Milhaud

Example 127 illustrates a division of the cornets and trumpets for different melodic strands. The clarinet-cornet combination in the melody is standard procedure. So, too, is the oboe-muted-trumpet doubling. Notice that the unmuted cornets have the melody, while the muted trumpets play an *obbligato*, not vice versa!

Jaromir Weinberger
Arr. by Richard F. Goldman

These two high-brass instruments can occasionally be given unrelated parts which have individual interest and importance. The following example is such a case. The trumpets in octaves here stand out with telling strength.

EX. 128. *AMERICAN JUBILEE, Overture*

Joseph Wagner

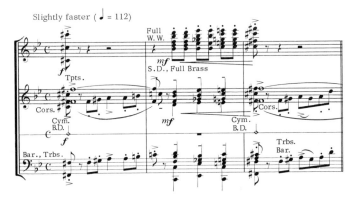

Fanfare flourishes have maximum brilliance when they are scored for the cornet-trumpet combination, as in Ex. 129. Delayed entrances, rather than unison doublings from the start, help to give them a cumulative thrust.

EX. 129. *FINALE from Symphony in B Flat*

Paul Fauchet
Revised by James R. Gillette

CHAPTER FOURTEEN

MIDDLE-RANGE BRASS INSTRUMENTS

Horn - Alto Horn - Melophone - Tenor Horn

RANGES, CLEFS, AND TRANSPOSITIONS

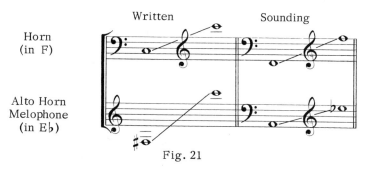

Fig. 21

Note: The lowest third of the horn in F is of little value in scoring music for the band, since these notes are not playable for the alto horn and melophone in E♭ which, as we have seen, play transposed F horn parts. Although occasional band parts for the horn in F are written in the bass clef, the practice is not widespread, since most nonprofessional players are unfamiliar with it.

The so-called tenor horn more correctly belongs to the tuba family. It has a semiconical bore and a set of valves and is played from an upright position. This instrument, used by some nineteenth-century composers of orchestral music, has not received very serious attention from writers of band music.

THE HORN IN F

The horn has a very long tubing, small in diameter, with a conical bore. It is coiled in a circle as a practical expedient. The use of a special funnel-shaped mouthpiece is an important factor in the production of its unique tone, although this mouthpiece is admittedly more difficult to control than the cup-shaped ones used for all the other brass instruments.

The first horns (natural and valveless) used for instrumental music were developed from the hunting horn. A set of crooks (tubular slides of different lengths) was inserted into the instrument, thereby establishing different series of fundamentals and keyed pitches which covered the circle of keys. Later, with the nineteenth-century invention of valves, the horn became a chromatic instrument rather than a diatonic one. (A detailed study of the horn and its evolution as an orchestral instrument can be found in the author's *Orchestration: A Practical Handbook*.)

From these rather complex beginnings, the *single* horn in F has emerged as standard for most ensemble work, including the band. This present-day instrument comes equipped with an E♭ crook which, when substituted for the one in F, makes transposition unnecessary for the reading of parts in E♭. A new *double* horn in F is gradually supplanting the single instrument. This double horn has a rotary valve which can throw the instrument into B♭. This fundamental gives the player more open tones [1] (tones played without fingered positions of the valves) than does the single horn and also extends the range, both high and low, by a fifth. The double horn also has the advantage of lessening the tension needed for playing range extremes.

It is, then, the horn in F that will be the chief concern of the band scorer, except when the transcription of orchestral music necessitates adaptations of horn and trumpet parts in many different keyed pitches. Although the rule given earlier for determining the intervals of transposition remains valid for most of the natural horn and trumpet parts, it cannot be applied successfully to all of them. Therefore, the student who is unfamiliar with this phase of orchestration should consult Chaps. 18 and 20 in the author's *Orchestration: A Practical Handbook*, where a full explanation of the perplexing matter is given, along with illustrative examples.

The horn, as distinguished from the alto horn or mellophone, is a middle-range instrument which serves as a tonal connecting link between the wood-wind and brass choirs. Its full, rich tone, with a slightly less precise attack than that of the other brass instruments, is perfect for supporting the wood winds, either separately or collectively. Although the horn is primarily an instrument

---

[1] Open tones on the horn require an extremely good embouchure, a combination of lip tension and blowing force.

with great sustaining potential, it can sound surprisingly clear and vigorous in rapid passages. Horn tone differs from that of other brass in that it is rounder, mellower, and more expressive. Accents are less sharp and biting: there is strength and weight without coarseness.

The tonal niche of the horn in the band deserves careful attention and understanding. It is an excellent solo instrument, ideal for supporting the wood winds, melodically or harmonically, and useful for middle harmony parts (fillers) with brass chords. Its firm tone quality carries well at all dynamic levels, either unaccompanied or with harmonic backgrounds played by the wood winds. The results are somewhat less satisfactory with the brass unless compensating dynamics and/or chord spacings are arranged accordingly. Since horn tone is less cutting and edgy than that of the other brass in its range, it is highly desirable to have important solo parts uncluttered by heavier timbres—brass or percussion.

The construction of the horn, its uniquely shaped mouthpiece, and its over-all range, exceeding that of any other brass instrument, pose something of a problem for the player of this instrument. These factors have caused horn players to specialize in medium-to-high or medium-to-low parts. This practice has led to a division of parts not encountered with any other wind instrument. Accordingly, parts for a horn quartet are written ordinarily as follows: high, I-III; low, II-IV, the voice parts not corresponding to the numerical order on the score page. This style of notation is shown in Fig. 22.

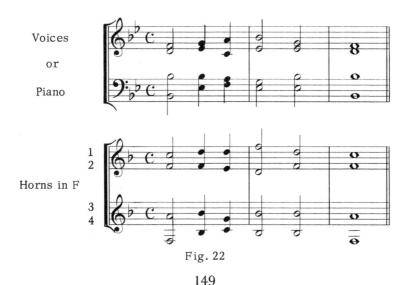

Fig. 22

149

The irregular instrumentation found in small bands has had a direct effect upon the voice allocation of horn parts by those interested in practical band scoring. Small bands—school and municipal bands or special military units—often have only two horns, sometimes three. With possible uncertainty of numbers, it is wisest for the scorer to select the best intervals of chords for the first and second parts, leaving the inside fill-in notes for the third horn. Then the part for the fourth horn may double the second or third horn, in unison, or be given a fourth chord tone, depending upon the harmonic texture of the passage. Chord progressions sound smoothest when there is a minimum of skips, with each part moving to nearest positions of chord tones; they frequently appear in close position.

Range Divisions

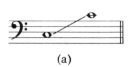

(a)

The lowest augmented fourth of this octave, starting on F, is noticeably weaker in carrying power than the middle or higher ranges, and this tonal difference prevails in loud passages, regardless of the dynamics or unison doubling. This range also presents intonation difficulties for the average player. For these reasons, the notes in the lower half of this register are more satisfactory when played either by the trombone or the euphonium. So-called pedal tones (fundamentals of each harmonic series) are excluded from use in the band as being ineffective. The upper part of this low octave falls naturally into the parts of the second and fourth horns. *Note*: The bass clef is used ordinarily for the lowest written notes in this octave in orchestration; G below middle C is the best starting written note in the treble clef for the horns in band scoring.

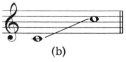

(b)

Horn tone has more authority and expressiveness, starting with this octave. Here, its evenness of tone makes it ideal for melody or harmony parts. Sustained chord tones or intervals with little or no movement are exceptionally effective as tonal pivots. Tempo, tessitura, and dynamics are important factors in determining the duration of the sustained tones. Of course, this is true for all wind instruments, including the horns. Very long, sustained, low tones require less lip pressure than higher ones. Also, loud dynamics require more breath than the softer levels.

150

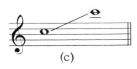

(c)

This octave is used almost exclusively by the first horn, with occasional support from the third part. It is the most eloquent range of the instrument and has real power for stating important thematic material The top fourth of this octave demands a firm embouchure and good breath control; these factors combine to make it a precarious *tessitura* for the average player using a single three-valve horn.

It should not be inferred from this resume that the second and fourth horns do not have occasional parts in the high octave, or that the first and third horns are not capable of playing in the lowest octave. In theory, the horns should have the same range freedom as do the other instruments. However, it is safest to avoid range extremes in practical scoring for the horns, while admitting some overlapping of ranges whenever advantageous to do so.

THE E♭ ALTO HORN AND THE E♭ MELOPHONE

The E♭ alto horn belongs to the saxhorn family, as determined by its bore and mouthpiece. In appearance, it resembles the familiar upright baritone and is about half its size. The melophone is shaped like the horn; otherwise it is the same as the alto horn. Both alto instruments have fingerings similar to that of the cornet and both are much easier to play than the horn. This practical matter of comparative grades of technical difficulty accounts for the widespread use of the melophone in many amateur bands.

Mixing horns with altos or mellophones poses a problem for the band director. The tone quality of the altos is definitely inferior to that of the horns, and any unison doubling by the two types thickens the sonority. In addition, their respective bells point in different directions.

The alto horns do not possess tonal beauty, expressiveness, or strength of the same degree as do the horns. Rather, their tonal characteristics may be regarded as similar to those of the cornet, but extended to the low alto register. They are strictly band instruments, used as practical substitutes for the horns.

The playing styles cited for the horns are also used for the altos. Hand stopping or muting is generally unsatisfactory and often disregarded in performance. Alto horns are preferred by some directors of marching bands because they are more easily used in performance.

Many of the examples used to illustrate the instruments of the wood-wind section have also contained parts for the horns in many playing styles. The supplementary excerpts given here show additional parts and further idiomatic usages of the horn.

When used as a solo instrument in the band, the horn retains much of its lyric expressiveness as it does in the orchestra. This quality is well represented in the opening unaccompanied passage in the following excerpt from a condensed score.[1]

EX. 130. *II.NOCTURNE from Symphony in B Flat*

The unaccompanied excerpt for horns in the next example comes between short answering phrases which are scored for the brass and low wood winds in chordal style. The passage carries out the intent of the title as given at the beginning of the movement.

---

[1] All illustrations for the horn which follow are excerpts from condensed scores with a sounding notation.

152

EX. 131. *II.RECITATIVE from West Point Suite*

Darius Milhaud

Moderato

Hns.1, 2

mf energico

Hns. 3,4

Themes with a strong rhythmic character acquire tonal profile when scored for horns in unison. This device, so common in orchestration, requires a quite different approach in the band, for the background sonorities and tonal strengths must be weaker than the horns if a suitable balance is to be achieved. In Ex. 132, the high rhythmic treble is scored for flutes and the high clarinets. Note the dynamic adjustment.

EX. 132. *I.OVERTURE from Symphony in B Flat*

Paul Fauchet

Allegro, molto deciso (♩ = 120)   Revised by James R. Gillette

Fls., E♭Cl., Cls.

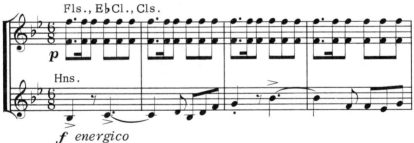

p

Hns.

f energico

Unison solo horns are also used for sustained melodic passages. The composer of the next excerpt alternates phrases for horns, starting in measure 56, with those for the euphonium and saxophone. The dynamics have been arranged to permit easy interplay of these melodic ideas.

EX. 133. *A SOLEMN MUSIC*

Virgil Thomson

Solo horn duets which follow interval patterns derived from the open tones of the natural horn (mostly thirds, fifths, and sixths) are quite common. They appear either in brass fanfares or as sustained melody parts, as in Ex. 134.

EX. 134. *CZECH RHAPSODY*   Jaromir Weinberger
                                                   Arr. by Richard F. Goldman

A few of the previous quotations from condensed scores have
shown the horn's potential for acting as a tonal pivot by means
of sustained tones (see Exs. 62 and 76). This effect can be accomplished by using stationary tones, intervals, or chords, or the
part may have minimum movement of independent interest. The
horn is unsurpassed for this purpose, especially when the texture
is quasi-contrapuntal. An application of this principle to a passage
having three separate strands of independent parts is shown in
the next example.

EX. 135. *IV. GIGUE from Concerto Grosso*

                                                          Joseph Wagner

Muted or stopped horns present something of a practical problem in band scoring, since horn parts sometimes are played by mellophones or alto horns, on which muting is impractical. Possibly this may account for the comparatively few muted-horn parts in the band repertory.

Two techniques are available for muting the horns. The most common technique consists of inserting a straight mute in the bell (*con sordino*), as in Ex. 136. A second method has the hand far into the bell, as in Ex. 137. Here a cross (+) indicates hand mutings; a circle (o) indicates open tones.

A more detailed discussion of muting is given in Chap. 24.

EX. 136. *I. JOHN HENRY from Railroad Suite*

Lyndol Mitchell

EX. 137. *FANFARE AND ALLEGRO*

Clifton Williams

Horns have long been typed for the afterbeats[1] of dance forms and marches. They are idiomatically suitable for this function when the parts remain in the middle register. Other winds are occasionally coupled with the horns when chord extensions are necessary. (More detailed data is given on this subject in Chap. 26 under the heading of Dance Forms.) The following examples have several settings for the horns with afterbeats. The rhythm parts in Ex. 138 have been scored for horns 2-3-4. The muted fluegelhorn on the melodic line is most unusual.

EX. 138. *LA BELLE HELENE Overture*

Offenbach
Trans. by Felix Greissle

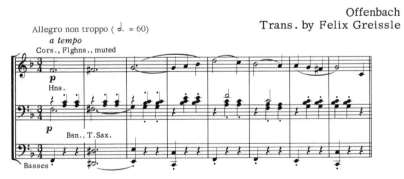

[1] The term "afterbeats," as used here, refers to intervals and/or chords which occur on the weak parts of beats or measures to complete characteristic rhythmic patterns.

157

EX. 139a. *THE HIDDEN FORTRESS*

Anthony Donato

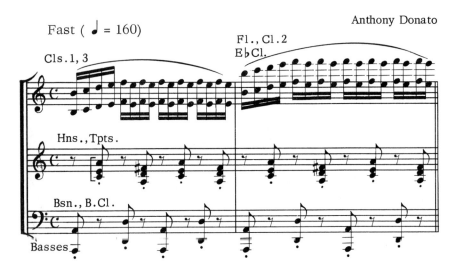

EX. 139b. *THE HIDDEN FORTRESS*

Anthony Donato

EX. 140. *TWO GERMAN DANCES, No. 1*

Beethoven
Arr. by Howard Kilbert

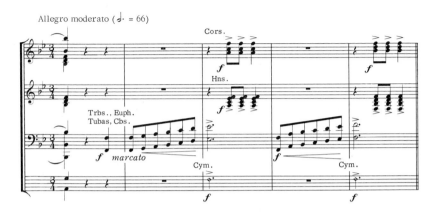

Before leaving the study of the horn, it is important to review its other potentials as illustrated in Exs. 10, 12, 13, 26, 35, 41, 43, 46, 59, 62, 65, 66, and 74. These excerpts should be reexamined for the discovery of other idiomatic playing styles and usages which can then be integrated with the more specialized ones given in this section. Muted horn parts are indicated in Exs. 4, 9, and 55.

CHAPTER FIFTEEN

LOW-RANGE BRASS INSTRUMENTS

Tenor Trombone - Bass Trombone - Euphonium - Baritone - Tuba

THE TROMBONES

WRITTEN AND SOUNDING RANGES

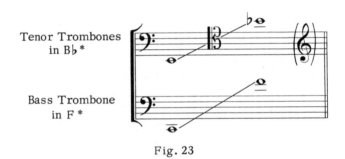

Tenor Trombones
in Bb *

Bass Trombone
in F *

Fig. 23

The use of the tenor clef, as a means of avoiding excessive ledger lines for high trombone parts, is desirable but not always practical, since many amateur players are not familiar with it. Undoubtedly, this situation will improve as more student players are taught to read it along with the bass clef.

As a practical expedient, tenor trombone parts are sometimes given in the treble clef (written a major ninth higher than they sound) to eliminate reading difficulties arising when cornet or trumpet players change over to the trombone.

The alto clef (middle C on the third line), as used for the alto trombone prior to the mid-nineteenth century, is of interest to the band scorer primarily in connection with band transcriptions of orchestral music.

* Non-transposing in the bass clef.

THE Bb TENOR TROMBONE

The slide trombone is a fully developed descendant of the medieval sackbut. It is the only wind instrument which can be manipulated to make all gradations of pitch. Stringed instruments with finger boards are also in this category. Variations of pitch in the slide trombone are regulated by means of slide positions which alter the length of the vibrating air column within the tube.

In construction, the trombone resembles the trumpet in that its bore is two-thirds cylindrical and one-third conical. Since the tubing of the Bb tenor trombone is twice as long as that of the trumpet, its fundamental is an octave lower in pitch. The shape of the mouthpiece is similar for both instruments.

The technical aspects of the slide positions are unique among the wind instruments. The other brass instruments produce a cycle of changing fundamentals and harmonic series by means of valve or piston combinations. The trombone accomplishes identical changes by means of altered slide positions. There are seven positions of the slide for the completion of a chromatic scale. Figure 24 lists slide positions, along with their corresponding fundamentals and harmonic series.

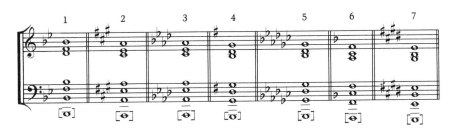

Fig. 24

In the first position, the slide is pulled up tight and then extended proportionately for the other six positions. These extended positions are not marked in any way; their accuracy depends entirely upon the ear and hand of the player. Adjacent positions can be taken almost instantaneously; others farther apart, require split seconds for their execution. Rapid passages requiring awkward slide positions should be avoided, since they are not playable with any degree of style, clarity, or good intonation (see Fig. 25).

161

CHANGING SLIDE POSITIONS

Fig. 25

On the other hand, rapid notes contained in one harmonic series do not need altered slide positions and are fairly easy to produce in most tempos.

CHANGING NOTES IN ONE POSITION

Fig. 26

Range Divisions

(a)

These bottom three notes require good breath control and are insecure both in attack and intonation for the average player. This is particularly true when a light attack is sought.

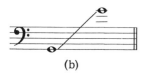

(b)

All the notes in this range are of excellent quality at all dynamic levels.

(c)

These three top notes should be avoided by all but experienced players. They require a well-trained ear plus a firm embouchure. The notes in the fifth above, starting on high B♭, are possible but beyond the realm of practical scoring for the band.

The trombones of the band are divided regularly into three parts, with occasional subdivisions in the first part, as with the cornets. These divisions overlap in the alto and tenor registers in the regular first and second parts with the third part remaining

162

mostly in the low tenor and bass ranges. Pedal notes (the fundamentals of each slide position) are of little value in the band as the tubas can produce these notes with far greater security and better intonation.

The bands of some European countries employ valve trombones in place of the more familiar slide model. The valve trombone produces its complete chromatic scale as do the other brass instruments. Both types of trombone have identical ranges and similar tone qualities. Although the valve trombone has some technical advantages over the slide instrument, it has not had wide acceptance by American instrumentalists.

THE BASS TROMBONE

The most commonly used bass trombone in America is pitched in F, a perfect fourth lower than the tenor instrument. Its first position has the same fundamental and harmonic series as that given for the sixth position of the tenor trombone in Fig. 24. The bass trombone has about three feet more tubing than does the tenor instrument and for this reason requires increased breath and embouchure control.

There is also a bass trombone built in B♭, which has a rotary device for changing the fundamental to F and a slide for lowering it to E. An F attachment for tenor trombones starts the range on C, while the E slide begins with B. Bass trombones are also built with other fundamentals, notably the one in G. This instrument can be found in some European and many English bands. All bass trombones are written in the bass clef and are non-transposing instruments.

The technical data given for the tenor trombone is applicable to the bass instrument. However, the more rapid tonguing styles for the latter are fatiguing and become sluggish, especially in the lowest register. The deep, full tone of the bass trombone makes it ideally suited to the bass parts of brass ensemble passages. Extremely rapid passages are more satisfactorily played by the smaller and lighter tenor instrument.

In scoring for the trombones, the scorer should not count on the availability of the bass trombone, desirable as it is for the band. This possibility should not be ignored, as the absence of the instrument can cause a serious problem. For example, chords might be positioned to give the bass trombone notes not playable by the tenor instrument. These notes must then be either inverted, omitted, or given to some other instrument. Should they be played

by a tenor trombone in an inverted position (played an octave higher than written), the chord positions become distorted. The other
two alternatives are equally bad. The band scorer who writes for
the bass trombone in the range below that of the tenor instrument
must be prepared for these eventualities. Figure 27 illustrates
how chords can become distorted if the bottom notes are inverted
an octave.

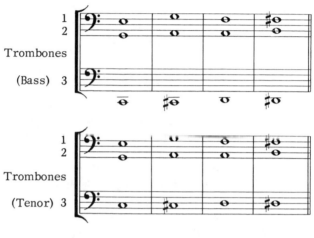

Fig. 27

THE TROMBONES IN COMBINATION

Hector Berlioz, in his monumental *Treatise on Instrumentation,*
referred to the trombones as "group instruments." This descrip-
tion is as pertinent for band scoring as for orchestration. The
trombones reach their maximum potential when they are playing
as a unit, either melodically or harmonically.

This characteristic is to be noted especially in connection with
the trombone as a solo instrument. Band music contains relatively
few strictly solo passages for *a single instrument.* Strangely e-
nough, the most extraordinary exception to this can be found in
the second movement of the Grand Symphony for Band, by Hector
Berlioz. This was an unprecedented work in the nineteenth century. The entire movement is scored for solo trombone with band
accompaniment. Examples 141a and 141b are excerpts from the
Recitative, the Prayer section being an extended lyrical movement,
appropriately eloquent but subdued. Another example of the trombone solo can be found in the Nocturne movement of Paul Fauchet's
Symphony in B Flat.

EX. 141a. *II. RECITATIVE AND PRAYER,*
  from Grand Symphony for Band, Funeral and Triumphal

Berlioz, Op. 15
Revised and edited by Richard F. Goldman

EX. 141b. *II. RECITATIVE AND PRAYER,*
  from Grand Symphony for Band, Funeral and Triumphal

Berlioz, Op. 15
Revised and edited by Richard F. Goldman

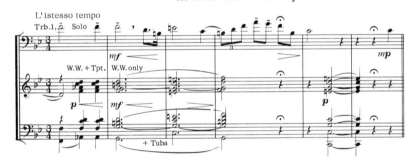

Solo parts for the trombones as a unit are, of course, both numerous and effective. There appears to be no apparent limit to the style of these parts, as they range from lyric phrases with considerable expressiveness to rhythmic tunes with suitable zest. The next excerpt illustrates the latter style with the tune in the high tenor register.

165

EX. 142. *3. CAKEWALK from Carnival Suite*

Alexander Tansman

The only true trombone *legato* phrasing is made by a lip slur applied only to notes in the high register of each harmonic series. All other *legato* phrasings are the result of lip slurs combined with changing slide positions. This technique produces a *portamento* style of *legato*, which is least good when used with rapid notations. Short slurs are preferable to long ones, as a general rule.

The next two examples illustrate *legato* styles for the trombones. The first one written by Milhaud, places the first and second trombones on a melodic line in octaves which span the instrument's tenor range. The tenor drum[1] is appropriately muffled here.

---

[1] A deep field drum.

Darius Milhaud

The second excerpt has a more sustained *legato* style which, it should be noted, is supporting the octave melody in the high treble. This is a device which is used quite frequently in band scoring. The broken chords here are scored for divided Bb clarinets.

EX. 144. *II. NOCTURNE from Symphony in B Flat*

Paul Fauchet
Rescored by F. Campbell-Watson

167

Unslurred *cantabile* melodies are played by tonguing each note. These notes can be connected in a characteristic style approximating the *legato* effect and at all dynamic levels. In the softer nuances, the tone is firm, but as if intoned. In the louder ones, trombone unisons or octaves are penetratingly strong and vigorous. This style is particularly effective for the emphasis of important thematic material which, in Ex. 145, is in the form of an *obbligato*.[1]

EX. 145. *SUNDAY MORNING AT GLION*

from By the Lake of Geneva

Franz Bendel
Trans. by F. Campbell-Watson

Unslurred unison or octave passages for the trombones, frequently paired with cornets and/or trumpets, are decidedly forceful as their combined sonorities have power and brilliance. Occasional passages of this kind introduce an element of contrast which is highly desirable in concert music for the band.

_____

[1] Examples 108 and 124 include <u>obbligato</u> parts for the trombones.

168

EX. 146. *THE HIDDEN FORTRESS*

Anthony Donato

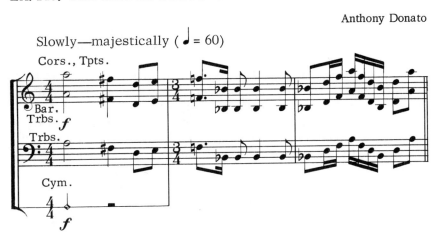

The trombones, as a unit, are indispensable for harmony parts in all styles. As such, they are often combined or alternated with the horns and/or cornet-trumpet units both to furnish contrast and to accommodate changing *tessituras*. However, chord positions directly affect the clarity and sonority of chord progressions for the trombones and should, therefore, receive special consideration.

Fundamental positions, with roots below C in the bass clef, sound thick and unclear.[1] Doubling the root an octave lower is of some help in relieving this condition, but it cannot remove the cause. First inversions in this register should also be avoided for the same reason. Second inversions, with the fifths in the bass, are less objectionable and are used occasionally for special effects made by the movement of blocked chords in this position.

Close-position chords placed in the tenor-baritone register sound extremely well with all dynamics but can be especially powerful in loud passages. Spreading the tones out in open position, spanning the tenor-bass registers, tends to disperse the sound. This is particularly well suited to passages with soft dynamics, where unit strength is not required. Chord progressions are smoothest in both positions when the movement of each voice is by nearest chord tones, with common tones being retained whenever possible.

[1] Chord placement is discussed fully in Chap. 25 .

169

The trombones of the band sustain harmony parts as regularly as the horns and with equally good results. Illustrations of this scoring device will be found in Exs. 42, 50, 73, and 102. Repeated chords are also idiomatically effective for the trombones, as shown in Ex. 26.

The trombones are good supporting instruments for melodic passages which are non-*legato* in style and set at loud dynamic levels. They are not used often for lyric bass parts, which require extended *legato* phrasing with soft nuances. Example 147 is somewhat unusual in that the melodic bass is for brass instruments only, the usual doubling reeds having an independent counterpoint.

EX. 147. *IV. GIGUE from Concerto Grosso*

Joseph Wagner

The following examples have been selected to illustrate varying styles of chord progressions as scored for the trombones. Example 148 is an illustration of unit playing in close position in the tenor range but at a soft dynamic level and without doubling.

170

EX. 148. *AMERICAN JUBILEE, Overture*

Joseph Wagner

The next excerpt has two-part interest. First, it shows an ascending range build-up in the brass to increase spread and volume for the *crescendo*. Second, it demonstrates one method of adjusting the trombone parts to accommodate the interchange of the harmony and bass parts in the tenor register, starting at N. These parts have been bracketed.

EX. 149. *WAKE ME UP FOR THE GREAT JUBILEE,*
Variations on an old American Song

George F. McKay

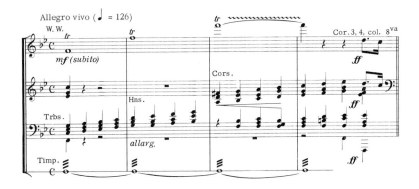

EX. 149 (continued)

The familiar rhythmic afterbeat patterns, generally associated with military marches, are frequently used in concert music for the band. These chords, usually scored for the horns, are often alternated with the trombones, either open or muted. This change frees the horns for melodic or harmonic parts in other styles without any loss of character in the rhythmic structure. The next two examples illustrate this disposition of the trombones for both styles of music.[1] Example 151 has a four-part division of the trombones.

EX. 150. *THE PRIDE O' THE LAND, National 4-H Club March*

Edwin Franko Goldman

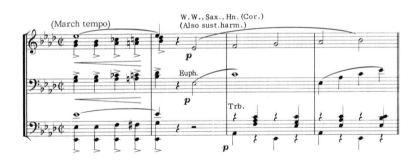

[1] Additional parts in this category are included in Exs. 34, 102, and 117.

EX. 151. *AMERICAN OVERTURE FOR BAND*

Joseph Wilcox Jenkins

The third trombone is sometimes used for bass parts with the
tubas when the euphonium is not available for this purpose. This
alternative in scoring is indicated in the next excerpt.[1]

EX. 152. *VIENNA 1913*

Bainbridge Crist

[1] A melodic and harmonic division of the trombones is shown in Ex. 20.

173

Finally, a word of caution is given here concerning an unusual aspect of the trombone's technical agility. The instrument should be scored idiomatically and not as an auxiliary euphonium or as a bass wood wind. The reason for this is perfectly obvious when one considers the slide technique of the trombone versus the keyed, valve or piston fingering of the other wind instruments. This peculiarity of the trombone accounts for its idiomatic playing styles and for much of its phrasing as well. Its technical limitation affects its execution of very rapid scale passages, diatonic or chromatic. Although no infallible rule can be given, some accepted practices can be offered as a safe guide and model.

The average trombone player can effectively manage three or four notes to one beat when that unit does not exceed the M.M. of 120-126, as in the following familiar excerpt.

EX. 153. *THE STARS AND STRIPES FOREVER*

John Philip Sousa
Arr. by Lucien Cailliet

The practicality of rapid note successions for the trombones may be further clarified by differentiating between passages with no or few changes of slide positions and those with several or many changes. An illustration of the former is given in Ex. 154a, and of the latter in Ex. 154b. The average player has little difficulty with repeated notes of the same pitch; difficulties arise in passages with rapid note changes of different pitches where awkward slide positions are required. (Review Figs. 24, 25 and 26.)

174

Example 154b, played non-*legato*, may be considered as a safe model. The storm section in the *William Tell* overture by Rossini also constitutes a good model where four notes to a beat are involved: ♩ =108.

EX. 154a. *CARIBBEAN CARNIVAL*

David Bennett

EX. 154b. *CARIBBEAN CARNIVAL*

David Bennett

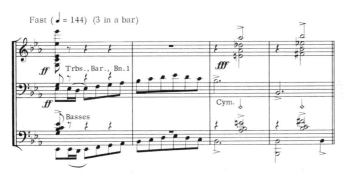

The last example graphically illustrates an idiomatic adaptation of very rapid scale passages for the strings and wood winds of an orchestra for the wood winds and brass of the concert band. Scales of this kind, at this or similar fast tempos, should never be scored literally for the trombones. Notice that the trombones here are confined solely to repeated chords. This *tutti* scoring may serve as an excellent model for future scoring for the full band, to be done in conjunction with the *Reference Chart of Keyboard Idioms and Patterns* (see Chap. 26).

175

EX. 155. *ITALIAN IN ALGIERS, Overture*

Rossini
Trans. by Lucien Cailliet

Allegro ($\quad$ = 138)

THE BARITONE AND THE EUPHONIUM (both in B♭)

RANGES, CLEFS, AND TRANSPOSITIONS

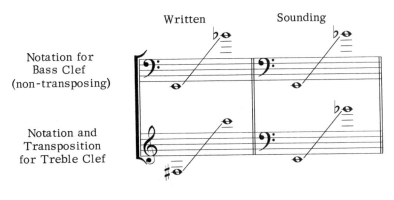

Written   Sounding

Notation for
Bass Clef
(non-transposing)

Notation and
Transposition
for Treble Clef

Fig. 28

THE B♭ BARITONE

The baritone, a member of the saxhorn family, has a tenor-bass range, and is pitched in B♭ with the same compass as the tenor trombone. Its position in the band is quite similar to that of the violoncello in the orchestra, since its functions and most of its range cover the same general area.

The baritone is built with three valves and played with fingerings that are identical to those for the cornet. It has a broad, melodious tone somewhat allied to those of the horns and trombones but with less distinctive richness. However, the baritone is a valuable band instrument because of its superior technical facility, fine blending potentials, and even tone throughout most of its compass. In this respect, it resembles the cornets, in that its parts can have a similar melodic and rhythmic content and importance.

The great majority of published music for the band is written for a single baritone part, with relatively few works indicating a two-part division. Although an occasional use of a baritone *divisi* may be justified, more or less continuous dividing thickens the texture and sonority beyond safe levels of artistic standards. Over-doubling the part may also cause problems of balance which should be considered by the band scorer. He can anticipate this situation

177

by indicating in the part the number of players which seems necessary and appropriate for the character of each passage. Failure to include this directive could lead to distortion of an otherwise well-balanced score.

Some players of the baritone, recruited from the ranks of the cornet section, are unfamiliar with the bass clef. Accordingly, publishers of band music issue separate parts for the baritone in both the treble and bass clefs. (Parts in the treble clef are written a major ninth higher than they sound, the same as for the B♭ bass clarinet and tenor saxophone.) However, baritone parts in the full score are ordinarily written in the bass clef. Although the very highest notes of the baritone can be correctly written in the tenor clef, it is inadvisable to do so, as the great majority of players are unfamiliar with this clef.

THE EUPHONIUM

The standard euphonium has three valves and is similar to the baritone, except that its larger bore makes for a rounder, more resonant tone. Models are made with an upright bell or in a bell-front position.

Some euphoniums are obtainable with a fourth valve which eliminates faulty scale gaps, improves tone quality, and increases its range in the lowest register by an augmented fourth. However, as this newer model has not as yet replaced the older one, it is unwise to extend the range for its parts beyond those given in Fig. 28. Although the names and parts of the baritone and euphonium are used interchangeably, the majority of published scores list only the baritone in the instrumentation.

Range Divisions

The range divisions previously given for the tenor trombone apply equally well to the baritone and euphonium. However, range extremes are somewhat easier and more reliable for the valve instruments. Their low octave is used mostly for bass parts, either melodic or harmonic, and only rarely for solo passages. The high octave has a full, round tone which carries well for melodic lines, *obbligatos*, and figurations.

Although the compasses of the baritone and the trombone are the same, we have seen one specific way in which their playing styles differ in Ex. 155. Further differences between these two instruments may be summed up as follows: the valve technique of the baritone makes it the preferred instrument in its range for

178

flowing *legato* phrases, harmonic figurations with large chromatic skips (notes not in a single harmonic series), and *staccato* passages in many forms.

Many of the previous examples have included parts for the baritone, but as secondary points of consideration. Of this number, the following should be restudied with the baritone as the instrument of major importance: Exs. 13, 14, 25, 34, 38, 42, 43, 50, 56, 58, 107, 108, 110, 113, 126, 127, 140, and 147. These excerpts show the baritone functioning in the following ways: supporting other instruments with melodic phrases, *obbligatos*, and scale passages; sustaining harmonic elements; carrying the bass parts, with or without the tuba; and filling in harmonic gaps with arpeggiated chords. Now it remains to examine a few more parts for the baritone as the leading solo instrument of the ensemble.

Baritone solos are much more frequent in concert music for the band than are trombone solos. This is because the baritone occupies the same relative position in the tenor-bass register as that held by the cornet in the treble range. Following are three excerpts from solo passages for the baritone. In this connection, it will be noted that the tenor range is used almost exclusively. Another point to be considered concerns the timbre of the accompanying parts.

The profile of melodic lines is clearest when the solo part has a contrasting timbre with, or a heavier tonal weight than the harmony parts. In the Creston excerpt (Ex. 156), both timbre and tonal weight serve to highlight the solo baritone. Note here also that the divided Bb clarinets are arranged to give a continuous repetition of the triplets but with a *legato* effect.

EX. 156. *LEGEND*

Paul Creston

EX. 156 (continued)

Cb. (pizz.), Tuba

It will be observed that the solo baritone in Ex. 157 crosses the sustained chords in the horns. The heavier tonal weight of the solo instrument makes this scoring possible. This arrangement would be decidedly less satisfactory if these harmony parts were played by trombones. The melodic profile would, of course, be more pronounced if the chords had been given to the reeds (see Ex. 158). The bassoon-horn combination is an excellent way in which to suggest the effect of a homogeneous timbre.

EX. 157. *III. RONDO from Royce Hall Suite*

Healey Willan
Edited and scored by William Teague

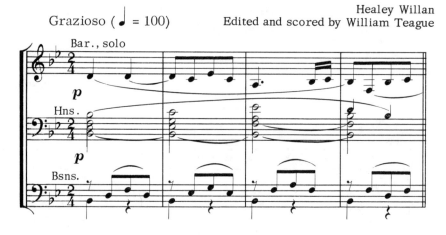

180

The euphonium solo in Ex. 158 has good tonal profile for the melody which is doubly important in this instance, inasmuch as it serves to introduce a theme for a set of variations. It is the only brass instrument in the ensemble.

EX. 158. *WAKE ME UP FOR THE GREAT JUBILEE*
Variations on an Old American Song
George F. McKay

Much early concert music for the band had the baritone typed for *arpeggios* as standard procedure. Mid-twentieth-century styles in composition have somewhat changed the value of this device and its scoring. *Arpeggios* are now scored more frequently for the lighter reeds rather than for the heavier baritone. Nevertheless, the baritone is still a useful instrument for the purpose, if it is not overdone. The *staccato arpeggios* in the next excerpt illustrate one of many patterns.

EX. 159. *III. SCHERZO from Symphony in B Flat*

Paul Fauchet
Rescored by F. Campbell-Watson

Some of the previous illustrations dealing with *obbligatos* included the baritone as a doubling instrument. The advisability of doing this must, of course, be determined by the total sonority level of each passage. The light reed-horn combination, used in the next example for the principal parts, permits the baritone *obbligato* to be heard clearly without doubling.

EX. 160. *POLKA AND FUGUE from the Opera*
Schwanda, the Bagpiper

Allegro moderato

Jaromir Weinberger
Arr. by Glenn Cliffe Bainum

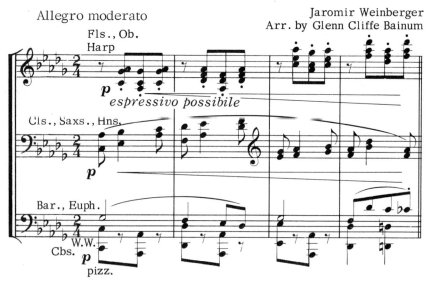

The baritone is preferable to the trombone for the scoring of bass parts with scale or chordal figurations. The reasons for this have been given previously. These same reasons apply here (Ex. 161), where a soft, *legato* phrasing is required. The bassoon doubling is a secondary consideration in this instance, it adds reedy quality to the baritone, but does not alter its tonal weight.

EX. 161. *E. F. G. OVERTURE*

Philip James

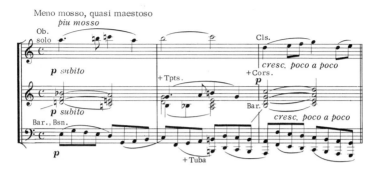

The next example continues the study of figurations, but in a different style and at a different dynamic level. The running eighth notes would be weak and ineffectual without the baritone. Important voice lines usually require the support of a brass instrument if they are to be heard in *tuttis* louder than *piano*.

EX. 162. *IN THE CATHEDRAL*

Gabriel Pierné
Trans. by Irving Cheyette

THE TUBAS

The E♭ Tuba - The BB♭ Tuba - The Sousaphone

WRITTEN AND SOUNDING RANGES

E♭ Tuba
E♭ Sousaphone
(Three Valve)

BB♭ Tuba[1]
BB♭ Sousaphone
(Three Valve)

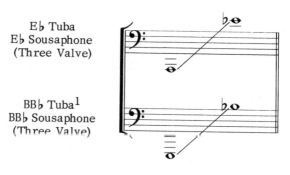

Fig. 29

The tubas are the lowest bass instruments of the saxhorn family. Their tube length is approximately twice that of the baritone and trombone and four times longer than that of either the cornet or the trumpet. This longer tube length places the fundamental of the tubas an octave below that of the baritone and trombone, and two octaves lower than that of the cornet and trumpet.

The instrument's very large conical bore, along with its equally large mouthpiece, produces a full, round, mellow tone with depth and firmness. Although the tubas require an enormous amount of breath to produce sound, they have much technical facility and are surprisingly flexible for dynamic changes.

The tubas for the band vary in size, shape, and construction. The small tuba is pitched in E♭, while the larger one has a fundamental of BB♭. These dissimilar pitched fundamentals determine the ranges of the tubas and, to some extent, the method of writing for them, as we shall see in some later examples.

---

[1] Some instruments have a low E♭ but this note is not considered practical.

184

Tubas are built in three shapes or models:[1] the upright, the standard tuba used both for symphony orchestras and concert bands, the circular or helicon model, with the bell slanting slightly to the player's left; and the sousaphone, with a removable bell facing forward. The last two models rest on the player's shoulder in playing position and are the most practical for marching bands.

Tubas, like the other brass instruments, are constructed with three or four valves which provide the means for changing fundamentals and harmonic series. The three-valve tuba is the more common of the two types and, therefore, the one to be scored regularly for the band. Four-valve tubas[2] are not used in sufficient numbers to warrant any extension of ranges beyond those given for the three-valve instruments.

The tubas occupy the same relative position in the bass register of the band that the string bass does in the orchestra. However, there is one major difference in the notation for the two instruments: the tuba is a non-transposing instrument, while the string bass sounds an octave lower than written (see Chap. 23). The violoncello-bass combination of the orchestra is carried out in the band either by a baritone-tuba pairing or by divided tubas.

In writing for the tubas,[3] it is most important to consider the range differential between the Eb and BBb instruments. The differential of a fourth in their respective ranges should be understood so that parts for divided tubas will be arranged to permit performance by both instruments. The necessity for these adjustments occurs most frequently with octave passages in the lowest register. The dividing process should be anticipated and managed smoothly so that there is no loss of strength or sonority.

Tubas are rarely divided for chord progressions in combination with other instruments. There are two exceptions. One is the occasional division of the tubas, with the baritone for chord sequences in open position; the other is division to provide the drone of sustained fifths in the low register.

These two usages constitute the scope of the divisions of tuba parts found in band scoring. The instrument is, after all, the chief

---

[1] A fourth type, called a recording tuba, has also been introduced. It is basically the same as the upright model, except that its bell faces forward instead of upward.

[2] The fourth valve increases the lowest range by an augmented fourth. It also simplifies complicated fingerings and improves intonation.

[3] The term "basses," as used in many condensed scores, is an inclusive one meaning tubas and string basses.

source of tonal strength, sonority, and support for bass parts; a support which may be that of the familiar chord notes in a military march, a melodic line, or the lowest harmonic parts in concert music. It is not necessary to mark divided tuba parts, as it is assumed that the highest part will be played by the Eb instrument.

THE Eb TUBA

Range Divisions

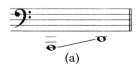

(a)

The lowest fourth has good tone quality but requires a good embouchure and breath control. Sustained notes are playable if they are not overly prolonged (see Ex. 167). Very rapid slurred passages, though possible technically, tend to sound blurred. Slowed-down notations with short slurs or detached notes come through clearly.

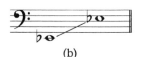

(b)

The notes in this register are the instrument's best for melodies and scales at all tempos and dynamics.

(c)

These top notes have good quality but do not retain a true bass tone. The tubas are essentially bass instruments and lose some of their characteristic tone quality if placed in the tenor range.

THE BBb TUBA

Range Divisions

This tuba, sometimes referred to as a contrabass instrument, is the largest member of the saxhorn family. Its practical range, a perfect fourth lower than that of the Eb tuba, is the same as that for the four-string contrabass.

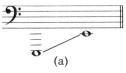

(a)

The same tonal characteristics attributed to the lowest notes of the Eb tuba apply equally well to the larger BBb instrument. Tone production in this register requires an enormous amount of breath, which is especially difficult to control in the lower fourth.

186

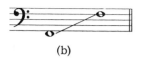

(b)

The upper half of this register is of better quality when played by the E♭ tuba or baritone. The lower half is used most frequently for melodic or harmonic bass parts.

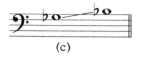

(c)

This highest third is of little practical value, as the tone is unsatisfactory and insecure.

THE TUBAS AS ENSEMBLE INSTRUMENTS

The tubas are the very foundation, not only of the brass section, but of the full band as well. All shades of dynamic tone control are possible and practicable with the tubas. They are capable of considerable technical agility, despite the rather ponderous tone of their lowest ranges. Large diatonic or chromatic intervals are no more difficult for them than they are for the other brass valve instruments. This technical facility permits reasonable variation of *tessitura* of bass lines, which might otherwise become monotonous.

Mutes for the tubas, though possible for the upright model, are not practical for most band music. Therefore, open or unmuted tubas should not be matched with other muted brass instruments if the effect of a homogeneous tone quality is desired.

Phrase markings follow the same general patterns suggested for the other brass instruments. The bright *staccato* notes of the tubas are the closest approach to the *pizzicato* of the string bass. Accented attacks carry conviction, if they are not overly extended. All tonguing styles are playable, but the most rapid ones cause some tonal sluggishness when applied to the notes in the lowest ranges.

Many of the examples dealing with the reeds and brasses included parts for the tuba, but as secondary points of interest. Inasmuch as these passages covered most of the instrument's playing techniques, they should now be reexamined and the tuba's place in the ensemble evaluated.[1] The excerpts which follow further illustrate some details of scoring for the tuba which heretofore have been only slightly covered.

[1] Review Exs. 2, 10, 13, 37, 48, 65, 72, 93, 102, 104, 113, 114, 117, 121, 134, 135, 137, 141, 155, and 161.

The tubas as a solo unit, without doubling, appear to be receiving more attention as the repertory of original music for the band increases. A rather extraordinary example of this kind occurs in Creston's *Celebration* overture. This work contains a solo passage of ten measures for tubas in octaves with an accompaniment of cornets and a tom-tom.

EX. 163. *CELEBRATION OVERTURE*

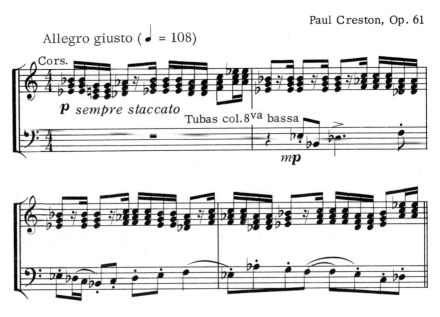

Another passage of sixteen measures for solo tubas is featured by Persichetti in his *Burlesque.* There can be no denying the humorous effect here as enlivened by its detached style of notation.

188

EX. 164. *IV. BURLESQUE from Divertimento for Band*

Vincent Persichetti, Op. 42

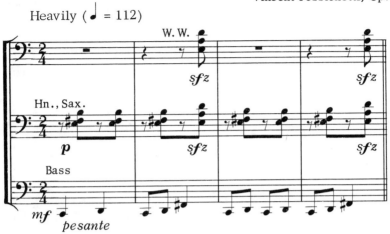

The band transcription of the following movement, *The Elephant*, originally scored for a small orchestra combination and two pianos, retains much of its droll humor, with the tubas substituting for the string basses. Notice that an optional high E is given in measure 2 for the E♭ tubas.

EX. 165. *I. THE ELEPHANT, Second Suite*
from Carnival of the Animals

Saint-Saëns
Trans. by Robert Cray

The tubas are often useful for outlining harmonic progressions derived from rhythmic patterns in the middle register. This is illustrated in Ex. 166. In this passage, the composer requests a field drum (F. D.) rather than the smaller side drum.

EX. 166. *III. FANFARE from West Point Suite*

Musical structure sometimes requires that bass parts be sustained over several measures. When this occurs, attention should be given to the tempo and dynamics, for both affect each wind instrument's sustaining potential. Example 167 contains parts for the tubas at about their maximum capacity, without resorting to alternating *divisi*.

EX. 167. *FUGUE No. IV from The Well-tempered Clavier, Book 1*

J. S. Bach
Arr. by C. K. Wellington

The final excerpts for the tubas illustrate a notation problem which results from dissimilar ranges.

EX. 168. *THE FORTY-NINERS: An American Rhapsody*

George F. McKay

191

EX. 169. *CHORAL PRELUDE: We All Believe in One God*

J. S. Bach
Trans. by James R. Gillette

Moderato ma energico (♩ = 60)

1, 2

Trbs.

3

Bar.

Tuba

Cb.

As condensed scores do not show adjustment of tuba parts, extracts from the full scores for the low brass instruments have been included for greater clarification.

The divided tuba parts in Ex. 168 are arranged to permit the Eb instrument to continue with the bass octaves by playing the top octave notes where they occur. *Note*: Conversely, it should be noted that many professional and school bands do not use Eb tubas, which means the loss of the highest fourth (Bb-Eb). The tuba part in Ex. 169 is obviously intended for the BBb tuba as the lowest notes, F and G, are not playable by the smaller instrument.

192

∞∞∞

CHAPTER SIXTEEN

THE BRASS SECTION AS
A COMPLETE UNIT

The Most Common Idiomatic Uses

The brass section of the band has far greater tonal strength and depth than does the wood-wind choir. Also, the number of doubled brass parts is usually larger than that of the wood winds, with the exception of the B♭ clarinets. These two factors are important in establishing the brass choir as the band's chief source of tonal solidity and power.

Although the brass instruments are now remarkably adaptable to many playing styles, there still remain certain types of melodic phrases and passage work which, though technically possible, are unidiomatic from the artistic standpoint. The brass instruments have many playing characteristics which remain fairly constant, regardless of the instrumentation of the ensemble. It is the matter of scope, both in the number and variety of ways the brass may be scored, that is of primary interest and importance to the band scorer.

The brass instruments are not always adaptable to parts regularly played by the wood winds or orchestral strings. In the band, when technical inadequacies are not an important consideration, scoring plans are determined by idiomatic effectiveness and appropriateness. For example, broken intervals and chords or *arpeggios* may be playable in some tempos by the cornets or baritones. However, the results would invariably sound awkward and unmusical, as these parts lie within the idiomatic playing styles of the clarinets or saxophones rather than those of the brass instruments. This and similar details of scoring are discussed in Chap. 26, which deals with the *Reference Chart of Keyboard Idioms and Patterns.*

The listing which follows summarizes the most common phases of scoring for the brass instruments, either as an independent unit or in combination with the wood winds. These ten points should be integrated with the analysis given for each instrument so that they will become an integral part of a practical scoring technique. In addition, each item is closely allied to corresponding entries of the *Reference Chart.*

THE MOST COMMON IDIOMATIC USES FOR
THE BRASS INSTRUMENTS

1. Solo and octave melodic lines at all dynamic levels
2. Chordal progressions in choral style
3. Unisons, intervals, or chords used for percussive accents
4. Sustaining with any dynamic
5. Rhythmic figurations
6. Outlining important melodies in the reeds
7. Doubling the reeds in unison or octaves for extra emphasis and/or tonal strength.
8. Increasing sonority, especially for climaxes
9. As an independent section for contrast of timbre and sonority
10. Coloristic effects

THE BRASS SECTION AS AN INDEPENDENT UNIT

The brass instruments of the band are scored as an independent unit somewhat more frequently than are the reeds. Their flexible dynamic range permits a diversity of musical styles and textures which shows to good advantage in the excerpts from full scores which are shown here.

Brass instruments sound particularly well in music of a chordal nature. Passages in this style are effective when played either *legato* or non-*legato.* The rather long slurs in Ex. 170 can be considered as exceptional though practicable. In Ex. 171, alternate notes for the third trombone are given, to be played in the absence of a bass trombone. The low D's for the baritone are, of course, playable only by a four-valve instrument.

GEORGE WASHINGTON BRIDGE

William Schuman

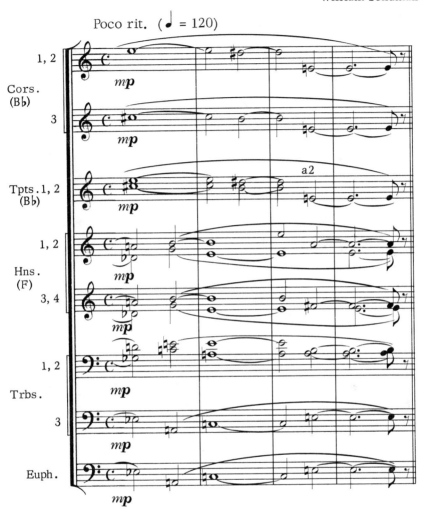

EX. 171. *THE HIDDEN FORTRESS*

Anthony Donato

The two following excerpts are representative scorings of homophonic and polyphonic styles of composition. In Ex. 172 which is homophonic, notice that there is only one melody part. The relatively high *tessitura* of the first cornet part has sufficient brilliance to carry above the harmony and rhythm instruments, notwithstanding the loud dynamic. This is a scoring peculiarity which applies more particularly to the brass section as a unit than to combinations of wood-wind instruments (see Ex. 178). Observe the dynamics in Ex. 173, adjusted to promote clear definition of the important thematic material in this contrapuntal passage.

EX. 172. *3.MARCH from First Suite in E Flat*

Gustav Holst

197

J. C. F. Fischer
Arr. by Keith Wilson

The next example has been included here to show a brass scoring of a melodic bass, combined with rhythm chords in the treble. The full score reveals this loud passage for the brass placed between softer ones for the wood-wind unit. It is a scoring device which ensures contrast through an effective interplay of timbres.

EX. 174. *TWO GERMAN DANCES, No. 1*

Beethoven
Arr. by Howard Kilbert

Antiphonal or answering phrases within the section are another means of securing contrast and variation of timbre. This scoring plan has been nicely arranged in the next example. The percussion instruments starting at G are used here as a solo unit.

EX. 175. *THE FORTY-NINERS, An American Rhapsody*

George F. McKay

The final excerpt contains several devices which are applicable to the scoring of dance forms and/or march-style passages with soft dynamics. The trumpets add extra pulse to the cornets, the trombones sustaining the harmony furnish resonance, while the baritone, doubled by one bass (tuba and/or string bass), provides a light, but adequate, bass part.

200

EX. 176. *POLKA II from Jugoslav Polka*

George List

Fast Polka Tempo

CHAPTER SEVENTEEN

SCORING THE BRASS AS AN INDEPENDENT SECTION

Scoring the brass as an independent section in concert music for the band differs considerably from the methods of scoring discussed for the wood-wind choir. First, the combined ranges of the two sections differ greatly. Second, the strength of the brass instruments is centered on the medium and low registers, while the wood winds alone are left to carry out range extensions above the treble clef.

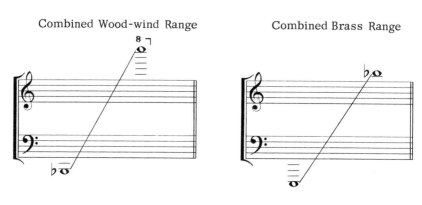

Fig. 30

From this range comparison, it is obvious that melodic extensions above the treble clef are not practical and that considerable unison doubling of the middle parts is inevitable. In addition, range divisions for four-part music can now be restated more specifically for the brass instruments as follows:

1. Cornets and trumpets encompass the range of women's voices.

2. Horns divide regularly for parts in the alto and tenor registers.

3. Trombones are adaptable to alto parts, as well as to those in the tenor and bass registers.

4. Baritone move freely between the tenor and bass ranges.

5. Tubas are strictly bass instruments.

Timbre distinctions, as discussed for the wood winds in Chap. 11, are not pertinent to or necessary for the scoring of brass instruments, as this section forms a reasonably homogeneous unit. Range differences are important, in that melodic lines sound best when they are carried out in their entirety by a single instrument. By way of illustration, the first strain of *America* in the key of G is playable by a horn, but the second strain goes higher than the advised safe range for this instrument.

This preceding data can now be applied to the scoring of chorals for brass instruments. The following are four of several possible settings available for four-part music. That for the horn quartet has been included to show the proper distribution of its parts (see Fig. 22). The movement of the harmony parts in Ex. 177d has been reduced so that the melody will have maximum clarity in this lowered register. The first two settings illustrate combinations within the section.

EX. 177. *AMERICA*

Example 178 is the setting for the brass instruments generally recommended for the basic and/or marching band. The voice pattern of the cornets here has been selected so that the duet parts will sound well with the trombones, and with or without the horns. When this plan is followed, the horn parts serve as harmonic fillers and are developed from the alto and tenor voices. Because of the position of the first cornet as the highest part, its melody will carry satisfactorily above the harmony instruments.

EX. 178. *AMERICA*

Scoring the brass of the full concert band presents several new points not heretofore discussed. In large ensembles, trumpet fanfares add a touch of brilliance, as in Ex. 179. However, in smaller bands, the cornet parts given in Ex. 178 should be used to ensure a stronger melodic line. The scoring of the four horns in two parts is both adequate and practical, especially when the complete tonal spread is as limited as it is here. The parts of the first and second trombones have been changed slightly from those given in Ex. 178 to clear the way for the melody in the baritone. Should this instrumentation be used for a minimum number of players, the notation given for the trombones and baritone in Ex. 178 could well be substituted for the one given below.

205

EX. 179. *AMERICA*

Scoring four-part music, other than chorals, serves a useful purpose by helping the scorer to differentiate between the functional and concert approaches to the brass instruments. In working with composed source material in the art forms, the finer points of balance, sonority, and contrast become major objectives. Obviously, none of these qualities can be achieved if a score is over-padded with unnecessary doubling. Some range extensions and occasional fillers are a legitimate means of increasing voice textures without causing tonal distortion. Limited contrast of timbres can be achieved through balanced sonorities.

Experience with this phase of scoring is both necessary and helpful, as shown in the previous chapter by the many passages for the brass as an independent unit. The following transcriptions are illustrative of the many possible methods for scoring the brass instruments with music primarily in four parts.

206

EX. 180. *IN THE CHURCH from Album for the Young*

Tchaikovsky, Op. 39, No. 24

EX. 181. *ROUNDELAY from Album for the Young*

Schumann, Op. 68, No.

The student should score chorals and four-part piano music for different brass combinations, using the source material provided for this purpose in the author's *Workbook for Band Scoring*.

207

⋘⋙

CHAPTER EIGHTEEN

THE PERCUSSION SECTION

Percussion Instruments Classified According to Pitch and Timbre
Vibrating Characteristics and Notation

Percussion instruments are unique in their pitch variance and vibrating characteristics. For this reason, it is advisable and practical to consider them according to their respective categories.

1. (a) Instruments with Definite Pitch
      Timpani, chimes, glockenspiel (orchestra bells and lyre), xylophone, marimba, and vibraphone
   (b) Instruments without Definite Pitch
      Snare drum (side drum and field drum), bass drum, cymbals, tambourine, triangle, wood block, castanets, tom-tom, temple blocks, maracas, claves, gong or tam-tam[1]
2. (a) Instruments Which Continue to Sound after Contact
      Timpani,[2] chimes, glockenspiel, cymbals, triangle, gong or tam-tam, vibraphone
   (b) Instruments Which Do Not Sound after Contact
      Xylophone, marimba, snare drum, bass drum, tambourine, castanets, wood block, temple blocks, tom-tom, maracas, and claves
3. Divisions by Timbre
   Divisions in this category are determined by the kind of vibrating surfaces—membrane, metal, or wood.
   (a) Membrane: All types of drums, including the tambourine
   (b) Metal: Glockenspiel (bells and lyre), vibraphone, chimes, triangle, cymbals, gong or tam-tam
   (c) Wood: Xylophone, marimba, wood block, temple blocks, castanets, maracas, and claves

---

[1] In practice, the larger of the two is usually known as the tam-tam.

[2] The continuing vibrations of the timpani are relatively short, but sufficient to warrant this classification.

A fourth grouping, variously known as "traps" or effects, in-cludes such noisemakers as the rattle, sleigh bells, anvil, wind machine, slapstick, whistle. Notation for these items is similar to that given for the other percussion instruments and in similar divisions.

Instruments with definite pitch are written on a staff with the proper clef. The use of key signatures is optional. Those without definite pitch may be written on a staff or a single line without any clef.

The vibrating characteristics of the percussion instruments differ considerably from those of the wind instruments. This, in turn, accounts for specific problems affecting their notation. In-struments made of metal continue to ring or sound in varying de-grees after contact. Those made of wood, and two members of the drum group, the snare drum and tambourine, cease vibrating im-mediately after contact. Only the timpani have continuing reso-nance of any consequence.

The effect of these vibrating characteristics on the notation of percussion instruments made of metal with definite pitch is illustrated in Fig. 31a.

ALL TEMPOS AND DYNAMICS

Fig. 31a

If this notation is used for a xylophone or marimba, the result-ing sound would be notated as follows:

Fig. 31b

For instruments with nonvibrating surfaces without definite pitch, the sounding notation is as given in Fig. 31c.

Fig. 31c

If the effect of continuous tone is required for instruments made of wood with definite pitch, the notation should read as follows:

Fig. 31d

Notation for the other instruments without definite pitch in this category is given in this manner:[1]

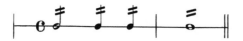

Fig. 31e

To summarize: percussion instruments made of metal continue to ring or vibrate after contact. Because this vibrating resonance is controllable, notation can be reasonably accurate. Rolled notes for the bells or chimes are not very satisfactory. Instruments made of wood, and the drum types, can maintain continuous sound only through the use of some form of repeated attacks.

---

[1] Two flags are sufficient for most moderate-to-slow tempos (style d and e), whereas three flags are recommended for slower tempos to ensure a true tremolo.

CHAPTER NINETEEN

THE DRUM GROUP

Timpani - Snare Drum - Bass Drum - Tambourine - Tom-tom

THE TIMPANI

Kettledrums, better known by their Italian name, timpani, are invariably used in pairs for twentieth-century scores; some scores call for three drums. These copper-kettle-shaped drums with calfskin heads are of two types: hand-tuned and the newer pedal-tuned drums. The hand-tuned drum, which was standard until the early 1900s, has a set of handles evenly spaced around the rim. One half turn of each of these handles alters the pitch by approximately one half tone. This technicality necessitates a few measures of rest in parts which require pitch changes during performance. The hand-tuned drums need more time for tuning than do those of the pedal type, on which pitch changes can be made almost instantaneously.

In practical scoring for the band, it is advisable to write for the hand-tuned drums, as the pedal type is not consistently available. The range compass of a pair of timpani covers an octave. The larger drum is always placed at the player's left. Supplementary larger and smaller timpani[1] are to be found in some of major symphonic bands, but they are not always available in the smaller organizations.

STANDARD TIMPANI RANGES

Large, 28 Inches   Small, 25 Inches

Fig. 32

[1] The largest drum has a 30-inch diameter (low: D–A); the smallest is 23 inches (high: D–G).

Timpani sticks are made of wood with mallet heads ranging from soft to hard. Considerable variation in tone and attack may be obtained through the interchange of sticks, a matter which is usually left to the discretion of the player or director. Stick technique employs single strokes with alternating hands for rolls and the more common rhythmic patterns. A skilled timpanist is a specialist, capable of performing surprising feats in applying stick technique to as many as four drums. A timpanist occasionally doubles on the other percussion instruments.

Old notation for the timpani had them tuned invariably to the tonic and dominant of each piece, with no pitch changes occurring in the course of a movement. This practice has been supplanted by a new approach which permits a completely free choice of initial tuning and subsequent tuning changes, as they may be needed. However, pitch changes should be arranged so that there will be a minimum of shifting from one drum to the other.

The equally important matter of notation for the timpani has also been affected by the early rigidity of pitch selection. Most band scores which were written prior to the 1940s specify exact pitch settings at the beginning of each movement but do not include accidentals as they occur in the part (see Ex. 172).

OLD STYLE OF NOTATION

Fig. 33

Since that time, there has been a noticeable and significant trend toward the elimination of the older method and the substitution of a more exact form of notation which includes all accidentals in each measure as they occur.[1] This method is consistently adhered to for all pitch changes made throughout each movement.

---

[1] Some band scorers use signatures in preference to accidentals.

212

Fig. 34

To summarize: notation for the timpani, as for all instruments, should be accurate. The newer harmonic content of most music and the freer use of the timpani indicate that the notation style illustrated in Fig. 34 is the one recommended as being both practical and definite.

The old style of writing untied rolled notes is confusing and should be discarded in favor of the newer one, which has all rolled notes tied. It is equally important that the starting and stopping points of all rolls be clearly marked.

Notation of rolled notes for timpani or the other percussion instruments may be written in either of the two ways given in Fig. 35a and Fig. 35b. The notation of Fig. 35a is the more common one and should include a minimum of three cross flags. Figure 35c gives the notation for a rolled interval.

Fig. 35

Inasmuch as the timpani have always been an integral part of instrumental ensembles, the band scorer should consider them as standard instruments and not as supplementary noisemakers. Although percussive to a degree, they do not belong in the same category with the other percussion instruments, which are considered with different musical values in mind.

Timpani parts in concert music for the band follow playing styles similar to those used in symphonic music for the orchestra. The chief difference may be that parts for the band are somewhat broader in scope. Nevertheless, the tendency to add timpani parts simply because key tonalities and tunings agree should be discouraged. Timpani parts should be carefully planned and spaced if they are to have their maximum effect.

The following list summerizes the most common playing styles and uses of the timpani:

1. Building climaxes either with a roll or the repetition of a rhythmic figure not necessarily doubled or derived from the other instruments (see Ex. 147)

2. For emphasis in all forms—melodic, harmonic, or rhythmic (see Ex. 155)

3. When played *staccato,* not unlike a string *pizzicato* (see Ex. 35)

4. Particularly effective when combined with brass instruments (see Ex. 183)

5. Solo rhythmic snatches of thematic bits, often arranged antiphonally (see Ex. 183)

6. Outlining the pulsations of rhythmic patterns (see Exs. 143, 172)

7. Long, sustained rolls as pedal points (a single, sustained note over which melodic or harmonic material is superimposed), usually for *crescendos* or *diminuendos* (see Exs. 28, 33, 79)

8. Intervals, played together or broken

9. Creation of tension through the use of *ostinatos,* preferably derived from the rhythmic patterns of principal thematic ideas.

Well-placed solo passages for the timpani have contrast value and often achieve a distinctive kind of brilliant strength which is not obtainable from the other percussion instruments. Example 182 illustrates this point and gives a slightly different version of the statement given in no. 9 in the list above.

EX. 182. *3. TRIBAL DANCE from Newsreel in Five Shots*

William Schuman

The next excerpt has been selected to illustrate nos. 4 and 5 in the list. This passage, in a fast tempo for three drums combined with the brass, provides a model for a variety of antiphonally arranged sequences for the timpani and wind instruments.

EX. 183. *I. PROLOGUE from Divertimento for Band*

Vincent Persichetti, Op. 42

THE SNARE DRUM

(Side Drum - Field Drum - Tenor Drum - Tom-Tom)

The snare drum, also known as the side drum, varies considerably in size and sonority. One of the popular models for concert music has two 14-inch membrane heads, is about 6 inches deep, and is played from an adjustable stand. It is equipped with a set of snares (wire-covered gut strings) attached to a clamping device which regulates their tension and contact with the bottom drumhead. The movement of the snares against the head accounts for the drum's characteristic dry tone quality. When the snares are released, the resulting sound is similar to that of an Indian tom-tom or other folk-type drums.

The military side or field drum is another type of small portable drum. It is usually equipped with snares and is played from a strapped shoulder position in marching bands. It has about the same diameter as the shallower snare drum but is several times deeper. This extra depth gives this drum a diffused, heavier sonority with a less bright, dry (*secco*) timbre (see Ex. 166).

The tenor drum, also belonging in this category, has interesting possibilities for the scoring of concert music. This drum, similar in size to the field drum, does not have any snares and has a rather deep tone, something like a miniature bass drum with a much higher timbre. Wooden or felt-headed sticks may be used—preferably whichever is specified by the band scorer.

Twentieth-century composers have experimented with combining these various types of drums in original ways. By the juxtaposition of high (snare drum) and low (field and/or tenor drums, with or without snares) sonorities playable by one performer, totally new and stunning effects have been achieved (see Ex. 204 for a practical method for notation). This is an area which offers possibilities for many novel effects, as different pitches, with or without snares, can be combined for more than one player, making independent rhythms both possible and practical.

The double-stroked roll is unlike that for the timpani and frequently ends on an accent. Notation for the roll is the same as that given for the timpani excepting, of course, the need of a clef or staff as previously noted. The termination of rolls can be clearly indicated by tying the last rolled note to an unrolled one as shown in Fig. 36. This style of notation is also correct for rolls on all percussion instruments.

(a)

pp   *cresc.*   *sfz*

(b)

f

Fig. 36

Two styles of stick technique, the flam and the drag, apply only to the snare drum. In both cases, one or more grace notes is prefixed to basic notations. Most band scorers usually leave the choice of the stroke to the player, simply indicating the essential rhythmic patterns. The following excerpt illustrates both the written and sounding notations for a "roll-off."

EX. 184. *A TRIBUTE TO SOUSA*

Maurice C. Whitney

Custom has established the practice of writing the snare drum, bass drum, and frequently the cymbals as a unit. The notation for this combination in much functional music for the band includes a staff and a bass clef. The snare-drum part is written in the third space (stems up), with single notes in the first space (stems down) for the bass drum and/or cymbals.[1] The abbreviations "B.D." (bass drum) and "cym." (cymbals) are used when either instrument is to play alone, while "tog." (together) is used when both play a single part. This last abbreviation is also used to indicate that two cymbals are to be struck together, as opposed to a single cymbal to be struck with a stick. This notation is, of course, more practical than correct for instruments without definite pitch.

[1] See Ex. 172, with double notes for the bass drum and cymbals.

217

Special effects have been introduced to vary the characteristic timbre of the snare drum. In addition to the tom-tom drum, they include several other effects which have been illustrated in earlier examples. One is the muffled head or cloth-covered batter head which deadens the tone (see Ex. 143). Another is the substitution of wire-spread brushes for sticks, a device used mostly for dance rhythms. Timpani sticks may be used in place of the regular wooden drumsticks to soften the attacks and the tone. Finally, rim shots—harsh, pistol-like sounds made by striking one stick against another in contact with the batter head and metal rim—may be used (see Ex. 115).

The snare drum, long identified with martial music and afterbeats in dance forms, has many other usages worthy of consideration. It is useful in supplying verve and zest to rhythmic patterns often derived from melodic or harmonic ideas, for projecting *ostinatos* with independent rhythmic interest, for supporting the rhythmic profilo of important thematic material, and for building big climaxes. The snare drum can be most effective at the softer dynamic levels when given rhythmic patterns of independent interest.

Parts for the snare drum are indicated in Exs. 21, 93, 107, 115, (rim shot), 155, 172, and 175; for the field drum in Ex. 166; for the tenor drum in Ex. 143; for the tom-tom (two sizes) in Exs. 62 and 72.

THE BASS DRUM

The bass drum is a noisemaker par excellence with a booming resonance of carrying power which is in proportion to its size. This drum has two membrane heads which are regulated to ensure resonance but not pitch.

The very nature of bass-drum resonance restricts stick technique to single, rather widely separated strokes in simple rhythmic patterns and the familiar roll. The notation for either playing style is the same as that for other percussion instruments without definite pitch.

Bass-drum beaters are available in two types: those with a large, moderately hard head; others with two heads, one large and rather soft and the other smaller and harder. By holding the double-headed stick in the center and using a wrist movement, a continuous roll may be played. Timpani sticks, when substituted for rolls, produce a more even, controlled roll comparable in effect to that of the timpani, which it often augments or replaces. Important timpani rolls are generally cued for the bass drum, as it is the best replacement.

218

Historically, the bass drum and cymbals have been paired as a unit in orchestral and band music. (The latter should be played as hand cymbals and not with one cymbal attached to a bass drum.) Although this combination is often necessary for functional music where strong-beat emphasis is important, it is less desirable in concert music where percussive timbres have coloristic value. Actually, there is much to be gained from separating the high-and low-pitch resonance of the cymbals and the bass drum.

Parts for the bass drum are indicated in Exs. 10, 21, 33, 62, 74, 93, 128, 135, 155, 172, and 175.

THE TAMBOURINE

The tambourine has one membrane head and is equipped with a set of metal disks called jingles. These jingles are in pairs and vibrate in proportion to the movement of the instrument.

Several types of playing techniques are used. Percussive strokes on the drumhead may be made with the fist or knuckles. Also, different kinds of drumsticks (timpani, snare drum, bell, or xylophone mallets) may be substituted, especially when tricky rhythms extend over many measures. Continuous jingle rolls are made either by shaking the instrument or by using the more difficult technique of rubbing a moistened thumb around the edge of the drumhead. Neither technique produces any percussive sound from the head. The notation for the tambourine does not differ from that for the other percussive instruments.

Tambourine parts in the band have generally carried connotations of the exotic in music. Actually, the characteristic dual percussive sound adds brightness and color to music which is rhythmic, gay, or festive, regardless of its national origin.

The tambourine may be considered as a unique miniature drum equipped with jingles and capable of splashy color effects at all dynamic levels. Parts for it conventionally follow the rhythmic patterns derived from the high-or middle-range instruments of the band and, because of its high-pitched jingles, it is frequently paired or alternated with the triangle. As with all percussion instruments, its effect is in proportion to the frequency of its use in each score. Tambourine parts are indicated in Exs. 113 and 117. The following excerpt illustrates a notation for the tambourine which was derived from the rhythmic pattern of the principal melodic line.

EX. 185. *CZECH RHAPSODY*

Jaromir Weinberger
Arr. by Richard Franko Goldman

~~~~~

CHAPTER TWENTY

PERCUSSION INSTRUMENTS
MADE OF METAL

Triangle - Cymbals - Glockenspiel (Bells and Lyre) - Vibraphone

Chimes - Tam-tam - Gong

THE TRIANGLE

The triangle is a steel bar bent in the shape of a triangle and having one open end. It varies in pitch in accordance with its variance in size (small–6 inches, medium–8 inches, and large–12 inches). The triangle is held by string or twine from a suspended position and a small steel rod or bar is used as a beater. Although band scorers do not, as a rule, stipulate desired sizes, there is no reason why this may not be done by the scorer as a means of securing contrast with this particular timbre.

The triangle's brilliant bell-like resonance makes it ineffective for complicated rhythms. Short, simple, basic patterns, tremolos, and single strokes at all dynamic levels can brighten up a passage considerably. Its sparkling timbre has piquant charm when used sparingly in soft passages. Conversely, rolls played strongly carry well in most *tuttis* and are particularly effective with wood-wind trills. Its brilliance is, therefore, the key to estimating the scope of its effectiveness. Parts for the triangle are indicated in Exs. 28, 45, 117, and 135.

THE CYMBALS

Cymbal resonance and tonal strength vary with the size and quality of the instrument. Turkish cymbals, made of a brass alloy and between 15 and 18 inches in diameter, are considered the best for the band. Matched pairs, played manually, are supplemented by a third suspended cymbal for use with different kinds of sticks, including soft-medium, and hard timpani sticks.

The cymbals, when played manually, are brought together with glancing blows which, contrary to casual observation, can be equally effective at *pianissimo* and at *fortissimo*. The old technique of rubbing the cymbals together for rolls has been displaced by the more controllable technique of using sticks on a suspended cymbal. When the stick technique is used, directions should include the kind of sticks desired—wood, metal, or timpani.

Notation for cymbals is now more detailed and diversified than it was prior to the twentieth century. Diamond-shaped notes have generally supplanted the old standard notation for the cymbals in concert music. The old notation, referred to in the previous chapter, remains unchanged for functional music. Some arrangers prefer to use crosses, with or without stems (x and/or x), for cymbal parts, especially when they differ from the bass drum part (see Ex. 62).

The notation for the cymbals should be accurate, as they have the strongest resonance and tonal depth of the common percussion instruments. Their tone can be "stopped" or "choked" almost instantaneously by bringing the two disks in contact with wearing apparel; a hand is used for a suspended cymbal. If, on the other hand, the cymbals are to continue vibrating beyond the limits of conventional notation (more than a measure), the words "allow to vibrate" or "let it ring" are then written into the part.

Loud cymbal crashes should be withheld for peak moments, climaxes with tonal and rhythmic tension; otherwise their explosive power palls quickly. A few well-placed and spaced crashes have real strength and character. Repeated crashings degenerate into mere noise which obscures musical values without increasing tonal volume.

Parts for the cymbals are indicated in Exs. 10, 21, 62, 66, 110 (roll), 113, 128, 135, 140, 146, 154b, 172, and 174. Example 191 and 205, call for a suspended cymbal with timpani stick.

THE GLOCKENSPIEL

The glockenspiel, more commonly known as the bells, is a set of chromatically pitched steel bars arranged in a playing position similar to that of a piano keyboard. *Note*: The bell lyre, as featured in marching bands, is a vertical model of the bells and has the same range as a small set.

Parts for these instruments are written in the treble clef with optional, though recommended, signatures. As ranges vary with the size of each instrument, the following compass is given as a practicable, safe compromise. The glockenspiel is a transposing instrument, in that its sounding range is two octaves higher than the written one.

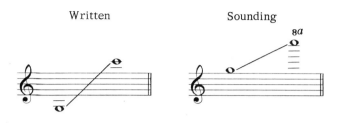

Fig. 37

The choice of mallets (yarn, rubber, wood, or metal) is usually left to the player, the selection being determined by the dynamic of the passage. Single notes, intervals, and three-note chords are playable, if confined to an octave. The instrument does not respond well to rapidly repeated strokes and is, therefore, not effective with ordinary tremolos.

The instrument has a bright sonority with penetrating carrying power which is stronger than that of the triangle. Accumulated, undampened vibrations from many overtones produce a tonal blurring which is, in this case, a characteristic asset. Its luminous resonance minimizes the percussiveness of attacks, except when steel hammers are used. Relatively short, solo melodic phrases have distinctive charm in the soft-to-medium-loud dynamic range. This instrument is well suited to outlining melodic or rhythmic ideas, short color dabs of single notes or intervals, and splashy *glissandos* on single-beat *crescendos*. Parts for the bells are indicated in Exs. 4, 10, 66, 106, 135 (outlining), 186, and 188.

The following excerpt shows an interesting use of the bells with the reeds as part of the harmony. It is taken from a work by a composer who pioneered valiently in the cause of original band music in the first decades of the twentieth century.

EX. 186. *SHEPHERD'S HEY*

Percy Aldridge Grainger

THE VIBRAPHONE

The vibraphone is an extra-large glockenspiel equipped with resonators, each containing a revolving disk which is operated electrically. These resonators produce an exaggerated *vibrato* which, in turn, causes continuous blurring and overlapping of sound. Sticks with soft mallet heads are ordinarily used, thereby precluding parts louder than *mezzoforte*. In rapid passages the vibraphone has tonal characteristics similar to those of the glockenspiel. The vibraphone is a non-transposing instrument, is built in two sizes, and has two ranges. The range in Fig. 38a is the more common of the two.

224

Practical   Occasional

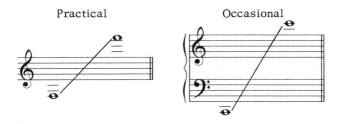

Fig. 38

This newest instrument of the percussion section is perhaps best known through its association with dance bands and orchestras in the field of "entertainment" music. Its unpredictable availability in concert bands hampers any real exploitation of its potentialities. For this reason, vibraphone parts are practically nonexistent in concert music for the band.

Single notes, intervals, or chords confined to an octave are played ordinarily without any form of repeated attack. The vibraphone lacks the brilliance of the bells, but it does have the advantage in its sustaining tone. The vibraphone is used as a coloristic touch on the second beats of measures 2 and 4 in Ex. 187. The instrument, without electric activation and played with hard mallets, becomes a steel (bell) marimba, capable of great brilliance and penetrating tone (see Ex. 188).

EX. 187. *ERIK THE RED*

Gene von Hallberg

225

Percy Aldridge Grainger

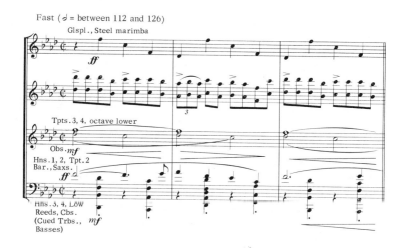

THE CHIMES

The chimes, also known as tubular bells, consist of a set of tubular metal pipes usually hung on a specially constructed rack or frame. Their range (non-transposing) covers an octave and a perfect fifth, with intervening chromatics as follows:

WRITTEN AND SOUNDING RANGES

Fig. 39

A gavel-like hammer is used for single strokes. Successive attacks pile up jangling overtones similar to those of a carillon.

226

As these large bells speak slowly, it is advisable to avoid any notation which would require attacks in rapid succession. Single strokes, well spaced, give the most satisfactory results.

The chimes, through their association with religious music, have been scored rather conservatively in the past. Although these heavy bell tones have obvious limitations in that they cannot be used too frequently, they can be most effective in music with a festive mood, where a varied but brilliant sonority is desirable. They are equally effective when combined with the other percussion instruments as an independent unit. The chimes at soft dynamic levels are quite attractive when used as a solo instrument for repeated notes or very short phrases. Parts for the chimes are indicated in Exs. 106 and 162.

THE TAM-TAM AND THE GONG

These large noisemakers of Far Eastern origin are the most powerful in the percussion section and, because of their size, speak rather slowly. Both are made of bronze, disk-shaped, have turned-down rims to minimize their low-pitched reverberating frequency, and vary considerably in size and sound. A large beater with a medium-hard head is used to produce sound.

Both instruments may be regarded as super-cymbals for use in the band. As such, they should be reserved for occasional moments when their great sonority can carry conviction unobtainable from the other percussion instruments. Single strokes with the dynamic extremes of *pianissimo* and *fortissimo* can be effective if used very infrequently; as yet, rolls have not been used extensively. Both instruments have extra-long continuing vibrations when struck strongly.

Most band scorers make no distinction between the tam-tam and the gong in their scoring. However, many conductors insist on having the large instrument with the right-angle, turned-down rim when the tam-tam is indicated in a score.

Parts for the gong are indicated in Exs. 156 and 191; for the tam-tam in Exs. 182 and 209. The following excerpt illustrates different dynamic levels for the tam-tam; the other percussion instruments are used to establish a mood with dark overtones preceding the entry of the principal motif.

227

EX. 189. *EULOGY*

Joseph Wagner

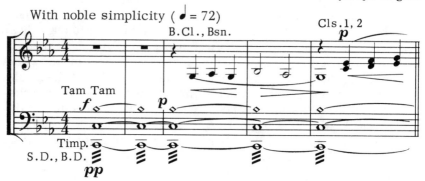

◇◇◇◇◇

CHAPTER TWENTY-ONE

PERCUSSION INSTRUMENTS MADE OF WOOD

Xylophone - Marimba - Wood Block - Temple Blocks - Castanets
Maracas - Claves

THE XYLOPHONE

The xylophone differs from the bells in that its bars are made of wood rather than metal. There are two types: a folding set without resonators with a small-to-moderate range, and a more elaborate set mounted on a special carriage with resonators and a range of more than three octaves. The ranges shown in Fig. 40 can be used with safety by the band scorer, with all notation being written in the treble clef.

A number of books on band scoring give written and sounding ranges as identical and recommend treating the xylophone as a non-transposing instrument. Since doing this would lead to the necessity for excessive ledger lines in the high register, it is more practical to follow a newer trend of notation, which has the written parts an octave lower than the sounding ones.

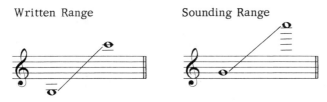

Fig. 40

The playing technique for the xylophone is approximately the same as that for the bells, the chief exception being one of notation, as explained in the text for Fig. 31. Xylophone tone is dry, brittle, and percussive. The highest tones sound somewhat metallic and lack resonance, the lowest ones have a decidedly wooden quality with considerable sonority. The best playing range lies in the middle compass, where the tone is strongest and sparkling.

The effect of sustained sound is possible only through the use of rapidly repeated attacks (rolls). Therefore, slow, sustained melodies are not very successful, as they require a constant tremolo. This instrument's best sounding parts include short rhythmic phrases, the outlining or embellishing of melodic lines, accentuation of melodic or harmonic ideas, and various forms of arpeggiated chords. Short, quick *glissandos* that end on an accented note add splashes of color. Intervals or three-note chords within an octave are also practicable.

A part for the xylophone is indicated in Ex. 82. The following solo part in Ex. 190 illustrates an alternative notation for the roll or trill and one for the *glissando*.

EX. 190. *SHEPHERD'S HEY*

Percy Aldridge Grainger

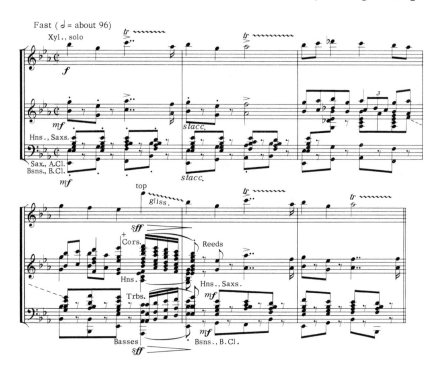

THE MARIMBA

The marimba is an extra-large xylophone equipped with resonators. It has a characteristic subdued mellow tone when played
with the customary soft mallets. As this instrument is conspicuously missing from the instrumentation of bands at all levels, it
is ordinarily inadvisable to include it in scoring plans. The ranges
of marimbas vary considerably, the following one being given as
a practical compromise for reference.

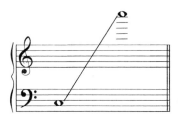

Fig. 41

THE WOOD BLOCK

The wood block is a hollowed-out rectangular piece of wood
with slots on each side near the top playing surface. Snare drumsticks or hard xylophone mallets are used with single strokes.
Its dry, brittle sound is used to point up accents or rhythmic figures and for tappings with a neutral percussive effect. Since wood
blocks vary in size and sound, it is entirely possible for two or
more of them to be used in juxtaposition or together.

The following excerpt shows an inventive usage of the percussion instruments with the wood block given an interesting two-
measure *ostinato*. Notice that all percussion continues the coloristic, rhythmic patterns established in the first two measures.
Exs. 195 and 197a are also of interest.

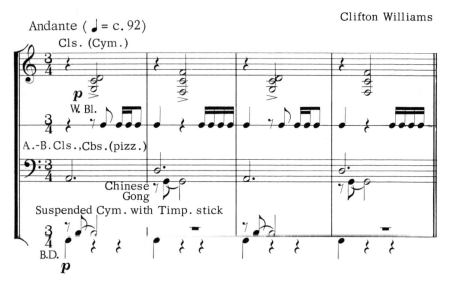

Andante (♩ = c. 92)

Clifton Williams

TEMPLE BLOCKS

Temple blocks, Chinese in origin, are round, brightly lacquered, wooden blocks. They are usually five in number and roughly tuned to approximate the tones of a pentatonic scale. Various sticks and mallets are used and the resulting sounds resemble those associated with gourds of different sizes. Temple blocks, long familiar in dance bands, are used only occasionally in music for the concert band. Notation is usually given as crosses with stems, written on a single line (see Ex. 192) or on a staff. It is to be noted in this example that the dissonances that occur here in the wind instruments are given to different timbres. This arrangement is less harsh and biting than when they occur in the same timbre.

EX. 192. *SYMPHONIC TRANSITIONS*

Joseph Wagner

THE CASTANETS

The castanets are shell-shaped pieces of hard wood in matching pairs. They are fastened together by string which is loose enough to permit manipulation with the fingers when they are held in the palms of the hands. However, as this technique is a highly developed skill, castanets are more frequently fastened to a wooden paddle which permits them to be played like a clapper or rattle.

Castanets have long been paired with the támbourine for music with a Spanish or Latin-American flavor. There is no logical reason, other than custom, why this pairing should continue. Each instrument has its own characteristic sound, which can be used whenever appropriate. Notation for the castanets should not include tremolos, as they are not practicable. The castanet part in Ex. 193 shows how decorative percussive parts can give added interest when their rhythmic patterns differ from those of the wind instruments.

F. M. Torroba
Arr. by Walter Beeler

MARACAS AND CLAVES

The maracas have gourdlike heads fastened to wooden handles. They are used in pairs and shaken like rattles.[1] The claves are two small, round wooden sticks, which are knocked together. These are strictly folk-type percussion instruments, indigenous to the music of Latin America, where they usually replace the drums in dance bands. They are invariably written as a two-part unit but with differing rhythmic patterns similar to those given in Ex. 194.

[1] The pebbles inside cause their characteristic sound.

EX. 194. *RUMBOLERO*

Morton Gould

CHAPTER TWENTY-TWO

THE PERCUSSION INSTRUMENTS
IN COMBINATION

Applied Usages - Origins of Rhythmic Patterns
Doubling Techniques - Scoring the Section as an Independent Unit

Band music has long relied upon the percussion section for a variety of extraneous effects, in addition to the more ordinary function of playing basic rhythms. This development was a natural one, inasmuch as the band repertory has always included novelty numbers featuring realistic effects ranging from whistles to anvils. However, as the artistic conception of concert music for the band increases, the percussion section can contribute new realizations of important rhythmic devices.

The variations of pitch levels, timbre juxtapositions, and tonal strengths are all characteristics of the section which are awaiting exploitation. The rhythmic freedom and vitality of twentieth-century music suggest directions for unprecedented polyrhythmic parts within the section as a unit. And the unusual potentialities of percussion instruments at soft dynamic levels promise to be equally rewarding.

It is the band scorer, not the director, who must determine the scope of percussion parts for each piece. Musical styles and textures are the guides which he must follow to determine the kind and number of percussion instruments to be used, as well as their appropriateness and effectiveness. In concert music, these instruments are to be studied and judged in accordance with their capacity to add dimensions of color and nuance, in addition to rhythmic emphasis.

The danger of overextending percussion parts beyond reasonable musical and artistic limits is one which requires constant attention and good judgment. Experience reveals that continuous percussive sounds reduce their intended effectiveness and dull the ear to the perception of juxtapositions of timbre and the power of tonal climaxes. Volume, if it is to be musical, must have instrumental balance as well as tonal strength.

The following list summarizes eleven ways to use the percussion instruments at all dynamic levels in concert music for the band.

1. Establish and maintain rhythmic patterns which can often be derived from principal or secondary thematic material.

2. *Ostinatos* are also effective for instruments without definite pitch, if they are not overdone.

3. Outline melodic ideas or figurations. Instruments with definite pitch are the most appropriate for this purpose. Those without definite pitch can, however, heighten rhythmic intensity.

4. Group scoring of mixed percussive timbres, either as an independent unit or combined with the winds, increases rhythmic vitality and tonal contrasts.

5. Coloristic effects derived rhythmically from melodic ideas supply continuity and interest.

6. Short color splashes, with or without rhythmic design, highlight nuances momentarily.

7. As an independent section with polyrhythmic patterns.

8. Point up the apex of tonal climaxes.

9. The effect of long percussive sound. Rolls on the timpani, snare and bass drums, and cymbal or triangle are the instruments most commonly used for this purpose.

10. Short, quick piling up of percussive timbres.

11. Carry out rhythmic patterns which may not be practicable or idiomatic for the wind instruments.

Percussion parts, when combined with those of the winds, often follow rather definite lines of doublings which increase rhythmic tension and permit considerable contrast of percussive timbres. This scoring technique can be achieved through the use of the following doublings:

1. The light, high-pitched instruments derive their rhythmic patterns from principal melodic lines and/or figurations or from middle harmony parts.

2. The heavier, low-pitched percussion instruments—other than the timpani—support, emphasize, or accentuate the pulsations or accents of the low bass instruments.

EX. 195. *AMERICAN JUBILEE Overture*

Joseph Wagner

Attention has previously been directed toward the desirability of occasional use of the percussion instruments at soft dynamic levels. The next excerpts from a condensed score and the percussion instruments from the full score have been selected to show the number of percussive timbres that are possible within a rather simple and limited melodic and harmonic structure. Notice the dynamic adjustments for all of the parts.

EX. 196a. *TANGO*

Albeniz
Trans. by F. Campbell-Watson

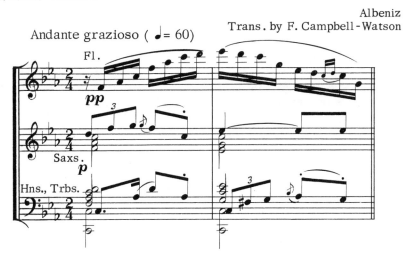

EX. 196b. *TANGO*

Albeniz
Trans. by F. Campbell- Watson

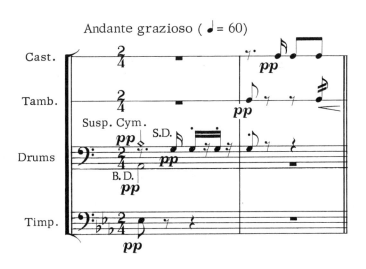

239

Some twentieth-century symphonic composers have experimented quite extensively with percussion instruments as an independent unit. Conceivably, the results of their efforts could be incorporated more frequently, with profit to concert music for the band. The two following excerpts, the first an introduction and the second an interlude, illustrate the direction that might be taken for scoring the percussion section as an independent unit. (Review the percussion parts in Exs. 62, 135, 155, 172, and 175.)

EX. 197a. *VI. MARCH from Divertimento for Band*

Vincent Persichetti, Op. 42

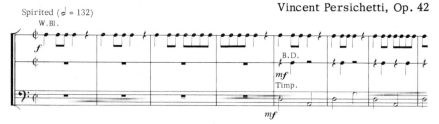

EX. 197b. *VI. MARCH from Divertimento for Band*

Vincent Persichetti, Op. 42

240

∞∞∞

CHAPTER TWENTY-THREE

SUPPLEMENTARY INSTRUMENTS

Harp · Celesta · Piano · Violoncello · Contrabass

The case against the use of the supplementary instruments has been stated in Chap. 3. Their inclusion appears to be a matter of personal choice rather than necessity of instrumentation. The following surveys are intended to clarify their potential assets for the concert band and to supply relevant data for their scoring.

THE HARP

The twentieth-century harp is a diatonic, double-action instrument which permits reasonably quick chromatic changes impossible with the earlier model. It is tuned in the key of Cb major and has the following compass.

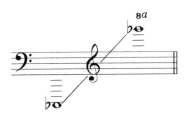

Fig. 42

Pitch changes are made by 7 foot pedals which operate a ratchet mechanism. These pedal positions carry through pitch changes from the tuned starting point (Cb major) in flats (b) through raised semitones in naturals (♮) and sharps (♯), thereby completing the chromatic cycle throughout the full compass of the instrument.

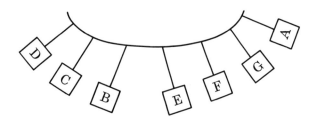

Fig. 43

Notation for the harp is similar to that for the piano with a few significant exceptions.[1] In the past, harp parts have been quite stereotyped, consisting chiefly of fill-in *arpeggios*, bass parts, occasional *glissandos*, and infrequent snatches of melody.

The harp is no longer considered either standard or necessary for the concert band. Its earlier inclusion was mainly a practical concession to a repertory drawn almost exclusively from orchestral sources. Band music, idiomatically conceived and scored, seldom provides opportunities for the inclusion of significant harp parts.

As music for the harp out of context is somewhat meaningless, the student wishing to pursue the subject should study the band parts for this instrument in the following full scores:

Beethoven–Kilbert, Two German Dances (Schirmer)
Campbell–Watson, *Cotton Moon* Overture (Remick)
Cowell, *Shipshape* Overture (Schirmer)
Crist, *Vienna 1913* (Witmark)
Franck–Gillette, *Finale Symphony in D minor* (Witmark)
Gillette, *Fugal Fantasia* (Witmark)
Grainger, *The Power of Rome and The Christian Heart* (Mills)
Hallberg, *Erik the Red* (Shawnee Press)
Humperdinck–Maddy, *Prayer* and *Dream Pantomine* from *Hansel and Gretel* (Remick)
Ingalls, Andante (Presser)
Kechley, Suite for Concert Band (Associated)
Rimski-Korsakov–Harding, *The Tsar's Bride* (Kjos)

[1] A comprehensive study of the harp can be found in Chap. 19 in the author's Orchestration: A Practical Handbook.

R. Strauss–Cailliet, Waltzes from *Der Rosenkavalier* (Boosey-Hawkes)

R. Strauss–Harding, *A Hero's Courtship* (Kjos)

R. Wagner–Cailliet, Excerpts from Act 3, *Lohengrin* (Remick)

R. Wagner–Cailliet, *Siegfried's Rhine Journey, Die Götterdämmerung* (Remick)

Williams, *Pastoral* (Summy–Birchard)

Work, *Portraits from the Bible* (Shawnee Press)

THE CELESTA

The celesta is generally classified as a percussion instrument because its tone is produced by felt hammers striking steel bars placed on a wooden frame. In appearance, it resembles a small harmonium or spinet piano. The tone quality of the celesta is light and subdued when compared to the more brilliant resonance of the bells. Actually, the dynamic range of the celesta is slight. For this reason, the celesta has not been considered adequate by the majority of writers of band music.

Notation is the same as that for the piano, with the bass and treble clefs used on one or two staves as needed. The celesta is a transposing instrument in that its written notation is one octave lower than the sounding one. The full compass is as follows:

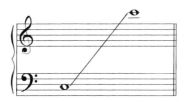

Fig. 44

The celesta is played with the same manual technique as that used for the piano but its usages follow styles associated with harp and bell parts. Its future potentialities in band music should not be compared to its position in the symphony orchestra because of the unequal tonal strengths in the basic sections of the two mediums.

No adequate examples can be given for the celesta in music for the band, since parts for it are practically nonexistent. Exceptions are found in the two following band scores which include a few passages for this instrument:

243

Grainger, *The Power of Rome and The Christian Heart* (Mills)
Kechley, Suite for Concert Band (Associated)

THE PIANO

The range, tone, and technical resources of the piano are sufficiently familiar to make detailed comment unnecessary.

Band parts for the piano as a supplementary instrument have not kept pace with parts in twentieth-century orchestral compositions. However, it would seem that these omissions have been due primarily to practical problems of performance peculiar to the band, not to any disinterest in the piano's value as a supporting instrument. Actually, the piano is far more suitable for band scoring than is the harp. Its greater tonal strength and almost limitless possibilities as a percussive string instrument await exploitation and application.

Many of the scores listed for the harp note that a piano may be substituted if necessary. The following full scores contain parts for the piano in a supplementary capacity. Those scores marked with an asterisk also contain parts for the piano as a quasi-solo *obbligato* instrument.

Falla–Greissle, *Fire Dance* from *El amor brujo* (Chester)
Kechley, Suite for Concert Band (Associated)
McKay, *Three Street Corner Sketches** (Schirmer)
Rogers, Three Japanese Dances* (Presser)

THE VIOLONCELLO

The violoncello (cello) is the real bass voice of the string section. Its playing range covers the bass and tenor *tessituras* with occasional reaches into the alto register. Excessive ledger lines are avoided by the use of the treble or tenor clefs for parts in high registers. It is a non-transposing instrument tuned in fifths and has the following compass:

Open Strings (Tuning)	Clefs Used	Professional Range	Practical School Range

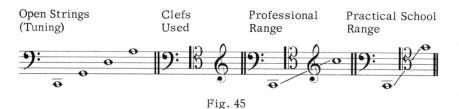

Fig. 45

244

The inclusion of the cello in the performance of band music appears to be by decision of band directors rather than by design of composers or transcribers. This is indicated by the almost total absence of parts for the cello in published band scores.

The cello, when brought into the band, doubles in unison baritone parts. Some directors feel that the cellos are invaluable in taking the edge off the tone of the baritones and tubas. While this may be, it would also seem that a line must be drawn somewhere if the band is to remain a distinctive wind ensemble rather than an unbalanced version of an orchestra.

The following works contain parts for the cello:

Jenkins, *American* Overture (Presser)
Kechley, Suite for Concert Band (Associated)

THE CONTRABASS

The contrabass (string bass) is the lowest bass voice of the string section. Its range is much more limited than that of the cello and its written notation is an octave higher than the sounding one. This instrument is tuned in fourths and has the following compass:

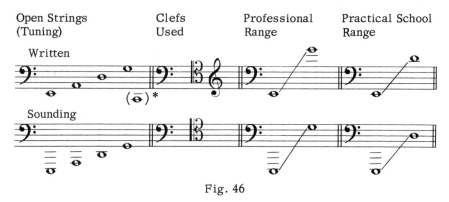

Fig. 46

* Five-string basses with the low C (and C extensions on four-string basses) are the exception.

There are two techniques for playing string instruments: drawing a bow across a string or strings (*arco*), and picking or plucking the strings (*pizzicato*). However, these two ways of producing tone are not exactly interchangeable, as momentary playing breaks are usually necessary for the change of techniques. The abbreviation "*pizz.*" is used to indicate the plucking of the strings, while "*arco*" is inserted for the resumption of bowing.

Phrase markings for the wind instruments usually cannot be applied as bowings for string instruments. This phase of scoring is one which requires specialized study which goes beyond the scope of our present analysis. (See Chap. 6 of the author's *Orchestration: A Practical Handbook*, for a complete explanation of bowing techniques for string instruments.)

The string bass does not occupy a position in the concert band similar to that of the violoncello, since parts for it are included in most published band scores. The directors of the first concert bands frequently used the string bass to smooth out tuba tone, to support it, and to substitute the string *pizzicato* for the tuba *staccato*. Later, when the band movement gained momentum and importance, the majority of composers and transcribers continued to include string-bass parts in the instrumentation along the lines established by the band directors.

Nevertheless, the string bass in the concert band should be considered as an optional supporting and/or supplementary instrument. All undoubled parts for it should be cued either for the tubas or low reeds as a precaution against voids of instrumentation. It is equally important to remember that the string bass is a transposing instrument, which automatically rules out playing from the sounding notation of most tuba parts.

Parts for the string bass are indicated in the following excerpts: Exs. 7, 34, 37, 50, 58, 59, 62, 65, 68, 72, 93, 104, 113, 117, 136, 140, 151, 152, 155, 156, 158, 160, 168b, 173, 174, 188, 191, and 211.

∞∞∞

CHAPTER TWENTY-FOUR

SPECIAL EFFECTS

Trills - Tremolos - Flutter Tonguing - Glissandos - Mutes
Slap Tonguing - Off-stage Players

The technical improvement of wind instruments during the twentieth century has contributed to a virtuoso style of playing heretofore only partially realized. This style, greatly expanded and developed by wind players in dance bands, has opened up new horisons for the writers of concert music for the band. Advanced techniques are no longer considered impractical, except for Grade C and D school bands.

Some earlier generalizations touched upon various forms of ornamental playing styles which, because of certain similarities, may be grouped together under the heading of Special Effects. The following commentary has been designed to help the student to become familiar with the notation for these effects and to view them in musical context.

The trill[1] is a form of ornamentation for the winds which may be employed advantageously to increase tonal tension and brilliance. It is, to some extent, the wind's most practical idiomatic means of approximating the *effect* produced by the unmeasured, bowed-string tremolo. Trills are also effective for long or short notes, especially when scored for the medium-high to high woodwind instruments.

Many trills formerly listed as impossible for the reeds are now considered playable, with special fingerings. However, trills in the lowest fifth of the wood-wind ranges, excepting the clarinet range, are not advisable. The starting and stopping points of all trills should be clearly indicated to avoid misinterpretation, as should the phrasing for grace notes terminating trills.

[1] The trill is always made with the next higher note in the same key, except when otherwise noted.

Although trills of minor and major seconds are playable by brass instruments, except for a few combinations, their effectiveness varies with each instrument and player. Trombone trills are made by means of lip slurs, but only in the high register. The other brass instruments use fingered positions of valves or pistons. Brass trills are somewhat more sluggish, blurry, and boisterous than those for the wood winds and generally lack clear intonation.

The following full-score excerpt (Ex. 198) is a good illustration of long trills for middle- and high-range wood winds. Observe the roll for the triangle as an additional source of brilliance. In this connection, it should be noted that brass trills are comparatively infrequent in band scores (see Ex. 199).

EX. 198. *HUNTINGTONTOWER, Ballad for Band*

Ottorino Respighi

EX. 199. *CONCERTO GROSSO*

Joseph Wagner

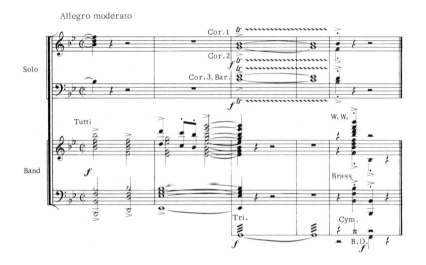

Trills or tremolos which extend over many measures constitute a scoring problem for wind instruments which does not exist
for the strings. The problem, of course, concerns breath changes.
The two-measure *ostinato* in the following excerpt with seventeen
repetitions is one such example. The transcriber has circumvented
the problem by alternating one-measure trills for the reeds in the
same timbre, thereby giving the effect of continuous trills, as in
the original orchestral score. This principle can be applied with
equally good results for extra-long, slurred tremolos or flutter
tonguing.

Manuel de Falla
Version for band by Felix Greissle

Allegro ma non troppo (♩= 126)

Bsn.

Cls.
(B♭)   2   3

T.Sax.
(B♭)

Hns.
(F)   2   4

The tremolo is a quivering or flutter effect similar to the trill. It is idiomatically better suited to the wood winds than to the brass and is easiest to play when confined to intervals of a third. Larger intervals, up to a sixth, are practical for the E♭ and B♭ clarinets. The tremolo, though playable by some brass combinations, tends to sound clumsy, heavy, and unclear. It is a device long associated with orchestral string parts and its adaptation to the wood winds of the band has been made with varying success.

Some band authorities believe tremolos, whether transcribed from keyboard music or orchestral string parts, should be scored as sustained notes for the winds, accompanied by rolls on one or more percussion instruments. Others take a more literal approach to their scoring, preferring to write out the parts in much the same way they do for string instruments. No doubt the final answer is a compromise determined by the idiomatic appropriateness of the tremolo as a contributing or substituting form of note repetition.

The notation for the slurred tremolo requires correct rhythmic representation of both notes of each interval, as shown in Ex. 202a. It is to be noted that trills are frequently combined with the slurred tremolo for the wood winds.

The tremolo in the following excerpt is a wood-wind adaptation of a measured, bowed, fingered tremolo. The one-measure slurs indicate that fresh attacks are to be given on the first beats of each measure. Notice here that there are few harmonic changes. Review Ex. 115 for another version of this style of tremolo. The phrasing in this excerpt requires two separate attacks for each measure.

Rossini
Trans. by Lucien Cailliet

Example 202a is an excerpt from the full score, designed to show the notation and changing chord positions for an unmeasured, slurred tremolo with the phrasing as given in Ex. 201. Trills and tremolos can be satisfactorily combined, as shown in Ex. 202b.

Two technical observations remain to be disposed of in this connection. The slurred tremolo is not well suited idiomatically to the brass instruments, as their tonal weight is too heavy for this style of note repetition. However, slurred wood-wind tremolos can acquire extra resonance if the chord progressions are reduced to part writing for sustained brass instruments.

EX. 202a. *Excerpts from Act One of LOHENGRIN*

Richard Wagner
Arr. by Lucien Calliet

EX. 202b. *Excerpts from Act One of LOHENGRIN*

Richard Wagner
Arr. by Lucien Caillet

Andante moderato

Flutter tonguing is a rather bizarre style of tonguing calling for an extremely rapid repetition of a note without rhythmic precision. It is playable at all dynamic levels. The notation for flutter tonguing is indicated by placing three flags or slanted lines across note stems, as with the bowed, unmeasured string tremolo. The effect of this style of tonguing is unique and coloristic. Richard Strauss used it in his *Don Quixote* to depict the bleating of sheep. It also can sound harsh, agitated, and flashy. Since the style is fatiguing to the player, comparatively short sections are preferable.

This playing style can be used with the non-reeds and the brasses. The single reeds can reproduce a reasonable facsimile of flutter tonguing with some difficulty, but it is technically impossible for the double reeds. Actually, flutter tonguing in the brass is best when scored for the cornets, trumpets, and/or trombones. The other brasses can manage a very fast kind of double tonguing which gives the effect of flutter tonguing.

255

It will be noted that the flutter tonguing in Ex. 203 has been arranged for alternating parts to relieve the strain on the players without losing the effect of the tremolo. Occasionally, flutter tonguing and trills are combined to produce a rather stunning brilliance, as shown in Ex. 204.

EX. 203. *LA BELLE HÉLÈNE, Overture*

Offenbach
Trans. by Felix Greissle

* or tonal repetitions, as rapid as possible

256

EX. 204. *1. INTRODUCTION from West Point Suite*

Darius Milhaud

257

The wind *glissando* has become increasingly conspicuous in concert music for the band, since jazz techniques have been adopted by wind players at most levels. This tonal slide effect, which ordinarily smears or blurs the tone from one note to the next, carries with it a sweeping, boisterous sound that can be quite novel in certain contexts.

The *glissando* can be used for the wood winds and the brasses without undue difficulty for the player, except in the cases of the horn and the trombone. *Glissandos* for these instruments are possible only by the use of lip slurs confined to notes in a single harmonic series of overtones. This technique is ordinarily used by the player when the *glissando* is indicated in the part. A wavy or straight line between two notes is the sign generally used to indicate a *glissando* (see Ex. 205).

There are two styles of *glissando* used for wind instruments. The most common one is that which places the slide effect between two notes separated by more than a second (see Ex. 205). Note that the *glissando* for the trombones adheres to the conditions given previously.

A second style adaptable more particularly to cornets, trumpets, and trombones is often identified as a "rip" *glissando*. It starts on an undetermined note and is indicated by an oblique line preceding each note, as shown in Ex. 206.

EX. 205. *TWINKLE, TWINKLE, LITTLE STAR,*
　　　　　　　　　　　　　　Variations for Concert Band

Frederick Piket

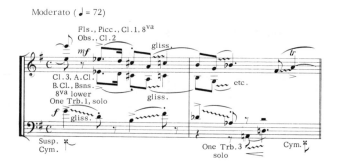

258

EX. 206. *PUPILS ROMP DANCES*
from the ballet Hudson River Legend

Joseph Wagner

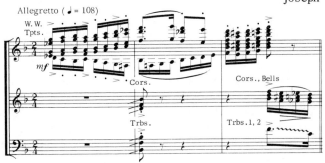

The mute is a device used primarily to soften tone for string and brass instruments; no practical way has been devised to apply it to the wood-wind instruments. However, the mute also alters tone quality to the point of producing changed sets of timbres, which are most valuable to the band scorer. It is highly desirable for the student to become completely familiar with both open and muted tonal characteristics of brass instruments, since these characteristics must be considered in scoring.

Only the cornets, trumpets, horns, and trombones are muted regularly in the band. The words *"con sordino"* or "muted" are used to indicate the muting of a passage. All notes following this direction are to be played muted until the words *"senza sordino"* or "open" are given. In scoring, a few seconds of rest should be allowed for placing and removing mutes.

Mutes are made in a variety of shapes and sizes to produce different sound effects. It is generally assumed that straight mutes will be used unless otherwise specified. Any deviation in mutes, such as cup, solo tone, or "shastock", should be indicated in the cornet, trumpet, and trombone parts. The horns use straight mutes only. Muted parts in range extremes, especially the low registers, are less satisfactory than those in the best playing range of each instrument.

The horn has a second idiomatic method for muting or stopping tone which is not used by the other brass instruments. This is done by combining lip tension and overblowing with the hand inserted more than normally far into the bell. Notation for this style of muting is indicated by placing a cross (+) over the note

259

or notes affected, usually with the word "brassy" or *"cuivré"* added to the part. A circle (o) is placed over the note on which normal playing is to be resumed. This method of muting produces a nasal, metallic twang with loud dynamics and a thin, distant tone with soft ones. When used for accents, the attack is sharp and biting (see Ex. 137). Horn parts in the band are not muted with the same frequency as are those for the cornets, trumpets, and trombones.

The two following examples have been included here to show that specific kinds of mutes are indicated in many condensed scores, as well as in the full scores (see Exs. 207 and 208). The notation for a trombone "laugh", muted or open, is given in Ex. 209. Also note another jazz technique—the use of wire brushes in place of sticks—employed in the Paul Yoder number; and a "Hi-Hat" cymbal.

EX. 207. *PORTRAIT OF THE LAND*

J. Mark Quinn

260

EX. 208. *HI-HAT*

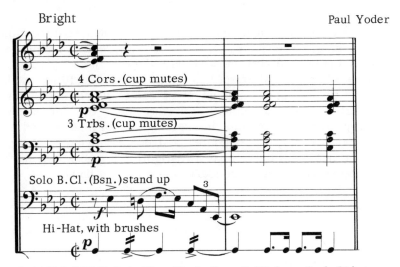

Bright   Paul Yoder

4 Cors.(cup mutes)

3 Trbs.(cup mutes)

Solo B.Cl.(Bsn.)stand up

Hi-Hat, with brushes

EX. 209. *POP! GOES THE WEASEL Variations on the Theme*

Adagio (♩ = 92)   Lucien Cailliet

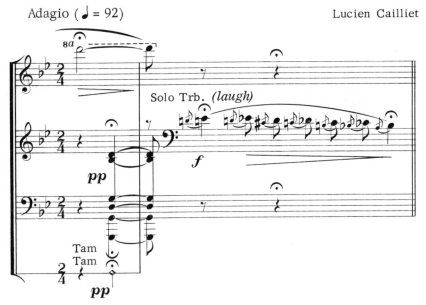

Solo Trb. *(laugh)*

Tam
Tam

Another playing technique appropriated for the concert band from the dance band is slap tonguing. This effect, used mainly for novelty and "show" numbers with a popular jazz flavor, gives each detached note a decidedly percussive attack. It is idiomatic for the single reeds only, and is most successful with the saxophones and only slightly less so with the clarinets.

One other special effect has yet to be tried and fully explored. This is the off-stage placement of one or more instruments for echo effects. David Bennett's arrangement of Morton Gould's *Cowboy Rhapsody* contains interesting use of muffled and unmuffled snare drums, with clarinet and cornet solos off stage. This is an area which might repay investigation and experimentation in connection with scoring concert music for the band.

CHAPTER TWENTY-FIVE

SCORING FOR THE FULL BAND

Chord Spacings and Resonance - Preparing a Score
Scoring Chorals

Scoring for the full band becomes a synthesis of the previous studies devoted to each section. It requires a review and reappraisal of instrumental values heretofore considered more or less within sectional limitations. This expanded creative process deals with multiple instruments and voice parts with an enlarged scope of combinations and potentialities. It necessitates the acquisition and application of some new and different scoring procedures quite apart from those associated with sectional arrangements.

Instruments acquire new standards of diversification when they are combined for full band scores. Idiomatic playing styles and techniques remain unaltered. However, the way in which these styles and techniques are employed involves the need for an expanded scoring technique, one that can cope with the creation of voice textures which can support balanced mixed groupings of unequal instrumental timbres and intensities.

The student of band scoring should avoid all superficial thinking of notes and music as synonymous. Notes are nothing more than the still-life aspects of music. The student's task is to ceaselessly develop his perceptive faculties so that the visual symbols of notation become inseparably associated with gradations of timbre and sonority. This is an acquired skill, indispensable to the successful band scorer and to the conductor. The writer of band music must be able to read *and hear* a score with the objective eyes and ears of the impersonal conductor who translates musical notation into living sound.

Three interrelated components of music remain to be discussed in detail before proceeding with scoring music for the full band. These are structure (or texture), balance, and resonance. The term "structure" refers primarily to the melodic and harmonic spacings of voice parts which affect tonal balance and resonance potentials. The interval pattern of the harmonic series (Chord of Nature) provides a ready-made formula from which certain practical principles of good instrumental spacing can be derived (see Fig. 1).

263

As an experiment, strike—*fortissimo*—one-line C, the fundamental in the series (Fig.1) on a piano, with the damper pedal depressed. Then press down silently any of the tones given as whole notes up to the eighth harmonic in this series. Release the key of the fundamental C, along with the damper pedal. The selected note in the series will continue to vibrate. (Tones above the eighth harmonic are too weak to be picked up.) The explanation lies in the fact that the complete series of overtones, now undamped, is allowed to vibrate freely. This phenomenon, multiplied many times over, accounts for the source of resonance of the piano and harp with the sounding board of each acting as a resonator. Further experiments will reveal that the lower tones in the harmonic series are stronger than the higher ones. *Note:* The quarter notes in the series are not exactly in tune with the tempered scale,[1] and therefore will not sound. The interval pattern of the series also reveals the absence of close-position chords in the low-bass register and a crowding of the overtones as they ascend to the highest note. Here, in this scale of nature, can be found the best pattern for doublings and fillers for all practical scoring purposes. Of the ten triad tones appearing in the series, there are five roots, three fifths, and two thirds. This proportion of triad tones will be generally acceptable in chordal progressions, regardless of the number of added doublings and/or fillers.

There is one more important lesson to be learned about the resonance of the piano that can be applied to the spacing, balance, and resonance problems of writing for the band. Play—*forte*—the C major triad in root position, but without the damper pedal. This

 chord will have a minimum of resonance with little or no vibrancy. Next, play the same triad with the damper pedal depressed. Now observe the change in sonority. The

Fig. 47   sound has come alive because the overtones of the full chord are free to vibrate, picking up sympathetic vibrations[2] from their fundamentals. Repeat this experiment, using an expanded chord of C major (see Fig. 48). Notice the increased resonance and vibrancy with the addition of more voice parts and a lower fundamental. From these experiments it will be obvious

---

[1] The tempered scale is represented by the octave, which can be divided into twelve equal semitones.

[2] The true notes in the harmonic series of each fundamental.

that piano music receives its resonance and brilliance in proportion to its range compass, and that the vibrancy of its sonority, is dependent upon the use of the damper pedal.

Fig. 48

At first glance, these elementary experiments may seem to be oversimplified and without relationship to scoring for the band. Nothing could be further from the truth. Actually, the connection between the piano and the band needs to be thoroughly assimilated and for this reason: there is no damper pedal in the band; it must be built into each score.

The band's equivalent of the piano's resonance can be secured best by proper spacing of all melodic and harmonic elements, along with a judicious arrangement of sustained harmony parts. Chord spacings similar to those shown in Fig. 49 may be permissible for piano writing but they are decidedly unidiomatic for band instruments. Keyboard music is written so that it can be played by ten fingers. Band music has an almost limitless number of voices to draw upon. The chords in Fig. 49 require further attention for an additional reason. Notice that these chords have large note gaps in the middle register.

SPACING FOR PIANO

Fig. 49

(Compare these spacings with those in the harmonic series.) Ordinarily, gaps of this kind would be most undesirable in band scoring and only a complete rearrangement of these chords could ensure tonal balance. Proceed on the premise that all notes sound exactly as written. Figure 50 gives these chords rearranged idiomatically for wind instruments.

265

SPACING FOR INSTRUMENTS

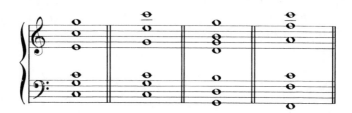

Fig. 50

Figures 51 and 52 are additional examples of chord spacings which should be studied and compared.

SPACING FOR PIANO

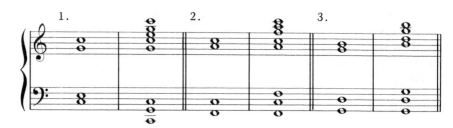

Fig. 51

SPACING FOR WIND INSTRUMENTS

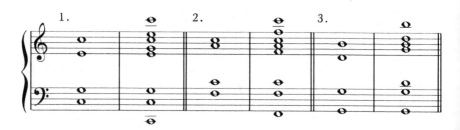

Fig. 52

It is evident from the study of these chord positions that idiomatic chord spacings are essential for balanced part writing. Doublings and fillers do not affect chord positions; rather they act as resonance factors only. Doublings are to be considered as additional voice parts in unison or octaves with existing chord tones.

Fig. 53

Fig. 54

On the other hand, fillers are to be regarded as added chord tones, notes not present in the original example. They may be in any register and should be considered as a means of extending the tonal spread as well as strengthening the middle-range harmonic spacings. In addition, fillers may, of course, be doubled.

Fig. 55

267

From these explanations it can be established that doublings tend to increase volume, while fillers serve to give sonority and balance to the harmonic structure. Neither addition should affect chord positions. In general, harmonic textures, once established, should be maintained until each phrase or passage has been completed. In this connection it should be recognized that chord positions above bass parts can be altered or expanded without changing the original positions of chord progressions.

Fig. 56

The applied principles, as derived from the foregoing uses of doublings and fillers, may serve as preliminary models in any rearrangement of harmonic progressions.

SUMMARY OF DEDUCTIONS

1. Avoid close-position triads in fundamental positions or first inversions in the lower part of the bass register.

2. Added doublings and fillers sound best in this preferred order: octaves (unisons), fifths, and thirds.

3. In general, it is advisable to keep thirds, sevenths, or ninths out of the bass parts when used as part of the sustained harmony. Moving melodic lines or scales with these intervals are not included in the category.

4. Downward from middle C, keep chord progressions in open position.

5. Upward from middle C, arrange extension in close position.

Previous study devoted to the scoring of the wood-wind and brass sections have included settings of *America* as a representative four-part choral. These examples should familiarize the student with some existing disparities of combined instrumental timbres and establish some workable distribution of voice divisions for the scoring of music with functional requirements. By combining the settings given in Exs. 97 and 178, including the revisions suggested in the text, and adding the percussion, we can achieve a scoring for the instrumentation of the small basic band.

A setting for the larger concert or symphonic band (Ex. 211) can also be similarly arranged by combining Exs. 98 and 179. This preliminary phase of scoring for the band is basic and should be carried out by the student with the source material provided in the author's *Workbook for Band Scoring*. These projects can be varied by supplementing vocal chorals with piano music which is essentially in four parts. All settings should be in full score if the full value of this work is to be realized. Both of these settings given for *America* are applications of the range divisions given in Table 5.

The approach to scoring varies with each individual composer. Some sketch their material for the piano; others prefer to set down their ideas in condensed score form; a small number work with a full score without any preliminary drafts. Any of these methods is, of course, acceptable if it produces the desired results.

The position of the transcriber is somewhat analogous to that of the student, since both use source material ordinarily derived from music for keyboard instruments or orchestral scores.[1] Keyboard music obviously presents certain problems of texture and spacing which must be resolved through adaptations for the potentialities of the wind instruments. Although the *Reference Chart* has been designed specifically to facilitate this type of transcription, its application, as illustrated by the many examples, can be equally helpful in band scoring, regardless of the form of sketches employed.

However, a condensed score is indispensable for band music, since many publishers do not issue full scores for their concert-music publications. (Full scores are rarely published for military marches.) Furthermore, preliminary sketches in this form often help to clarify the range, scope, and voice leading of parts, thereby permitting a better appraisal of their fluidity when viewed horizontally.

The following example shows an adaptation of a piano excerpt which is idiomatic for wind instruments. The four necessary and principal elements of the composition have been arranged to convey the *effect* intended by the composer (1) melody, (2) rhythmic design, (3) sustained harmony parts, and (4) bass parts. Sketching scores in condensed form often suggests contrapuntal possibilities which can provide part interest without distorting the flow of the principal melodic lines. The canonic imitation used for the entrance of the third treble voice at 5 in Ex. 212 gives this part melodic profile and makes the transition to the last measure less abrupt than would have been the case if the part had been omitted.

[1] Band transcription of orchestral music is discussed separately in Chap. 28.

EX. 212. *SONG WITHOUT WORDS*

Mendelssohn, Op. 85, No. 4

∞∞∞

CHAPTER TWENTY-SIX

THE REFERENCE CHART OF KEYBOARD IDIOMS AND PATTERNS

Standardization of Transcription Media as a Basic Formula Applied to Band Scoring

---

The exploratory subject matter given thus far has covered technical data concerning the band instruments, including a detailed study of their potentialities, appropriateness, and position in various ensemble combinations from quartets to the full band. Attention has also been directed toward range, timbre, and intensity considerations. These qualities and characteristics have been illustrated in both condensed- and full-score examples. Separately and collectively, these examples constitute a valuable perspective and reference source for band scoring.

Chapter 25 contains preparatory reference data on various working procedures in preparing scores for the band. Pursuant to this discussion, it is generally conceded that music for keyboard instruments (piano or organ) furnishes the most accessible and practical source material for band scoring, either as an entity or in combination with work in original composition. This material is likewise advantageous inasmuch as the great majority of students of this subject are prone to do their musical thinking in terms of a keyboard instrument. The considerations embodied in the studies devoted to the *Reference Chart* can be of inestimable value to the composer of original band music as well, regardless of his instrumental experience or composition habits.

Music for the piano and the organ can be considered as similar only in so far as the digital techniques used for performance of both are essentially interchangeable. And this fact in actual practice does not alter the basic considerations governing the necessity of securing idiomatic modifications of chord spacings as discussed in Chap. 25. The major objective in transcribing keyboard music for the band is not only involved with technical matters of adaptation, but with providing the means of resonance as well. This matter of resonance should be inseparably linked to all scoring plans so that it will become an integral part of a serviceable scoring technique.

Previous studies devoted to piano resonance in Chap. 25 have considered the source and means of amplification. We have seen how chord spacings affect resonance potentials and what modifications are necessary to achieve them for wind instruments. We have further established that the band transcriber is not handicapped by the digital considerations of keyboard music, as he has numerous instruments and voice parts at his command.

However, the transcriber using organ music as source material must, of necessity, differentiate between its tone quality and the method of producing it as opposed to entirely different characteristics of the piano. The organ has a non-percussive tone with practically unlimited powers of *sostenuto* which can be varied and controlled by means of stops and pedals. Piano tone, on the other hand, is basically nonsustaining and percussive.[1] Another differentiating factor concerns the possible tonal spreads of the two instruments. A single note in the piano's middle register may be expanded by as much as four octaves by means of couplers and stops when played on the organ. These are two elements which can directly influence the structural distribution of voice parts in the art of transcription.

Tone quality of the organ is determined by the choice of stops used and the ways in which they are combined for the manuals (keyboards) and foot pedals. These stops vary, not only in timbre, but in pitch and volume. Dynamics are, therefore, somewhat misleading and decidedly comparative when considering band transcription of music for the organ and piano.

The organist and the band scorer function along similar lines in one respect. The former sets his stops at the beginning of each piece and subsequently adds or releases them as determined by the music's character, dynamics, and stylistic features. He seeks appropriate registration (stop settings) with due regard for tonal balance, and avoids those stop changes which would contribute abrupt levels of timbre and volume.

The band scorer executes his task similarly, but on paper, behind the scenes. He does, of course, have greater freedom and artistic license in the manner of handling his materials and resources, but the same unwritten rules of taste in arranging instruments in combination apply equally to him. The organist carries out the musical implications of the printed page; the band scorer defines and decrees his intentions in score form.

[1] The effect of the damper pedal on piano tone has been discussed in Chap. 25.

In one respect, the transcriber of band music is in a totally different position from that of the orchestrator using the same source material. The latter has to consider more than two centuries of tradition derived from a repertory with established styles and textures. The band scorer, on the other hand, has no such equally inclusive guide or library.[1] Nonetheless, the implications derived from certain artistic principles and practices—as culled from the art of orchestration—would seem to have some validity and place in considering band transcriptions of music taken from different periods. (These considerations are particularly pertinent to band transcriptions of orchestral music.) A band transcription of a Bach prelude needs a different kind of texture and treatment than does a prelude by Shostakovitch. This is an area of artistic accomplishment which is dependent upon good judgment, taste, and musicianship.

The *Reference Chart* represents a collective standardization of the *most common idioms and patterns* to be found in music for the piano and organ. In some instances, purely technical considerations may be isolated from their musical context for reasons of clarification when they do not affect structural textures. However, the majority of entries are left in context to show not only all necessary idiomatic modifications but to illustrate the resultant effect upon total voice parts and resonance factors as well. The subject matter of the *Chart* does not neglect the discussion of purely musical values associated with keyboard idioms and patterns. On the contrary, it seeks to develop the material with structural textures suitable for idiomatic band scoring. The scoring of each technical problem in the *Reference Chart* thus becomes a model for all subsequent use of identical or similar subject matter.

Although each example used serves to illustrate a specific major entry of the *Chart*, it will be observed that other entries, shown in parentheses, are constant factors and considerations in all scoring plans. These couplings of entries demonstrate the interrelationship and interdependence of most of the subjects listed in the *Chart*, for the acquisition of a good scoring technique lies in the ability to combine successfully many isolated considerations into a well-organized and unified whole. The texture and part distributions of the music examples in most categories are often suitable for sectional scoring as well as for mixed-timbre ensembles.

Literal transcription of keyboard music for the wind instruments is often rather futile, since the parts for the two types of

[1] This reference is to band music, not to chamber music for wind instruments.

instrument are not always interchangeable idiomatically. The scorer's task is to rearrange characteristic keyboard idioms and patterns as though they were originally conceived for the wind instruments.

Many of the examples which follow illustrate this concept. Often they take the form of divided single-voice lines, either melodic or harmonic, into two or more parts as a practical solution for achieving idiomatic voice textures. This compositional device is often given precedence over any instrument's potential capacity to play unidiomatic keyboard parts; a necessary distinction for the proper approach to the study and analysis of the examples which follow.

The prospective band scorer should keep in mind that a considerable amount of keyboard music does not lend itself readily to transcription for other media. The experience gained from studying the following scored exercises and actual scoring of similar examples provided in the *Workbook* will be helpful preparation for selecting source material—original sketches or keyboard music—suitable for band scoring.

REFERENCE CHART OF KEYBOARD IDIOMS AND PATTERNS

I. BROKEN INTERVALS

    1. Broken octaves (treble and bass)
    2. Broken octaves with embellishments (treble and bass)
    3. Broken octaves combined with other intervals
    4. Broken sixths
    5. Broken thirds
    6. Broken sixths and thirds combined

II. BROKEN CHORDS

    1. Broken chords in close position (treble and bass)
    2. Broken chords in open position (treble and bass)
    3. Mixed chord positions
    4. Broken chords spaced for two hands
    5. Broken chords with implied melodic lines
    6. Broken chords with blocked melodic and rhythmic patterns
    7. Arpeggiated chords

I. BROKEN INTERVALS

Broken intervals are a technical device which enable the composer of keyboard music to establish and maintain certain rhythmic patterns within idiomatic limitations. They are, in effect, used to replace or substitute for repeated intervals and are frequently found in sequence. Because of technical difficulties, they are usually written with *legato* phrasing, especially in fast tempos. The process of transcribing them for wind instruments must, of necessity, include considerable compromise in achieving practical and playable modifications.

Literal transcription of some broken-interval patterns is often possible for single wind instruments under certain conditions.

Tempos, *tessituras*, and dynamics are the important factors to be considered, as is the technical skill of the player for whom the passage is intended. Obviously, rapid tempos, difficult *tessituras*, and dynamic extremes directly affect the practicality of passage work in this category. So, too, must the size of the intervals be considered and sometimes rearranged.

The phrasing styles of broken intervals also require attention, since many of them need revision for performance by the wind instruments. The objective in their transcription should be to preserve their basic interval and rhythmic patterns whenever possible. Non-*legato* single notes which are repeated in a harmonic context are rarely effective except for rather short passages. Detached intervals, on the other hand, sound good when they are properly spaced in good playing *tessituras*. The *effect* of *legato* phrasing can be achieved by combining one slurred part with a more rhythmically active, unslurred part. In addition, it should be remembered that broken intervals, when divided for wind instruments, retain tonal continuity only when they remain in one timbre; mixed timbres result in unequal colors and intensities.

The transcribing process of broken intervals for band scoring is not comparable to that for orchestration, inasmuch as the wind ensemble does not possess a satisfactory equivalent or substitute for the measured string tremolo[1] (a style of repeated notes which may be played either *legato* or *staccato*). As a result, intervals in this category are to be considered and modified according to their over-all *musical effect*. When this has been accomplished, suitable idiomatic adaptions can be made without loss of stylistic features.

The following examples illustrate the many modifications and adaptions which are possible and practical within variable tempos, *tessituras*, and dynamics. They are also intended to stimulate creative musical thinking along similar lines for *they do not constitute the last words on this subject*.

The Roman numerals shown in parentheses, along with their corresponding entries from the *Reference Chart*, indicate their numerical position in the chart and not their technical importance in scoring. The letters RC, when combined with example numbers, refer to subject matter of the *Chart* and are given to facilitate easier identification of music examples and illustrations in this section.

---

[1] The author's <u>Orchestration: A Practical Handbook</u> carries a full explanation of this form of tremolo, with illustrations keyed to the <u>Reference Chart</u>. Also see Section XII of the <u>Reference Chart</u>.

1. Broken Octaves (Treble and Bass Registers)

(Broken Chords, II-1; Outlining, III-2; Two- and Three-part Music, VI; Sustained Intervals, VII-2; Obbligatos, X)

EX. RC1-a-b-c. *TURKISH MARCH from Sonata XVI*

Mozart

1. The repeated octaves double tongued in the treble wood winds[1] are possible at this tempo but not entirely necessary as the alternate setting at (b) is less fatiguing and more idiomatic for multiple units and therefore the one to be used ordinarily. The version at (a) illustrates how sustained notes (cornets) can supply strong *legato* support.

2. The percussion unit is the same as that found in some of this composer's orchestral works.

3. The alternate setting at (c) is one which can be effective for relatively short passages or where the part can be divided within one section of the wood winds.

4. Grace notes, as given in this excerpt, should be incorporated as part of the harmonic texture.

5. The inclusion of an *obbligato* part in this scoring is a matter of personal preference. Purists believe *obbligatos* should not be introduced unless included in the original source material. Others working with the medium feel that occasional interpolated melodies add considerable part interest, especially when there may be frequent repetitions of unchanged thematic material, which is the case in this example.

EX. RC2-a-b. *SONATA PATHETIQUE (bass part only)*

Beethoven, Op. 13

---

[1] This is a recognized technique for piccolo, flute, and bassoon; it is still in the experimental stage for the clarinet, saxophone, and oboe.

1. The *effect* of these broken octaves is as given at (a) and is one of several modifications for wind instruments in very lively tempos. It illustrates the band's inability to cope literally with the problems of rapidly repeated notes which are, of course, quite easy for keyboard instruments and the string instruments of the orchestra.

2. The modification at (b) is not advisable except at moderately fast-to-slow tempos and then only for rather short passages.

2. Broken Octaves with Embellishments(Treble and Bass Registers)

(Melodic Lines, III-4; Two- and Three-part Music, VI-1; Sustained Notes, VII-2; Voice Leading, IX)

EX. RC3. *SONATA No. 17*

Haydn

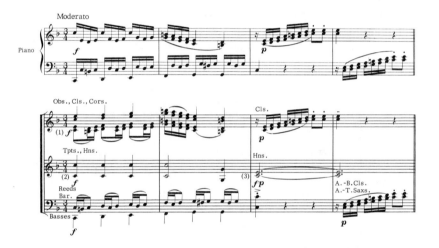

1. A literal approach to scoring embellished octaves, as shown here, is to be avoided as being generally impractical. Octaves in this category are best divided into two parts in a manner which will approximate both interval and rhythmic patterns, regardless of their positions in either the treble or bass registers.

2. Notice that the cornet parts at (1) complete the sixteenth-note figuration derived from the embellishing notes of the alto and bass parts.

3. The full-voice implications of two- and three-part music should be developed whenever the dynamic range is indicative of the need for more than average resonance. In this instance, these required parts are shown at (2) and (3). Notice how the horns at (3) in the middle register bind together the thirds of the treble and bass parts. This is a scoring device deserving special attention, for it illustrates the first lesson to be learned in working with sustained notes in the middle register.

4. Timpani could be added with the trumpets and horns as far as (3).

EX. RC4-a-b-c. *WITCHES' DANCE*

Edward MacDowell, Op. 17, No. 2

Secondary Considerations: (Implied Bass Parts, IV; Spacing Problems, VII-2; Voice Leading, IX; Antiphonal Effects, XI)

1. Broken octaves or other intervals with embellishments in this
arrangement function primarily as a modified form of a trill. Settings for wind instruments must, however, recognize certain player
difficulties directly allied to the necessity for adequate breath
breaks.

2. The setting at (1) can be effective over many measures only if the parts are arranged with *divisis* within each section. The
four-measure slur for Cl. I at (1) is consistent with the higher
trill in the flute.

3. The arrangement at (b) has greater rhythmic interest than
that at (a) and suggests the 2/8 rhythmic pattern found in the original. Notice that the bells (2) have accents with a 2/8 outlining
pattern, as in the original.

4. The antiphonal effect shown at (c) is still another variant
form for embellished intervals. It has the added feature of being
useful as an added form of ornamentation when combined with
either (a) or (b).

5. The melody-harmony spacing with pedal marking at (3) furnishes the clue to the distribution of voice parts in transcribing
passages in this or similar passages.

3. Broken Octaves Combined with Other Intervals

(Implied Bass Parts, IV; Spacing Problems, VII-I; Voice Leading, IX)

EX. RC5. *HUNGARIAN RHAPSODY No. 8*

Liszt

1. Broken intervals in this category, and more especially those in very fast tempos, are best modified for wind instruments along the lines previously discussed for Exs. RC1 and RC2. Inclusion of trills, as seen here, is a useful idiomatic device for increasing rhythmic momentum within restricted technical limitations.

2. The horns at (1) provide pivotal harmony in the middle register which does not interfere with the more rhythmic parts in the trombones and baritone.

3. In much slower tempos, the treble part, as given here, could be developed along lines shown in Exs. RC1 and RC9.

4. Broken Sixths

(Melodic Settings, III-5; Contrast Problems, VIII)

EX. RC6. *WALTZ No. 3*

Dvořák, Op. 54

1. Broken sixths are definitely best for wind instruments when they are divided into two parts, as in Ex. RC6. This rearrangement of the voice textures is a good model to follow for most instrumental combinations, except for the very lively tempos. (Review Ex. RC5.)

2. The opening chords of this excerpt amply illustrate one phase of concerted brass playing which is all too frequently overlooked, namely, *staccato* chords at soft dynamic levels.

3. An element of contrast is introduced at (1) by providing an interplay of timbres between the reed and brass instruments.

287

5. Broken Thirds

EX. RC7-a-b-c-d. *CHARACTERISTIC PIECE*

Mendelssohn, Op. 7, No. 4

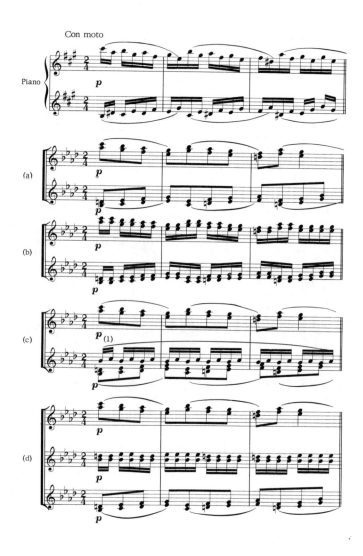

1. Modification of broken thirds for wind instruments follows lines similar to those already established for octaves and sixths. The version at (a) would be the most practical and desirable one for very quick tempos, whether played *legato* or *staccato*. The reduction of the rhythmic pattern does convey the interval effect intended by the composer, notwithstanding the difference in rhythmic notation.

2. The repeated thirds at (b) can be used at very rapid tempos only for relatively short passages where they may add contrast and/or brilliance without fatiguing the player. Technical difficulties of this kind are minimized, of course, in proportion to the speed, dynamic, and rapidity of tongue action required for each passage.

3. The added part at (1) in Ex. RC 7-c restores the basic rhythmic pattern of the original, as in the version given at (a), and retains its *legato* phrasing. This new approach to broken intervals illustrates how embellished notes can be used to vary a rhythmic pattern in a *legato* style. It is a device frequently possible and often more desirable than resorting to repeated notes, which may distort phrasing styles.

4. The setting given at (d) is included here to show how repeated notes can be combined with *legato* phrasing, should it seem to be appropriate or necessary.

6. Broken Sixths and Thirds Combined

Wind transcription of combined broken intervals presents no new procedures beyond those already discussed here. The final choice of modification of all broken intervals will be dependent upon and determined by its appropriateness and practicality, as it pertains to the playing style in the context of each passage. The settings shown in the next two examples indicate the scope of modifications that are playable for wind instruments.

In Ex. RC 8, the added chords at (1) are included here to show one method of supporting higher chords with more rhythmic activity.

The four modifications given in Ex. RC 9 should be studied, appraised, and compared to the other settings in the category as a final exercise in transcribing broken intervals in a variety of interval patterns.

Weber, Op. 24

290

EX. RC9-a-b-c-d. *SONATA*

Beethoven, Op. 26

II. BROKEN CHORDS

The function of broken chords in keyboard music is basically similar to that described for broken intervals, in so far as their use permits chordal representation in rhythmic patterns adapted to a keyboard technique. However, chord placement and spacing are obviously designed for the fingers of two hands and are, therefore, subject to considerable modification before they can be considered as acceptable for the wind instruments of the band. (Review Chap. 25 on chord spacings.)

Chords in this category are generally written as a single voice line from which harmonic progressions can and must be deduced and rearranged to fit known requirements of spacings. This phase of transcribing requires constant vigilance if good voice leading is to be established and maintained (see Section IX of the *Reference Chart*). Here too, the band scorer will note certain limiting factors which are peculiar to wind instruments and not associated with the strings of the orchestra. The ultimate objective is that which achieves the best sounding voice textures for wind instruments without sacrificing a loss of the music's stylistic features.

1. Broken Chords in Close Position (Bass Register)

(Melodic Settings, III-5; Implied Bass Parts, IV; Three-part Music, VI-1; Sustained Notes, VII-2)

EX. RC 10. *HUNGARIAN RHAPSODY No. 7*

Liszt

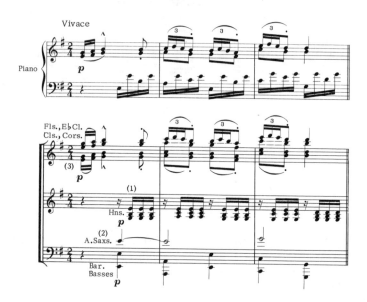

1. The fast, dance-like character of this excerpt suggests a need for afterbeats (1) rather than a broken-interval treatment for the middle harmony parts.

2. Notice how the lowest bass notes of the piano part are here extracted from the broken chords. This technique is one to be encountered frequently in the process of establishing bass parts implied in the harmony of broken chords of piano music. Usually the lowest notes in the figurations are the ones to be selected for this purpose.

3. The sustained part at (2) adds harmonic cohesiveness without assuming *obbligato* significance.

4. The cornets at (3) give necessary support to the higher and weaker wood-wind parts. *Note*: The afterbeats for the horns in this *vivace* are entirely playable since both beats will be given. See text and examples for Ex. RC 41-a-b-c.

EX. RC 11. *PIÈCE HÉROÏQUE*

César Franck
Trans. by Joseph Wagner

293

1. This scoring illustrates how broken chords can be combined with sustained chords to carry out a specific rhythmic pattern. Observe the manner by which these parts at (1) alternate within the B♭ clarinet section, thereby relieving the player of unnecessary fatigue and difficulty. Clarinets II and III are combined here to match the frequently larger section assigned to the first part.

2. The expanded melodic line at (2) is desirable as a means of ensuring balance between the melodic and harmonic parts.

3. The *crescendo* in the harmony parts is marked *poco* to restrain the dynamic potentials of these heavier instruments.

EX. RC 12-a. *POLONAISE*

Beethoven, Op. 89

Secondary Considerations:(Outlining, III-2; Repeated Phrases, III-5; Spacing Problems, VII-1, 2; Antiphonal Effects, XI; Two-part Music, VI-1)

1. These broken chords, transcribed as repeated chords, promote a rhythmic lift needed for this dance movement. From the foregoing examples, it can now be established that broken chords in the bass register can ordinarily be readjusted for two different functions, namely, middle harmony progressions and separate bass parts. Subsequent examples will reveal that considerable freedom may be taken in transcribing these chords for wind instruments. Example RC 12-b is given here to show how repeated chords may be further modified for *legato* phrasing, preferably by wood winds.

EX. RC 12-b. *POLONAISE*

Beethoven, Op. 89

2. The cornets at (1) in Ex. RC 12-a serve the dual role of outlining the melodic line and sustaining middle harmony parts. Notice how these parts form a firm brass core as combined with the trombones.

3. The trumpet notation at (2) is an antiphonal effect derived from the wood winds.

4. The repeated chords at (3) are not difficult at this tempo and they brighten the end of the phrase preceding a bridge passage.

5. This excerpt demonstrates the need of and the manner for establishing melody, harmony, rhythm, and bass parts from most keyboard music in two or three parts.

1. Broken Chords in Close Position (Treble Register)

Chords in this classification are somewhat more problematical in transcription than those in the bass register. They too have a dual purpose and function, in that they are generally designed to complete harmonizations, while simultaneously maintaining rhythmic momentum. It is an area where the transcribers of band music have displayed and exercised considerable artistic license. Nonetheless, the band scorer should seek the idiomatic adaptations which most approximate the *effect* of broken chords, retaining their interval and stylistic features while circumventing all attempts at literal transcription.

Here too the importance of the damper pedal as a contributing factor to piano resonance (see discussion in Chap. 25) is often of significance in scoring some chords in this category. When these chords occur in passages showing a need for resonance as well as rhythmic elements, in the treble register, the scoring plan can resemble the methods used for chords in lower registers, as previously discussed. Basic rhythmic implications are to be retained while outlining and/or sustained harmonic parts are fitted in as background elements.

EX. RC 13-a-b. *PASSACAILLE*

Handel

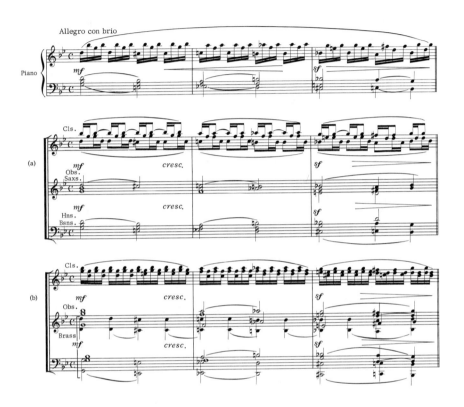

Secondary Considerations: (Spacing Problems, VII-2; Voice Leading, IX)

1. This strictly chordal excerpt has been scored at (a) to illustrate the manner in which broken chords in the treble register may be divided into two parts. It can be considered as a satisfactory model for all tempos.

297

2. Example RC 13-b presents a wood-wind version of the measured tremolo combined with an expanded harmonic texture. Notice
the outlining parts in the soprano and alto registers. The student
is advised to remember that many of the embellishing devices
used in some of the examples illustrating the *Reference Chart*
(canonic imitation, chordal figuration, embellishments, and so
forth) have been given, not necessarily because they are indispensable in any specific scoring, but rather to indicate ways and
means of developing parts to increase melodic, harmonic, or
rhythmic interest. The final decision about their inclusion must
remain the prerogative of each band scorer as it concerns what
is best for the band—best technically for the players and best
musically for the listeners.

The scoring of the following excerpt reveals the extent of change
that is sometimes deemed necessary to secure idiomatic representation of chords in this classification.

EX. RC 14. *TROÏKA EN TRAINEUX, Sleigh Ride*

Tchaikovsky, Op. 37a, No. 11
Trans. by Charles O'Neill

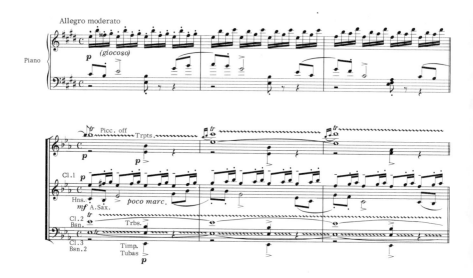

2. Broken Chords in Open Position (Bass Register)

Broken chords in this category are transcribed similarly to those already examined in close position. The lowest notes are usually extracted from these chords to form independent bass parts, while the remaining notes are rearranged and spaced advantageously for wind instruments.

EX. RC 15. *INTERMEZZO*

Brahms, Op. 119, No. 3

Secondary Considerations: (Melodic Settings III-5; Implied Bass Parts, IV; Spacing Problems, VII-1, 2; Voice Leading, IX)

1. This setting should be studied from two points of view. First, consider the method used at (1) for sustaining and outlining the full-chord progressions as indicated by the pedaling *col Ped*. Second, observe the manner by which the rhythmic parts at (2) are spaced and kept in a single timbre. The voice texture of this setting is a good working model for most chord progressions in this category, regardless of the instruments used.

2. The harmony parts in the treble (3) will carry well with the melody instruments at (4).

3. The sustained bell tones will brighten the melodic line without distortion, which would occur if it were played with a roll.

2. Broken Chords in Open Position (Treble Register)

Little change in scoring these chords will be necessary from those studied previously in the bass register. In this connection, it will be remembered from the interval pattern of the harmonic series that chord tones in the treble range become close together as the higher registers are reached. (Review spacings in the series in Chap. 5, Fig. 1.)

Schubert, Op. 120

Secondary Considerations: (Chord Repetitions, V; Two- and Three-part Music, VI-1; Contrast Problems, VIII)

1. The phrase repetition here suggests a change of *tessitura* for the melodic bass and broken chords in the treble. The repeated chords in (a) at (1) need the sustained support shown at (2) while those at (3) will also have better harmonic continuity by continuing the sustained wood winds as at (4). The repeated chords, as scored here, are typical of much of this composer's orchestral writing.

2. An alternate modification of these chords is given at (b).

3. Although the *legato* style of phrasing at (5) is often desirable and effective for the Bb clarinets, the change to cornets shown at (6) is rarely used, as it would be decidedly cumbersome. Brass instruments, though technically equipped for playing chords in this manner, are rarely so employed because their tonal spreads are heavier and thicker than those of the wood winds.

3. Mixed Chord Positions

EX. RC 17. *SONATA No. 3*

Schubert, Op. 120

Secondary Considerations: (Outlining, III-2; Melodic Settings, III-5; Implied Bass Parts, IV; Sustained Chords, VII-2; Voice Leading, IX)

1. Chords with mixed positions (close and open) differ from those previously analyzed only in that further modifications are often necessary to ensure consistent voice textures and good voice leading.

2. The outlining by a double reed at (1) provides good contrast with the harmonic figuration and sustained chords in the single reeds.

3. Notice that the bass part has been modified to fit the ranges of the baritone saxophone and the bassoons, thereby permitting the excerpt to be played solely by the wood-wind section.

4. Although the voice textures here would allow the scoring of some brass instruments in place of those indicated, the character of the phrase suggests lightweight timbres, with the heavier ones reserved for subsequent repetitions of the main thematic material.

4. Broken Chords Spaced for Two Hands

EX. RC 18-a-b-c. *LITTLE STUDY*

Schumann, Op. 68, No. 14

This piano excerpt, though illustrating this subject in its most elementary form, does not appear as encouraging material for band transcription. Yet it actually contains, by implication, all of the necessary elements for instrumental textures: melody, harmony, and rhythm. These potentialities will now be examined step by step.

1. Chords in this style should first be reduced to part writing as shown at (a).

2. Once this has been accomplished, the characteristic rhythm of the phrase can be added to either the alto and/or tenor parts, whichever seems most appropriate, as in (b).

3. The voice texture may then be further expanded, as shown in (c), and the part interest increased by the addition of a counterpoint or *obbligato*, as at (1) (see Section X of the *Reference Chart*).

This simple exercise not only provides pertinent information on the modification of broken chords spaced for two hands, but also illustrates how a single line or part can often be expanded and developed to meet the multiple voice requirements for the wind instruments of the band.

EX. RC19. *SONG WITHOUT WORDS*

Mendelssohn, Op. 62, No. 1

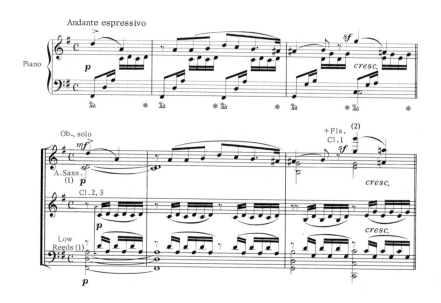

304

Secondary Considerations: (Melodic Settings, III-5; Implied Bass Parts, IV; Two-part Music, VI-1; Sustained Notes, VII-2; Voice Leading, IX)

Keyboard music abounds in this style of writing from which harmony and bass parts must be extracted, rearranged, and combined with essential rhythmic patterns. Although the working details for these assignments will vary with each piece, the fundamental objectives and methods will remain quite regular.

1. Note how the sustained notes at (1) fill in the harmonic gaps caused by the rhythm of the B♭ clarinets II and III.

2. This is still another example illustrating the manner in which two-part music can be reworked to meet the requirements of band textures.

3. Also, observe the entrances at (2) to support the subsequent *crescendo*.

4. Finally, follow the voice line of each part in considering the voice leading.

5. Broken Chords with Implied Melodic Lines

EX. RC 20. *MOMENT MUSICAL*

Schubert, Op. 94, No. 1

Secondary Considerations: (Sustained Notes, VII-2; Voice Leading, IX; Secondary Parts, X)

Composers of piano music often turn to this technical device as a means of securing melodic-harmonic combinations playable by one hand. Modifications of it for wind instruments can best be secured by first extracting the melodic line in its entirety and then completing the harmonic-rhythmic parts.

1. Chordal pivoting[1] around one or two notes or chords often

---

[1] Harmonic progressions which gravitate toward one tonal center, usually a principal triad.

306

permits the arrangement of flowing parts within a limited framework, as shown at (1).

2. The first measures of the phrase here in the wood winds is answered by the brass at (2), while the continuation of the triplet figuration at (3) supplies continuity and part interest.

3. Notice the sustained alto part at (4), as reduced from the lowest treble notes.

4. The bells give a piquant, percussive tint which brightens the wood-wind timbres.

6. Broken Chords with Blocked Melodic and Rhythmic Patterns

Chords in this form, often in two parts and generally associated with pre-twentieth-century composers, are only partially successful when transcribed for wind instruments. They are especially troublesome when they extend over many measures in quick tempos. The following settings illustrate one practical approach to this scoring problem.

Secondary Considerations: (Implied Melodic Lines, II-5; Outlining, III-2; Implied Bass Parts, IV)

1. Chords appearing in two parts must first be rewritten with consistent voice textures, as shown at (a). By so doing, the implied melodic line and bass parts become apparent and the middle harmony parts are easier to manipulate.

2. After this reduction has been made, characteristic rhythmic patterns (1) can be idiomatically modified for wind instruments and positioned advantageously. This accomplished, the other necessary component parts can then be added without difficulty, as shown at (3) in (b).

3. The triplets given in (c) are a useful alternative version for very vigorous passages with strong dynamics. If this form is used, the instruments at (1) should be shifted to the higher treble shown at (2). These triplets, thus combined, would have both brilliance and tonal strength. An alternative melodic line (2) is permissible to reproduce the rhythmic pattern of the original; it would not be necessary for the soprano part at (3).

Mendelssohn, Op. 7, No. 4

Secondary Considerations: (Broken Thirds, I-5; Outlining, III-2; Spacing Problems, VII-1, 2)

Blocked chords, often in sequence and with few harmonic changes, can be modified idiomatically for wind instruments in several ways. The two settings given here are suggested as both practical and representative. Notice that there are alternating parts in both (a) and (b). These parts would regularly be given to wood winds rather than brasses, for the latter are more useful when outlining and/or sustaining the basic notations of the broken blocked chords.

7. Arpeggiated Chords

Band transcription of arpeggiated chords differ somewhat from the other kinds of broken chords inasmuch as they must be idiomatically revised and then placed in good playing ranges adequately supported by sustained harmony; otherwise they will sound weak and ineffectual. And these considerations remain valid, regardless of the dynamics employed. The addition of sustained tones is a direct application of the lessons learned in Chap. 25, which dealt with the subject of resonance and its importance in arranging the right kind of textures for band music.

A distinction has been made between chords in this category and those previously discussed as broken chords since the arpeggiated variety ordinarily spans considerably more than an octave. The earlier examples applied primarily to chords of not more than a tenth.

Grieg, Op. 54, No. 4

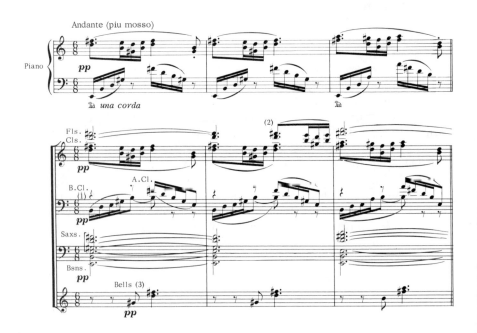

^{i} Secondary Considerations: (Outlining, III-2; Implied Bass Parts, IV; Three-part Music, VI-1; Spacing Problems, VII-1; Antiphonal Effects, XI)

1. This scoring for the wood-wind section at a *pianissimo* level demonstrates the value of sustained chords for *arpeggios* as shown at (1) for, without them, the effect would be that of chamber music style[1] rather than band music. This distinction is one not to be overlooked or slighted. It reverts to the discussion of resonance examined in Chap.25.

2. Notice the sustained flutes outlining the Bb clarinets and

[1] Music for winds intended for small groups of players without doublings.

312

subsequently acquiring independent part interest by the antiphonal effect at (2).

3. The bells at (3) have an outlining function in addition to their coloristic value.

EX. RC24. *PIÈCE HÉROÏQUE*

César Franck
Trans. by Joseph Wagner

Secondary Considerations: (Three-part Music, VI-1; Spacing Problems, VII-2; Voice Leading, IX; Antiphonal Effects, XI)

1. The band transcription of this organ excerpt carries over the essential points made for Ex. RC23. Observe the manner by which the *arpeggios* at (1) are supported by the horns at (2).

313

2. The antiphonal effects starting at (3) contribute thematic interest and continuity with lighter timbres than the melodic lines they imitate (see Section XI).

EX. RC25. *PIÈCE HÉROÏQUE*

César Franck
Trans. by Joseph Wagner

Secondary Considerations: (Melodic Settings, III-5; Three-part Music, VI-1; Spacing Problems, VII-1, 2; Contrast Problems, VIII; Voice Leading, IX)

1. The three-part *arpeggios* are indispensable here, if a maximum sonority is to be achieved for the *fortissimo*.

2. Observe the tonal strengths for the melodic phrases at (1) and (2). Evaluate the comparatively weak highest part at (2) as compared to the equal-strength octaves at (1). This comparison will illustrate the point made frequently in earlier chapters concerning the lack of brass timbres in the high range of the treble clef.

3. Compare this scoring with the previous one for the purpose of determining the scope of resonance needed for each band score.

EX. RC26. *SONATA No. 3*

Schubert, Op. 120

Secondary Considerations: (Spacing Problems, VII-1, 2; Contrast Problems, VIII)

The pianistic version of these arpeggiated chords, though technically playable by the reeds, present something of a problem if used literally in octaves. Their rearrangement, as given, lies in better *tessituras* for the instruments indicated as combined with the outlining sustained chords.

315

III. MELODIC LINES AND FIGURATIONS

We have seen in Section II-5 (specifically in Ex. RC 20) how idiomatic parts for wind instruments can be developed from chords with implied melodic lines and rhythmic figurations. The observations given there may be applied equally well to the creation of similar parts in original music for the band. The chief concern in both instances is to devise smooth-flowing lines with good voice leading and then select instrumental timbres which will provide the best representation for each part.

The band scorer seeking wide acceptance of his work is advised to familiarize himself with the various intonation difficulties that may be encountered with the wind instruments, since their performance varies considerably with the technique and musicianship of each player. Rimski-Korsakov advised having instruments playing in their best registers in preference to forcing others into uncontrolled ranges. This advice still remains valid for successful writing for wind instruments.

A pertinent example in this instance could be the scoring of a passage with large chromatic intervals for a double-reed instrument when a single-reed instrument would ensure far better results tonally. Forcing instruments into ranges where dynamic extremes cannot be played without forcing is another illustration. Awkward slide positions and other technical data have previously been cited for each instrument as a guide to prevent both technical difficulties and tonal distortions. Such passages, written without due regard for each instrument's technical capacities, must be attributed to the scorer even though he cannot be held responsible for poor intonation resulting from technical shortcomings of the player.

1. Large Melodic Skips

Melodic lines, when combined with broken chords, often contain large melodic skips that are generally unsuited to performance by wind instruments. Passages of this kind can usually be modified idiomatically by dividing the melodic line into two or more parts. The band scorer's task is to rearrange these parts so that they will retain the general *effect* of the original rhythmic and interval patterns, but always in terms of voice textures which will sound well alone and when combined as a unit. Example RC 27 shows six styles of melodic lines in this classification with suggested practical voice divisions which may be applied to the scoring of the wood winds whenever appropriate.

316

EX. RC27-a-b-c-d-e-f. *PERPETUAL MOTION (treble only)*

Mendelssohn, Op. 119

Although large melodic skips are somewhat less hazardous for most winds than for the strings, the risk of poor intonation nevertheless exists whenever awkward fingerings are present. Example RC 28 is a case in point. The eighth-note figuration (1), though idiomatically playable by a few wood-wind instruments (flutes or clarinets), would ordinarily be ineffective if transcribed literally because the two *implied* voice lines would lack proper melodic definition. This phrase is a good example of a melodic line combined with an embellishing figuration. An idiomatic modification of it for wind instruments requires a two-part division as shown at (2).

EX. RC28. *VALSE CAPRICE No. II.*

Grieg, Op. 37

Secondary Considerations: (Melodic Setting, III-5; Contrast Problems, VIII)

The dynamic change in measure 4 has a direct effect upon the fullness of the scoring and the arrangement of the brasses and percussion. Notice how this point is reflected in the percussion parts, as well as those for both wind choirs. (Consult Section VIII, with its suggested voice allocations covering the entire dynamic range.)

EX. RC29. *VALSE CAPRICE No. II.*

Grieg, Op. 37

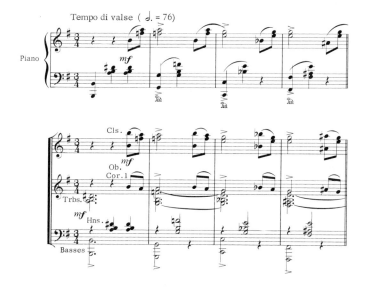

Secondary Considerations: (Spacing Problems, VII-2; Voice Leading, IX)

1. This excerpt is another variety of melodic line with large pianistic skips and irregular voice leading. Wind settings of this style of writing can often be modified so that consistent voice textures will have good voice leading (see Section IX). Notice the manner in which the principal and secondary melodic lines are arranged as a three-part voice progression in good registers for each instrument.

2. The disposition of the bass parts merits attention, as the pedal markings indicate the necessity for a changed notation which will accurately represent the exact rhythmic values that are required.

3. Once again, compare this setting with Ex. RC 28 so that the tonal spreads of each may be evaluated in terms of comparative dynamics

Note: Example RC 29 illustrates a point made earlier about the possibility of several satisfactory settings being made for the same piece. This excerpt could be scored quite literally for the wood winds with a pleasing effect. However, the intervals in the treble (unisons and thirds), though not difficult, would have better voice leading if consistent voice textures were arranged as given.

2. Outlining a Melodic Line

EX. RC30. *BAGATELLE No. 9*

Beethoven, Op. 119

Secondary Considerations: (Broken Chords, II-4; Spacing Problems, VII-1, 2)

1. The broken-chord figuration in the first two measures here is an excellent illustration of a pianistic passage in need of outlining which leads to a division of parts as shown. The scoring presents still another example aimed at demonstrating how *legato-* outlining parts may be successfully combined with non-*legato*

321

repeated notes, yet producing an over-all slurred effect which is ordinarily quite acceptable.

2. Observe the manner in which the sustained parts at (1) function to support those at (2) and the way they fill in the harmonic gap present in the original as the melodic line ascends.

EX. RC31. *PUPILS' ROMP DANCES from Hudson River Legend*

Joseph Wagner
Trans. by the composer

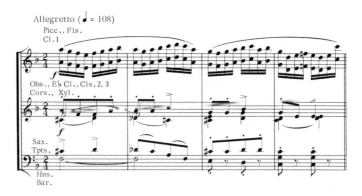

Outlining will frequently cause dissonances, as is the case in this excerpt. In this connection, it should be noted that the rapid figuration—with the dissonances—is confined to the light wood winds, while the outlining part is given to the heavier cornets with the xylophone accenting this part with coloristic spice.

Outlining is also a useful device for rapid scale passages without harmonization (1). This is an area which can sound hopelessly weak, especially in small bands, unless outlining or harmonic support is present. Chords are also often employed for outlining as at (2). These high harmonic parts contribute cutting brilliance not obtainable from the soprano-range cornets and trumpets. Note the interchange of the cornet parts starting at (3) as a support for the weaker wood winds for this sweeping scale passage.

Schubert, Op. 120

3. Dividing a Melodic Line

EX. RC33-a. *LITTLE PRELUDE*

J. S. Bach

EX. RC33-a (continued)

Example RC33-a serves to confirm an earlier assertion to the effect that occasional keyboard figurations can be adapted for the winds with only slight alterations. This setting has been left simple and direct in keeping with the Baroque style.

Example RC33-b has been included here principally to demonstrate how the same source material can be rescored with greater fullness, brilliance, and sonority, due to better idiomatic writing for the brasses. The analysis which follows it accounts for the various interpolated parts.

Purists will prefer the first version, since it is nearer to the spirit of the original. Others with different leanings may respond equally well to the second setting. In either case, the latter should be considered as serving its purpose of illustrating ways and means for dividing a melodic line in the treble or bass register.

J. S. Bach

326

Secondary Considerations: (Broken Chords with Implied Melodic Lines, II-5; Implied Bass Parts, IV; Two- and Three-part Music, VI-1; Spacing Problems, VII-1; Voice Leading, IX)

1. Band transcriptions of music in this two- and three-part style sound best when full advantage is taken of the implied voice potentialities, as shown here (see Section VI). Literal settings, though often possible and sometimes desirable, tend to ignore the fundamental principle of developing voice textures in keeping with the instrumentation of the band. This is particularly applicable when melodic lines are combined with chordal figurations.

2. Sustained chords which outline, as at (1), often clarify and support harmonic implications of divided melodic lines.

3. The chords starting at (2) support harmonically the melodic line, provide middle-range resonance, and fill the harmonic gap caused by the ascending treble parts.

4. The trumpet parts at (3) illustrate how thematic interest—often antiphonally arranged—may be developed from chordal progressions. Notice that the added tenor part at (4) carries out the octave patterns used in the two previous measures.

5. Observe the way the rhythmic feel of the mordent at (5) is realized by the snare drum. This is particularly effective here in building up the *stretto* effect of the *crescendo*. In this connection, it is to be noted that embellishments, such as mordents, trills, turns, and so forth, are better for the wood winds than for the brass.

6. The bells at (6) outline the melodic figuration and consolidate the two treble parts.

7. A final examination of this setting should be devoted to the matter of voice leading for all parts, alone and in combination.

327

4. Melodic Lines Combined with Repeated Note Patterns

EX. RC34-a-b. *SONG WITHOUT WORDS*

Mendelssohn, Op. 19, No. 2

Secondary Considerations: (Dividing a Melodic Line, III-3; Single-note Repetitions, V; Two- and Three-part Music, VI-1)

1. The scoring objective for music in this category entails the arranging of divided voice parts so that they will, when combined,

preserve the musical and stylistic features of the original.

2. The technique used for dividing a melodic line can usually be applied here with satisfactory results. This procedure is similar to that used for extracting implied bass parts (see Section IV).

3. The rhythmic pattern, continuous sixteenth notes in this instance, can be arranged in two ways: first, by embellishing pivotal repeated notes as in Ex. RC34-a which permits *legato* phrasing; a second, by substituting chord tones for embellished notes, as in Ex. RC34-b. Ordinarily, the style shown in Ex. RC34-a is preferable because of ease in playing.

4. This excerpt, as scored for a wood-wind ensemble, utilizes the good sustaining qualities of the saxophones for middle harmonies with the higher-pitched instruments reserved for the *sforzando* in the third measure.

5. Melodic Settings: Contrasts, Comparative Strengths, and Repeated Phrases

The subject of melodic settings in band scoring is one of paramount importance inasmuch as principal thematic material must have adequate timbre definition if is to be heard in its proper perspective and balance. Tonal profile can be secured by achieving a distinctive balance between melodic lines (principal and secondary) and all accompanying parts.

The scored examples here contain a variety of melodic settings which should be studied and analyzed in their musical context. Some of the factors which make this definition possible will now be examined as separate entities.

Contrast. The element of contrast is essential to all concert music for the band if it is to have clarity and distinctiveness. This quality is particularly applicable to melodic settings which must dominate all combinations of instrumental distributions for *tutti* passages. In addition, it is worth noting that melodies lose their effectiveness if confined to a limited *tessitura*, color, and range over extralong passages.

Tonal Strengths. Clarity of tonal definition is obtainable through an understanding of comparative instrumental strengths. Previous study of each instrument's strong and weak ranges has shown that many factors in these areas are to be considered in appraising their relative values because of the variance in tonal strengths and timbre intensities.

Spacing. Melodic lines reach maximum effectiveness when their accompanying parts are spaced so that they permit freedom of movement without clashes with conflicting and stronger tonal strengths. Here, too, strong and weak ranges, timbres, and doublings play an important part when considering scoring plans for band music. (See Section VII dealing with spacing problems.)

Repeated Melodic Phrases. Repeated melodic phrases can often be given renewed interest by the juxtaposition and/or alternation of timbres and *tessituras*. Short answering phrases with alternating mixed timbres may be arranged as a continuous single-line melodic part or may introduce a higher or lower octave for this purpose. Melodic phrases with little rhythmic activity and/or phrase endings with similar movement may also be advantageously embellished by the inclusion of very short canonic phrases, preferably in a contrasting timbre and *tessitura*. (See Section XI for illustrations of this point.)

Note: Each of these four elements is to be found in varying degrees of emphasis, style, and form in practically every illustrative example in this text. The student should learn to recognize these points as each new score is studied.

6. Nonmetrical Passages

Short, semi-cadenza-like passages without actual metrical divisions are the most practical when they are scored for a single solo instrument. Often these passages can be transcribed quite literally and should be scored for an instrument which can perform it in its entirety. Some liberties with notation are permissible when pianistic idioms do not conform to those for wind instruments.

The following example is a representative passage in this classification. *Note*: This scoring advice does not refer to small groupings of grace notes which are an integral part of a melodic line.

330

Jean Sibelius, Op. 85, No. 3

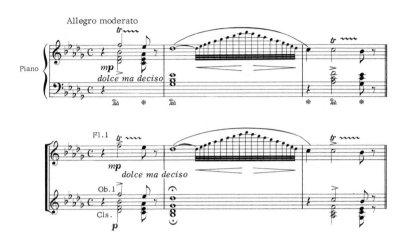

IV. IMPLIED BASS PARTS

Whereas the extraction and use of implied melodic lines (Section II-5) is indispensable, their counterparts in the bass register—implied bass parts—must be appraised and applied somewhat differently because their functions are not always the same. The band scorer must, in each instance, decide what advantages are to be gained by the use of implied bass parts before proceding with the extraction of these parts, *for their inclusion is not always desirable*. The deciding factors generally arise from the following considerations:

1. In what context do the passages occur—two, three, or four parts?

2. Would the division of a bass part help or hinder the fluidity of a melodic-bass phrase?

3. Can the scoring of implied bass parts contribute support

to the melodic and harmonic structure and is it needed for this purpose?

4. Should extracted bass parts be doubled with revised *tessituras*?

The answers to these questions can help to determine the advisability of including implied bass parts when opportunities arise.

A number of the excerpts shown thus far have included the application of this technique. (Review Exs. RC1, RC3, RC10, RC12, RC15, RC17, RC18, RC19, RC21, RC22, RC23, RC26, RC33, and RC34.) Others that follow will further explore this subject, but as a secondary entry of the *Reference Chart*. Examples RC36 and RC37 are two widely different instances where the extraction of implied bass parts is a decided advantage to the arrangement of the voice textures for the instruments of the band.

EX. RC36. *GAVOTTE from English Suite in D minor*

J. S. Bach

Secondary Considerations: (Dividing a Melodic Line, III-3; Three-part Music, VI-1; Spacing Problems, VII-2; Contrast Problems, VIII; Voice Leading, IX)

1. The bass part starting at (1) illustrates the point that the lowest notes in a florid bass line are not always the proper ones for an implied bass part. However, when properly chosen and scored, they will furnish adequate bass support for treble parts without detracting from the rhythmic flow of chordal figurations (2).

2. This example further demonstrates some of the possibilities available in this category for developing voice textures from three-part music.

3. Notice how the parts at (3) in the middle register supplement and support those in the higher treble at (4).

4. Observe the manner in which the tonal spread and strengths in the opening measures marked *forte* are reduced at (5) to ensure contrast for the dynamic change of *mezzo forte*.

5. Follow the voice-leading pattern of all parts.

EX. RC37. *AUTUMN SONG, October*

Tchaikovsky, Op. 37a, No. 10

333

Secondary Considerations: (Sustained Notes, VII-2; Voice Leading, IX; Obbligato, X)

1. This excerpt has been selected primarily to clarify the significance of some grace notes when they occur in the bass register. These notes are ordinarily inserted as a technical expedient to ensure the continuity of bass parts. Grace notes in this category, when transcribed for wind instruments, should be incorporated as integral notes of the bass line and notated with proper rhythmic values.

2. Rolled chords, as in the second and third measures, have no place in band music unless scored for the harp, piano, or celesta.

3. Sustained notes, as at (1), provide a degree of harmonic continuity not obtainable from the chords in the trombones at (2).

4. The *obbligato* at (3) is continued in the last measure to finish out the phrase with the melody. Note that this part at (4) is slowed down rhythmically to compensate for the melody triplets (see Section X).

V. SINGLE-NOTE, INTERVAL, AND CHORD REPETITIONS

Previously exploratory studies have included some discussion of this subject, but coincidental with other entries in the *Reference Chart*. The examples which follow are intended to reexamine the variety of ways by which parts in this classification may be modified for wind instruments.

1. Repeated Notes (without Rests) (Treble and Bass Registers)

EX. RC38. *FIESTA MORA EN TANGER from Album de viaje*

Joaquin Turina

Secondary Considerations: (Sustained Notes, VII-2; Obbligato, X; Antiphonal Effects, XI)

1. Although there will be times when passages of this kind might be scored quite literally, there will be an equal number of instances when their transcription will have far greater effect if they are

modified to benefit from the resources inherent in the band's instrumentation. The scoring above is intended to exemplify one such modification.

2. Repeated single notes are not as successful for the winds as they are for the orchestra's strings (see Ex. RC39).

3. The principal octave melody at (1) benefits from the different timbre of the parts at (2).

4. *Obbligatos* in the tenor register are effective if not overdone. The one at (3) has thematic interest, being a canon in the octave with the melody. (This subject is discussed in detail in Sections X and XI.)

5. The timpani part extends the B pedal point [1] to another timbre in character with the original.

---

[1] Long, sustained or repeated note or notes over which other material is superimposed.

EX. RC39. *BEAR DANCE*

Béla Bartók
Arr. by Erik Leidzen

The difficulties involved in the scoring of repeated notes for wind instruments, as opposed to the strings, is well illustrated here in full score. It is concerned with arranging divisional parts for instruments in the same or similar timbres, but so that the total effect will be of one continuous instrument and timbre. A second and equally important point concerns player fatigue. Repeated notes, intervals, or chords which present this problem should be recognized and removed from wind parts.

2. Single Notes, Intervals and Chords (with Rests)

EX. RC40. *POLONAISE*

Beethoven

Rhythmic elements in this classification are not idiomatically effective if transcribed literally. The rest-note pattern, so common in keyboard music, needs to be modified considerably for wind instruments, with the rests removed, as shown in Ex. RC40. The rest-note pattern is valid only when it is an integral part of the rhythmic scheme of afterbeats, as found in marches and dance forms.

3. Melodic Lines Combined with Interval and Chord Repetitions

This melodic-rhythmic combination is one which has extra-special difficulties concealed by its apparent simplicity. These difficulties revolve around problems resulting from dissimilar idioms for unlike media. Various factors are involved in this scoring category for wind instruments, as will be seen in the next two examples.

The first problem arises when intervals or chords *cannot be treated as afterbeats* in the general acceptance of this term. This takes place when a strong beat or pulse does not precede each group of notes with the rest-note pattern. It is especially applicable when there is only one strong beat in each measure. When this happens, melodic lines must first be divorced from the rhythmic elements and then notated with proper form. After this has been completed, the accompanying rhythmic parts (intervals or chords) can be arranged with full representation without rests, as shown in Ex. RC41.

Three versions have been given here to indicate the scope of voice textures and their arrangement, as derived from source material in this style. Example RC41-a or any similar passage is playable by several wind combinations if the passage occurs in a moderate *allegro* or slower tempo that can be conducted "in three" or with three beats to a measure. A passage of this kind in a much quicker tempo, such as *allegro molto, vivo, vivace* requiring but one beat or several strong beats for each measure, causes the afterbeats to be relatively difficult rhythmically and could be scored similarly to Ex. RC41-b or RC41-c. This is an area where the scorer must decide on what is best for the band and its players while adhering to the basic spirit and style of the original source material.

EX. RC41-a-b-c. *BAGATELLE*

Beethoven, Op. 33, No. 2

340

A second style of rhythmic elements requiring considerable modification concerns passages with alternating hand patterns. These passages should be rearranged so that melodic, harmonic, and rhythmic parts will have consistent voice textures, each complete in itself and with good voice leading. The following example illustrates the method to be used for isolating these three elements. The passing dissonances are of no significant consequence.

EX. RC42. *MARCHE GROTESQUE*

Christian Sinding, Op. 32, No. 1

A reduced rhythmic plan (Fig. RC1) of music in this classification can be decidedly helpful in making adaptations for wind instruments. Compare this one-line outline with the snare drum part in Ex. RC42.

Fig. RC1

EX. RC42 (continued)

341

Repeated notes, intervals, and/or chords often appear with the rest-note pattern in *bravura* passages for the piano as in Ex. RC 43. In this particular instance, it is significant that the composer indicated his harmonic intentions by including a chord with the first treble octave. Obviously, attempted literal transcription of this and similar passages would be decidedly impractical. Accordingly, modification for these passages should aim to produce the *effect* of the over-all rhythmic pattern which, in this instance, is realized by the wood-wind trills and percussion rolls. This scoring combination is the one most generally employed to generate tonal tension for passages of this kind.

EX. RC43. *RONDO CAPRICCIOSO*

Mendelssohn, Op. 14

VI. TWO- AND THREE-PART MUSIC

Music in this category requires further classification in terms of its styles—homophonic, polyphonic, and style mixtures. A large part of the music repertory for keyboard instruments contains passages for two and three parts. Sometimes these voice lines are intentional, while at other times they are the result of technical considerations peculiar to the media.

Band transcriptions of music with these textures necessitate an appraisal of several primary considerations. Is a voice texture of two or three parts maintained consistently, or does it alternate with more parts? Do these limited voice textures appear to be an interlude between fuller voice writing with harmonic, not contrapuntal, progressions? Is the style of the music homophonic (one-voiced melody with harmonization) or polyphonic (many-voiced, part against part)? These are the questions which must be settled at the outset before proceding with scoring plans.

There can be no denying the fact that occasional two- and three-part passages, not whole compositions, have good contrast value in concert music for the band. The scorer's task is to select, retain, or insert these thin-voice passages where they would be appropriately effective. However, most two- and three-part music must, of necessity, be revised to meet the instrumentation capacities of the band if a reasonable amount of resonance, tonal strength, and solidity are to be realized.

1. Homophonic

Homophonic music has a single melodic line with harmonization. The harmonic elements may be simple chord progressions or a complex accompaniment without altering this concept. This music is usually conceived and developed with vertical movement of parts rather than composed of combined individual voices moving with horizontal implications.

This style of music requires suitable melodic profiles with proper harmonic spacings for its effectiveness. Its scoring does, of course, allow for considerable freedom in the use of doublings and fillers, especially in the middle register, as has been shown in many of the previous examples. Harmonic additions, when employed with modified two- and three-part homophonic music, are to be determined by harmonic analysis and their inclusion rarely necessitates the moving of either the melody or bass *tessituras*.

The following excerpt, scored primarily for reeds, is drawn

from music most commonly associated with this style (homophonic) for two voices. The student is urged to reexamine the other examples of this kind in this text in order to reevaluate scoring methods for limited voice textures as source material.

EX. RC44. *SERENATA ANDALUZA*

Manuel de Falla

A second style of two- and three-part homophonic music is that which has greater horizontal freedom for the parts and consequently fewer chordal figurations. Although these voice textures may frequently give the impression of polyphonic music, they remain in the homophonic category just so long as one or more voices

344

can be considered as chordal figurations. Here too, the student should study and account for the many added parts in Ex. RC 45 and be able to justify their inclusion.

EX. RC45. *RIGAUDON*

Rameau

2. Polyphonic

Polyphonic music's strength lies, not primarily in its harmonic implications, but in the deft management of its voice parts. Its compositional aspects include a comprehensive application of the principles of counterpoint defined as "the art of adding one or more parts to a given part according to certain rules." Time has relaxed the rigidity of rules for applied counterpoint in favor of the freer adoption of basic principles.

Polyphonic music is, therefore, exactly the opposite of the homophonic style, since it achieves its status when two or more melodic voices progress with horizontal movement in harmonious combinations. The number and complexity of the voice parts in no way alter this distinction. Individual voice parts are not harmonized as done for most homophonic music. Yet some harmonization may be introduced as a means of increasing sonority and/or as an independent rhythm unit without altering the contrapuntal style. Vertical harmonic considerations are brought into play in the actual manipulation of the voices and whenever harmonizations may be developed.

Band scoring of music in this style and texture can be aided by incorporating the following suggestions:

1. Principal thematic material needs superior tonal strengths for acceptable part definition and clarity. This may be achieved through contrast with other voice parts and by unison and/or octave doublings.

2. The selection of instruments for each counterpoint should be governed by their range capacities, if complete phrases are to be playable in their entirety.

3. Subject-and-answer counterpoints fare best when there is a distinct differentiation of timbres and strengths. Phrases in this category are not effective when scored for identical timbres.

4. Dynamics should be adjusted to clarify the relative importance of each voice part.

5. Harmonizations in fugal passages are inadvisable unless indicated by the composer.

Resonance and brilliance for this style of music can usually be achieved through the interpolation of sustained tones, outlining, and some increases in the tonal spread of its different parts. Actual harmonizations in chordal style are sometimes valid when advantageously arranged for peak climaxes. (See the full score of Bainum's transcription of the Fugue from *Schwanda* by Weinberger.)

346

Some of these scoring techniques are illustrated in the following examples. For additional illustrations of scored polyphonic music see Exs. 30, 33, 78, 83, 135, 147, 167, and 199.

EX. RC 46-a-b. *CAPRICCIO*

Handel

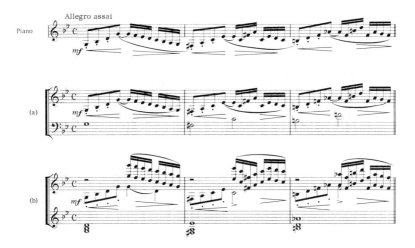

The scoring of Ex. RC 46-a shows how sustained notes, outlining the melodic line, create a second voice which is often useful for increasing resonance and tonal strength. The version at (b) is further evidence that single melodic lines can frequently be developed into several-voice patterns *without* sacrificing their characteristic individuality. The principles used here have many potentialities in the scoring of polyphonic music.

The reader is reminded that voice divisions and developments, as given here, are designed to show how compositional techniques

347

can be applied to band scoring. *The appropriateness of their usage will be dependent upon the form and style of each piece.* But it must also be remembered that two- and three-part music for the harpsichord or piano was never intended by its composers as source material for band music. Therefore, the scorer needs to adapt this material and to condition his musical thinking in working with original material in terms of forms and textures that are suitable for the wind instruments.

EX. RC46-c. *CAPRICCIO*

Handel

This two-part excerpt combines the points made in the previous example and includes another *Reference Chart* entry (see Section IV) as a logical means of securing an increased number of voice parts and resonance for polyphonic music.

Music in this category often yields the potentials of many implied voice parts, as shown in the setting of the next excerpt by Bach. The scorer's task in such instances is to extract and develop these voice potentials while adhering to the spirit of the original material. It is recommended that the student analyze this setting by accounting for proper identification with pertinent entries in the *Reference Chart.*

EX. RC47. *GAVOTTE AND MUSETTE from English Suite No. 3*

J. S. Bach

The scoring of fugues, *fugatos*, or bridge passages with fugal textures in two or three parts can ordinarily follow suggested plans given for the previous examples in this classification. Example RC48 introduces octave extensions of the melodic lines as a means of increasing the tonal spread, thereby extending the resonance factor as determined by dynamic considerations. Ordinarily, the stylistic character of fugal music can help to determine the extent to which its textures may be expanded and/or developed. Conservative scoring, appropriate for music of the Baroque or Classic periods, would hardly be typical of the Romantic or Modern periods. A good example of twentieth-century scoring of the fugue may be found in the final movement of Paul Hindemith's Symphony in B Flat for Concert Band.

3. Style Mixtures

From its earliest beginnings, symphonic music for the concert hall has been characterized by its frequent juxtapositions of the homophonic and polyphonic styles. Music in this category has the advantage of having organic unity blended with stylistic contrast. The scoring of music in this category remains basically unchanged from the methods used heretofore for the homophonic and polyphonic models respectively. The one significant difference in the scoring here concerns the matter of voice leading when the two styles are brought together.

The following Schubert excerpt is a good example of the juxtaposition of these two styles of composition. The voice textures have been arranged to blend the changes of style mixtures with a restraint characteristic of the period.

351

Schubert, Op. 94, No. 1

In the next excerpt, the range of scoring possibilities has been increased in accordance with the composer's implied intentions, as indicated by the pedal markings. Here is source material which requires sustained chord progression to support the canon in the octave in the treble parts. Its freer and bolder character permits a full-band sonority with appropriate brilliance.

EX. RC50. *FANTASTIC DANCE NO. 3.*

Dimitri Shostakovitch, Op. 1

VII. SPACING PROBLEMS IN THE MIDDLE REGISTER

Music for keyboard instruments, especially that for the piano, is replete with passages which spread the treble and bass parts far apart from each other. Although this distribution works out more or less satisfactorily for these instruments, the same cannot be said for these structural divisions when applied to the instruments of the band. It is advisable to approach settings of music in this category with the intent of eliminating and replacing these parts with other voice distributions which will remove large harmonic gaps from the middle register.

Modifications ordinarily required to bring about the relocation of parts can be accomplished usually by rearranging close-position chords in the bass register to open position, often in conjunction with the addition and/or rearrangement of existing harmonic elements in the middle-to-low treble range. Any and all modifications should, of course, remain faithful to the original in matters of harmonic and rhythmic content. This phase of scoring is of the utmost importance if there is to be a proper balance between the melodic and harmonic elements.

There is a second reason why this subject has extra special significance in scoring for the band. The exploratory studies carried out in Chap. 25 are most pertinent to the elimination of middle-harmonic gaps because properly arranged parts in this register promote the band's chief source of resonance. Furthermore, sustained notes, intervals, and/or chords here act as tonal pivots around which higher and lower parts can move with complete rhythmic freedom.

This subject has been alluded to as a secondary consideration of the *Reference Chart* in many of the preceding excerpts. Examples RC51 and RC52 have been selected primarily to show one method of redistributing voice parts for the elimination of large harmonic gaps.

1. Large Harmonic Gaps

EX. RC51. *OXEN MENUET*

Haydn

This typical bit of Classic piano music lends itself very well to band scoring, providing the middle-range harmonic gaps are eliminated. Notice the melodic-harmonic usage of the cornets and the quasi-fanfare octaves for the trumpets. Also, observe the separation of the baritone and tuba parts. In this connection, it is to be noted that the tuba, though technically capable of playing fast figurations, are often given outlining parts when a semitransparency of sound is desirable for certain styles of light music, which is the case here. Finally, consider the pattern and consistency of the individual voice parts which provide the middle-range textures for the *tutti*.

355

Ernst Dohnányi, Op. 2, No. 2

The necessity for filling in the middle harmonic gaps in the middle register is even more obvious in this music than was the case in the preceding Haydn excerpt. Here too, study of the structural textures will reveal several points of interest not to be overlooked.

First, consider the descending melodic phrase and the manner by which the cornets compensate for changing *tessituras*. Next, observe how the melodic line, at first above the cornet range, is alternated in the three parts, thereby ensuring the retention of the melody in the soprano brass instruments. This principle of scoring can be most useful for retaining essential voice parts within the limits of individual sections.

The disposition of the bass triplets illustrates one method of completing and modifying harmonic elements when scored for brass instruments. The low reeds could, of course, be given these triplets literally or expanded as chord formations, as shown in the original piano part.

2. Sustained Notes, Intervals, and Chords

Practically all of the scored *Reference Chart* examples have contained some mention of the place and value of sustained parts as one sure means of securing cohesive resonance for band music. Actually, no specific recommendations can be given for the inclusion of these added parts; they can be determined only by the style and distribution of voice parts in each passage. There is always the danger of overloading the middle register and this should be avoided since the instrumentation of the band is overly heavy in this range. The purpose of sustained middle-range parts should be regarded distinctly as a means of providing idiomatic parts which will contribute harmonic continuity and resonance. It should not be assumed from this emphasis that middle-range parts are indispensable, for there will be times when their inclusion may detract from a transparency of textures conceived strictly as linear voice parts without sustained harmonizations.

In the consideration of much piano music as source material, it is advisable to bear in mind that it was written for an instrument that is essentially percussive and decidedly limited in sustaining powers. Composers using this medium must, therefore, incorporate harmonic implications which may often prove to be obscure to the beginning transcriber who has had little experience in going beyond surface considerations. Difficulties of this kind can perhaps be best resolved by the style and character of each piece serving as a guide to representative modifications which will recognize the full implications of each passage and transform these elements in terms of voice textures suitable for wind ensembles.

Some idea as to how these modifications may be worked out in practice is illustrated in the two following examples. The Brahms transcription aims to retain the characteristic *staccato* style intended by the composer yet has some resonance built into the middle register by the sustained trombone parts.

357

Brahms, Op. 118, No. 3

In pursuing this point, it should also be established that sustained single-line parts (see the first two measures of Ex. RC 54) or extended *obbligatos* give a similar cohesive effect which is often desirable as a substitute for sustained intervals or chords.

EX. RC54.   *PUPILS' ROMP DANCES from Hudson River Legend*

Joseph Wagner
Trans. by the composer

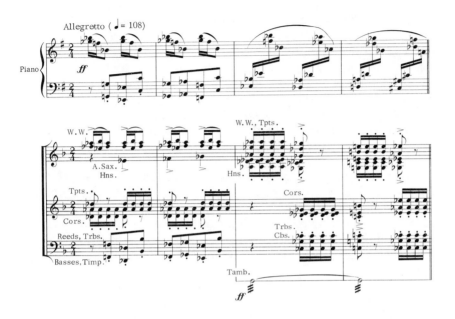

VIII. CONTRAST PROBLEMS CONDITIONED BY DYNAMICS

Considerable attention has been given to emphasizing possible potentialities of contrasts resulting from juxtapositions of strong and weak timbres and their respective intensities. A second and equally important element in this consideration deals with contrast as required for structural modifications necessitated by unequal and/or changing dynamics.

The composer of keyboard music not infrequently presents identical or similar passages with differing dynamics as one way of indicating contrast. The band scorer can, and sometimes does, use this same device in dealing with passages where extenuating circumstances preclude structural changes or changes of instrumentation.

However, the great majority of composers for all media vary their structural textures in accordance with dynamic implications. This technique of the craft is particularly applicable when dynamic extremes are employed for similar or identical melodic, harmonic, and rhythmic materials. Here too, the band scorer utilizes his forces in accordance with the theory that limited tonal spreads produce limited resonance, sonority, and brilliance.

The following chart (Fig. RC2) is intended to show the comparative positions of various chord extensions with their preferred spacings, doublings, and fillers, as might be employed for a gradual *crescendo* and *diminuendo*. Chords in brackets are given to suggest alternate spacings when fewer notes are desirable.

Fig. RC2

Many of the examples illustrating *Reference Chart* categories include direct application of the principles of tonal extensions, as shown in the above chart. The two following settings continue to develop these ideas as one practical way of securing contrast for music conditioned by dynamics.

EX. RC55. *DANZA LUCUMI*

Ernesto Lecuona

EX. RC56. *DANZA LUCUMI*

Ernesto Lecuona

Contrast may also manifest itself when alternating timbres and *tessituras* are in juxtaposition, as shown in Ex. RC 57. This simple device is always effective for unlike ideas highlighted by sudden dynamic changes. Indeed, alternating the wood-wind and brass choirs antiphonally—in all but the loudest passages—may be successful in music which suggests this style of scoring (see Ex. RC 58).

EX. RC 57. *JUGOSLAV POLKA No. 2*

George List

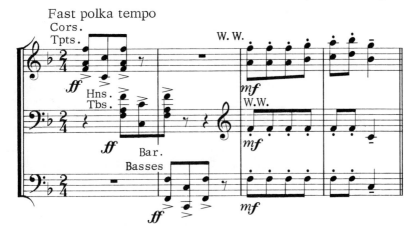

Mendelssohn, Op. 54

IX. VOICE LEADING

Good voice leading, a mark of distinguished craftsmanship, separates the amateur from the professional scorer. The study of musical theory, particularly style, harmony, and counterpoint, is a good preparation for the acquistion of this technique, although many self-taught composers and arrangers have displayed a mastery of it in their works. In order to attain it, one's musical thinking must be directed toward the concept of horizontal voice progression, rather than considering chord tones in vertical blocked movement. Its application is a skill which can be acquired.

Voice leading is perhaps nowhere more apparent than in scoring for wind instruments. This is particularly true with the wood winds because of their collective heterogeneous tonal characteristics. The heavier tonal strengths of the brasses are another factor which cannot be overlooked, as their entrances and releases are even more conspicuous. Singly or collectively, the voice movement of all wind instruments needs to be constantly evaluated in context of the structural textures of each passage. The following suggestions are given as aids for facilitating and promoting satisfactory habits for good voice leading.

1. Consider each voice part as a separate entity with horizontal, not vertical movement.

2. Treat each chord tone as an integral part of a consistent voice texture in all chord progressions.

3. Evaluate in context the function of all harmonic fillers as independent voice parts whenever possible.

4. Apply contrapuntal devices when appropriate.

5. Remember that the inconsistent voice patterns and textures of much keyboard music cannot be adapted literally. However, they can be modified to provide logically developed voice parts without giving the impression of static immobility.

6. Endeavor to retain consistent voice textures for complete phrases. Do not add or subtract notes because the source material does so for no reason other than technical expediency. Retain only those notes which are necessary for harmonic clarity and which can provide voice progressions with logical, smooth voice leading.

Good voice leading is an important phase of a compositional technique and should, therefore, be painstakingly developed for band scoring in all forms. Band transcription of orchestral music presents comparatively little difficulty in this regard, as most orchestral voice textures are ordinarily adaptable as acceptable voice parts for the wind instruments of the band.

Voice parts can have continuity of line if they are playable in their entirety by one or more instruments of similar timbre and tonal strength. In some instances melodies, counterpoints, figurations, or *obbligatos* exceed good playing ranges. In such cases, overlapping and continuation by instruments with similar tonal strengths—and timbres, if possible—constitute a practical means of securing the *effect* of continuity and smooth voice leading.

Practically all of the exploratory examples given for the *Reference Chart* thus far have cited Voice Leading as a secondary entry for consideration. All examples so marked should now be reviewed with attention focused on the working out of these parts.

The following examples are given here primarily to reemphasize the difficulties which can be expected in transcribing piano music for the band and to show modifications which would be suitable under most conditions. The scoring for wood winds in Ex. RC 59 demonstrates the necessity for modifying inner parts so that the ensemble will have consistent voice parts with clarity, resonance, and style. The second example by Grieg gives further elaboration of these ideas as they pertain to origin and development of all voice parts needed for the many-voiced texture of this setting.

EX. RC59. *HERBERGE*

Schumann, Op. 82, No. 6

Grieg, Op. 37

X. OBBLIGATO OR ADDED SECONDARY PARTS ARRANGED FROM HARMONIC PROGRESSIONS

The addition of *obbligatos* or secondary parts (melodic and/or rhythmic-harmonic figurations) is an efficient way of increasing part interest in music which is essentially homophonic. The extraction of independent voice parts from harmonic progressions is a practical application of a contrapuntal technique as its many species are applicable in this category.

Obbligatos, in the accepted meaning of the term in band music, are ordinarily placed in the middle register where the instrumentation is the strongest. Overwriting and/or overloading these parts has been a characteristic fault of much band music in the past and one which should, therefore, be attempted only occasionally. On the other hand, melodic and rhythmic-harmonic figurations can be placed in any register, although it should be observed

367

that such parts appear quite often in the high ranges and only a little less often in the medium and low registers. Caution is advised for scoring which would overemphasize any added secondary parts to the detriment of the principal melodic lines.

The band scorer is free to use embellishing parts wherever they seem appropriate. The process for securing their ultimate form can frequently be approached by applying—in reverse—the technique used for *Chart* entry III-2, Outlining a melodic line. Parts so manipulated within the framework of homophonic music often add considerable luster, brilliance, and rhythmic activity to passages that might otherwise sound rather dull and colorless. The student should experiment with this style of writing in working with the many examples provided in the author's *Workbook*.

The value of these added parts often lies, not only with their effectiveness as individual counterpoints with the original melody, but with their aptness to combine with each other as well. This duality of purpose is to be observed in the following examples, as these counterpoints have been arranged so that any two can fit simultaneously with each other in any range, as well as with the original melody. It is imperative to realize in this connection that such part additions are to be used sparingly, since overelaboration, though intriguing on paper, may result in a meaningless jumble of sounds in performance.

The variant embellishments which follow are given here primarily to show existing possibilities for most source material. Obviously, anything approaching continuous use of them would be as unwise as their complete absence. They have been designed to demonstrate one practical method of extracting *obbligatos* or secondary parts, first, in their most elemental form, and later, in a more developed style with melodic profile.

The three *obbligatos* in Ex. RC61-a-b-c, are first shown in their simplest form. They were made by starting with different chord tones and zigzagging to subsequent chord tones always differing in direction and design from the original melody whenever possible. Notice that the rhythmic patterns of the phrase repetitions in the original melody automatically suggest a similar treatment for the various versions of all added parts in this category. The application of this technique is a reliable means of securing both continuity and homogeneity.

EX. RC61-a-b-c. *DANCE CAPRICE*

Grieg, Op. 28, No. 3

The following graphs show the optional lines of direction taken for the basic interval patterns of these voice parts.

EX. RC62-a-b-c. *DANCE CAPRICE*

Grieg, Op. 28, No. 3

In Ex. RC63-a-b-c, these parts have been developed so that they now have independent melodic profile. This final transformation is an area which permits the band scorer considerable inventiveness, with an opportunity for creative melodic writing. Although the initial work may seem to be somewhat mechanical, the final result should be as distinguished as the melody it adorns.

EX. RC63-a-b-c. *DANCE CAPRICE*

Grieg, Op. 28, No. 3

Secondary parts in the form of rhythmic melodic or harmonic figurations are idiomatic and quite common for much band music. Inasmuch as their function is chiefly one of ornamentation, they are ordinarily placed in the high register. Figurations may, of course, be placed in any range, providing they are scored for weaker tonal strengths than the principal melodies. The following examples are two of several figurations which might be developed from the harmonic progressions of this Grieg excerpt.

371

Grieg, Op. 28, No. 3

Obbligatos and rhythmic-harmonic figurations are quite frequently combined, with stunning effect when properly scored, for
all forms of band music. This combination is particularly effective
for loud *tuttis* where part interest might otherwise be negligible.
Note: All phrasing has been intentionally omitted from the illustrative parts here, as this phase of scoring is closely allied to and
dependent upon final scoring plans. However, it is to be noted that
staccato or non-*legato* figurations go very well together with more
sustained lyric parts when they are scored with proper balance
(light wood winds for figurations with the heavier reeds and brasses for basic parts). The phrasing of all component parts should
always be thoroughly considered, for it can become the means of
providing considerable *contrast* when the scoring is well regulated.

EX. RC65-a-b-c-d-e. *DANCE CAPRICE*

Grieg, Op. 28, No. 3

XI. ANTIPHONAL EFFECTS

The term "antiphonal effects," as used here, refers to brief answering phrases which are added to the original source material, thereby contributing part interest with an ornamental or embellishing value. These answering phrases may attain significant status when they repeat or imitate melodic and/or rhythmic characteristic features of principal thematic ideas in differing timbres and *tessituras*. In this form, they have an extra advantage of enlarging thematic interest.

There are several conditions under which antiphonal phrases serve a useful purpose. One such instance occurs when melodic lines become momentarily inactive rhythmically. Sometimes this condition exists as an inherent part of a phrase, while at other times it will be more noticeable at phrase endings. The application of these ideas can be seen in Ex. RC24. (Review the comments given for this example.)

It is frequently possible to exercise a transcriber's privilege of enhancing structural textures for the full band by introducing answering phrases of thematic material, rather than resorting to padding with chordal fillers. This is an area where the creative faculties of the band scorer can function to the fullest. It is particularly applicable to scoring the high winds where the mere doubling of soprano range parts in the octave would be dull and uninteresting. The following excerpt illustrates this scoring technique.

EX. RC66. *PRELUDE in B Flat Major*
from *"Three Preludes and Three Studies"*

Mendelssohn, Op. 104, No. 1

Many of the preceding examples, including those for the *Reference Chart*, have indicated antiphony in a variety of forms and styles. The band scorer is, of course, at liberty to integrate these effects in a score whenever they seem to be musically justified.

375

This subject matter is also closely allied to the element of *contrast*, for antiphony can likewise be obtained with a juxtaposition of timbres and choirs. Antiphonal effects in this category should now be reviewed in Exs. RC55 and RC56, as well as in the many scored excerpts where this subject received special consideration. Caution is advised in the writing of these parts, for over-elaboration can become as deadly as a lack of genuine part interest. Develop the necessary skill for the usage and then employ it wisely.

XII. TREMOLO TYPES

Earlier discussion of this subject examined the technical aspects of the wind instruments in relation to the execution of various styles of tremolos as found in music for the band. In addition, some scored examples of tremolos—unmeasured and measured, tongued and slurred—have been considered and evaluated. It remains now to correlate this material with the various tremolo styles as found in some keyboard music and to further adopt methods of modification in accordance with procedures which are best for the band. (Review No. 2 in Chap. 7 and No. 110 in Chap. 13.)

The following review is given now to reestablish certain facts peculiar to the tremolo in music for the band.

1. The band tremolo cannot equal the string tremolo of the orchestra. It is a makeshift device at best and should, therefore, be approached on the basis of what is best for the band in performance, rather than seeking modifications based on string techniques used in orchestration.

2. The wood winds alone are adaptable to slurred tremolos, per se, the brass being accessible for flutter tonguing when a non-*legato* style is desirable.

3. Wood-wind trills are frequently combined with slurred tremolos—less so with flutter tonguing, when the full choir is employed. Trills for the brasses are hardly ever used with tremolos in any form.

4. The place and position of the percussion instruments take on significant importance for the band tremolo. It supplies rapid reiteration of sound so necessary for the accumulative effect of the tremolo without the need for considering the player's fatigue. It is in the effective combining of the various potentials that the band

scorer can achieve diversification of idiomatic tremolos for the band.

The following scored excerpts examine several technical considerations which must be determined in the scoring of tremolos; actual or implied in some source material. In Ex. RC67 the *effect* of a tremolo is achieved solely by the percussion instruments. It is, perhaps, the most common way to secure continuous rolled sound and has the extra advantage of being accessible for all percussion instruments which can be rolled. The low-range chord in the second measure has been repositioned for the brass choir, thereby eliminating a meaningless rumble of sound which would result from any scoring in its original position. The full woodwind chords are reserved for the climactic first beat in the last measure.

EX. RC67. *HUNGARIAN RHAPSODY No. 12*

Liszt

The second example here deals with a rather impossible set of scale figurations which produce the effect of accumulated resonance within the technical limitations of a piano technique. Considerable blurring of sound is inevitable with this notation: it was not intended to be otherwise. Both settings of this excerpt have been designed to capture the general *effect* of these scales in terms of the band's potentialities, rather than to experiment with any form of literal adaptation. Significantly, it is to be noted that an idiomatic literal setting of these scales, though technically possible for a few bands, would be highly impractical for most; hence the practical approach is both preferable and necessary in this instance.

The first version, given in Ex. RC68-a, combines wood-wind trills with brass flutter tonguing, the percussion instruments supplying rolled sounds continuously. This scoring, though rather boisterous, would have maximum sonority. The style could be adapted to scoring similar types of music where this *effect* might be appropriate.

Liszt

A second version (Ex. RC68-b) combines slurred tremolos with trills for the wood winds and discards the brass flutter tonguing. It also substitutes lighter percussion rolls, in keeping with the altered wind scoring of the tremolo. This model is the one to follow ordinarily. Other scoring combinations may, of course, be tried, but those presented here are the ones most frequently employed for the band tremolo.

XIII. DANCE FORMS (Afterbeats)

The subject of Dance Forms has been included in the *Reference Chart* primarily because of problems arising for the disposition of afterbeats as they occur in much music for the piano. Most music in this form can usually be divided into three parts: the melody, the rhythmic afterbeats, and the bass part. (Sustained parts, though often employed, are being considered as optional for this discussion.) In these respects, dance forms may be said to resemble the basic parts of military marches and can, for this reason, be used as good preparatory material for their scoring at this point. As no new scoring procedures are involved in the setting of melodic lines and bass parts for dance forms, attention can now be directed toward some of the more basic questions concerning the disposition of afterbeats.

The chord positions and register placements of afterbeats have a direct effect upon the balance and clarity in band scoring. In the matter of chord positions, it is to be noted that second inversions of triads and seventh chords are best as starting positions for afterbeats. It also is necessary to establish that chord progressions in this form should always move to nearest chord tones, retaining a maximum of common tones whenever possible. Obviously, all chord positions may appear in progressions involving afterbeats, but these positions will sound best when they occur between well-sounding inversions. Chords in this category should retain consistent voice textures and not be shifted in register simply because the source material may do so as a technical expediency.

The *tessituras* of afterbeats is another factor to be studied. Low-register, close-position chords, as we have seen in Chap. 23, sound thick and heavy and are, therefore, to be assiduously avoided. Afterbeats sound best ordinarily when confined to the medium-low alto and medium-high tenor ranges.

There can be no inflexible rules given for the scoring of afterbeats, as they are to be found in almost limitless combinations in band music. Nevertheless, the horns generally carry the brunt of these parts with the cornets and/or trombones often appearing as a second unit. Needless to say, some compositions require scoring by the full wood-wind section or the partial brass choir for the proper presentation of some afterbeats, especially in loud passages. In this connection, the student is reminded that the voice allocation for three and/or four horns is not the same in band scoring as it is in orchestration. (Review the first part on the horns in Chap. 12.)

With this information established, the student should now restudy the scoring of afterbeats as they are given in dance forms in the following examples: RC 5, RC 10, RC 12, RC 28, RC 29, RC 30, RC 37, RC 41, RC 59, RC 60, and RC 65.

The Rachmaninov excerpt which follows should prove instructive as a final study in this category. It is a practical illustration of a point made many times in this text, namely, band scoring should be based on scoring plans which are best for the band. The arrangement here by an expert craftsman shows how afterbeats have been introduced to retain the rhythmic scheme so characteristic of this dance form as used quite continuously in the preceding sections. Obviously, this setting is one of several which would be possible for this source material, but it is a clear example of artistic licence based upon sound scoring methods and one which will reward careful study and comparison.

381

EX. RC69. *ITALIAN POLKA*

Rachmaninov
Scored for band by Erik W. G. Leidzen

∞∞∞

CHAPTER TWENTY-SEVEN

SCORING MILITARY MARCHES

MARCHING AND SYMPHONIC BANDS

Marches can, for all practical purposes, be divided into two distinct categories: grand or processional concert marches with two or four moderate beats to each measure; and military marches, sometimes called quick step, with two beats to a measure with the unit of beat usually varying from 120–126. *Note*: The much quicker tempos used by some marching and "show" bands make rhythm parts or afterbeats impossible for the winds; they can be played by the percussion.

The concert march, as the name implies, is designed primarily for concert programs, although it is used upon occasion for stately processions when a rather slow pace is desired. For either usage, the performing band ordinarily has the advantage of indoor acoustics or an outdoor shell. The composition and scoring of this march form are basically the same as those of concert music, which have been previously examined. There are no new or unexplained problems.

These conditions do not prevail in scoring military marches. Several dissimilar factors necessitate the acceptance of certain limitations which are not associated with concert music. The marching band, regardless of its instrumentation, performs regularly out of doors, where it is exposed to the elements. It does not have the advantages of acoustical amplification and an audience of silent listeners. Its function is utilitarian; its purpose is to provide martial music which will enthuse and exhilarate large groups of marchers. Accordingly, the directors of marching bands seek music which can best fulfill these requirements.

The primary objective in scoring marches for the marching band should be acquisition of a maximum volume from a minimum of parts—*not instruments*. Rhythm and melody are the two principal elements to be featured in the scoring—*not the harmony*.

First, consider the composition and effectiveness of some of the accepted marching units. The drum corps is an old and honorable unit which has functioned successfully *without* melody or harmony instruments. It is strictly a rhythm outfit, efficient but musically colorless. The bugle and drum corps and the fife and drum corps represent concessions to the addition of melody, not harmony. Part writing for bugles or fifes does not alter this fundamental concept. The purpose and function of these units is to maintain simple but basic march rhythms.

A second and important consideration is that of volume. Obviously, the drum corps (snare and bass drums with cymbals) has the power to carry the rhythm without other instrumental support and is not easily overpowered by any combination of wind instruments. This fact has a direct bearing on the band scoring of marches, as the following text will show.

Military marches have always been a regular part of most band programs and in consequence have been scored for the instrumentation of the full or standard concert band. In addition, the concert band was the only marching band until the second quarter of the twentieth century. Therefore, marches were scored for three-part divisions of B♭ clarinets, cornets, and trombones. (Lucien Cailliet's revised scoring of Sousa's march *The Stars and Stripes Forever*, published in 1954, includes two-part divisions for flutes, oboes, bassoons, and alto saxophones, in addition to the three-part divisions cited above.)

Philip J. Lang in his book *Scoring for the Band* advocates the elimination of all three-part divisions and the adoption of two parts only for B♭ clarinets, cornets, and trombones, along with an instrumentation revised to coincide with that of the basic band (see Table 3, Chap. 3). Scoring with this instrumentation would give maximum volume with a minimum of parts. Table 3 is now repeated, in alternate form, as Table 6, to show several practical considerations not previously cited and to use in conjunction with the scoring given in Ex. 216.

TABLE 6

BASIC BAND INSTRUMENTATION—MARCHING BAND

Wood Winds	*Brass*
D♭[1] and C piccolo	B♭ cornets I-II
Flute[2] (playing the C picco- lo part)	B♭ trumpets I-II (playing cornet parts)
B♭ clarinets I-II	E♭ and F Horns I-II
E♭ alto saxophones I-II	Trombones I-II
B♭ tenor saxophone	Baritone (euphonium)
E♭ baritone saxophone[3]	Tubas (sousaphones)

Percussion

Snare drum, tenor drum, bass drum, cymbals, and bell lyre

The marching band, as it is now constituted, has been affected by several practical considerations which deserve attention, since they are concerned with the portability of instruments and their usefulness in performance on the march.

1. Double reeds (oboes, English horn, and bassoons) are not well suited to the rigors of a marching band.

2. The large single-reed instruments (bass clarinet,[3] baritone[3] and bass saxophones) are also not portable.

3. French horns in F, though used occasionally in some marching bands, are less practical than the easier-to-play melophones in E♭ or upright altos.

4. Timpani, notwithstanding their infrequent appearance mounted on mobile platforms, belong in the concert band.

5. Sousaphones in E♭ are used by many bands with young players. Some college bands have many BB♭ sousaphones and a few in E♭, while most service bands rely on only those in BB♭. The variability of these pitches needs consideration in the scoring of marches, since it affects the range and divisions of the cued parts.

Obviously, much can be said for the advantages of both large and small instrumentations for scoring marches. Some willingness to compromise would seem to be in order if marches are to be played by units of both sizes. Perhaps the difficulty can be

[1] Fast becoming obsolete.

[2] Generally considered ineffective on the march.

[3] Regarded as portable by some band directors.

resolved by arranging scores for the instrumentation and divisions of the basic band (see Table 3) to which supplementary parts for the concert band (see Table 1) can be added. This method need not necessarily impair the effectiveness of either unit. However, some crossing of divided parts in the larger instrumentations would be inevitable.

The scope of color contrasts and instrumental effects for marches is naturally limited. However, contrasts and effects should not be regarded as a prime requisite in scoring marches. Marching units thrive on music which has clear rhythms and simple, catchy tunes with a big sonority.

Following are some practical suggestions for scoring marches:

1. Do not rely on the piccolo, flute, or Eb clarinet to carry the melody alone. Use these instruments in unit combinations with the other soprano reeds.

2. The first Bb clarinets should not be assigned to second soprano parts above melodic cornets. Keep them on the melody or figuration.

3. Three-part afterbeats in the middle register are adequate.

4. Use two-part trumpets on the melody and best-sounding second soprano or high alto parts, or for embellishing fanfare flourishes.

5. Keep the first (melody) and second (harmony) soprano parts, along with high alto parts, in the cornets when possible.

6. Vary the trombones with countermelodies, occasional afterbeats, and sustained harmony parts. Only the third trombone should be given unmelodic bass parts, and this very infrequently.

7. Score all major parts, melodic and harmonic, for the brass section.

8. Give variety to baritone parts with principal melodies, *obbligatos*, and occasional harmony parts—rarely unmelodic bass parts.

9. Allow the percussion section to carry the major part of the rhythm. It can do so without assistance from the other sections.

10. Use the trio of saxophones (two altos and a tenor) as a close-position chord unit. These instruments may be given melodies, *obbligatos*, figurations, and harmonic progressions.

11. One countermelody at a time is ample; do not overelaborate.

12. Keep all instruments in their best playing ranges by avoiding extremely high and low registers.

13. Do not rely on the wood winds to carry important parts without some support from the brass.

14. A safe scoring plan is one which will sound complete with brass and percussion instruments only. Use the wood winds for

extra brilliance and sonority.

15. Coloristic effects will be limited in scope. Secure contrast by means of dynamic changes rather than timbre subtleties.

16. Rely on considerable unison and octave writing with a minimum of harmonic divisions.

17. Avoid simultaneous divisions in the B♭ clarinets, cornets, and trombones.

18. Keep the rhythm of afterbeats simple and clear. Snare and tenor drummers on the march should not have to decipher complicated rhythms.

19. Diversify horn parts by giving them sustained harmony progressions and occasional melodic and *obbligato* parts as a relief from uninteresting afterbeats.

The march excerpts that follow illustrate many of the points given above. Example 213 is a typical march introduction with its antiphonal octaves aided by the sustained middle parts. The last two measures starting at the double bar show the voice distributions which are retained for most of the first strain. Note that the soprano wood winds double the cornet parts an octave higher, thereby adding an incisive kind of brilliance. This scoring technique has, of course, been shown in many of the examples of concert music, but it is particularly effective for marches. The four-voice horns with the afterbeats are to be regarded as the exceptions rather than the rule.

Edwin Franko Goldman

388

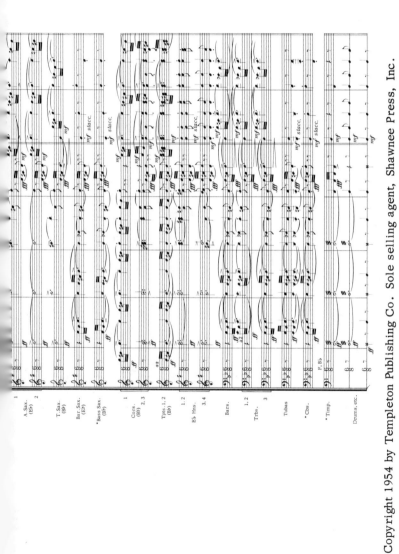

*Instruments not listed in "standard" instrumentation.
**Not included in the original scoring. Added by the author.

389

The next excerpt, with its reduced over-all range, ensures contrast in keeping with the softer dynamic, as do the percussion parts marked "for marching only." It should also be noted that the scoring here is complete without the reeds (recheck numbers 13 and 14 in the list).

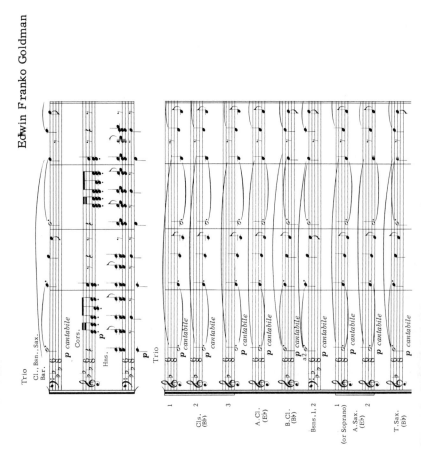

EX. 214. *ON THE HUDSON*

Edwin Franko Goldman

390

Compare the *tutti* scoring given below with that for Ex. 214. The soprano wood winds have been raised to the high register as they were in Ex. 213. Observe how the rhythm pattern of the *obbligato* or countermelody varies from that of the main theme. This scoring technique is based on the workable theory that one part should have rhythmic motion when its counterpart is comparatively inactive. (Review Section X of the *Reference Chart*.)

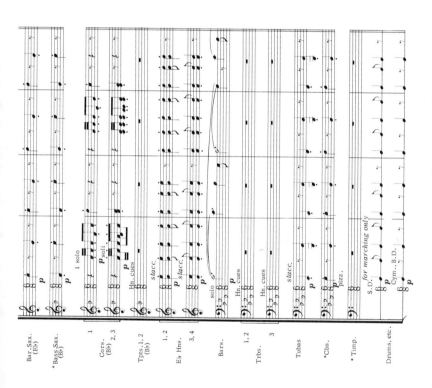

EX. 215. *ON THE HUDSON*

Edwin Franko Goldman

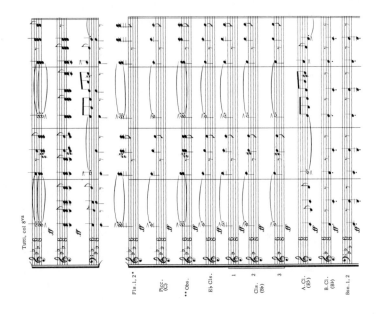

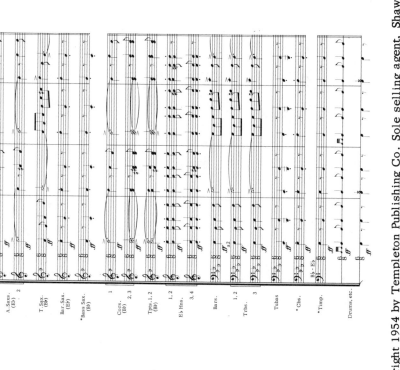

The three preceding examples have been scored for the symphonic band, the few supplementary instruments omitted from the standard listing being of secondary importance in the overall scoring plans. As a final scoring project in this category, let us consider a rescoring of Ex. 215 in accordance with the instrumentation of the marching band. (Review Table 3.)

For this study, compare the respective voice parts of Ex. 216 with those of Ex. 215. In the former, the voice lines have been thinned out for two- rather than three-part divisions. The middle harmony parts are no longer written as afterbeats, but as integral harmony notes which complement and fill out the higher soprano parts. The rhythm is entrusted entirely to the percussion instruments, as shown in the full score.

EX. 216. *ON THE HUDSON*

Edwin Franko Goldman

These brief but typical examples contain the basic scoring formulas, whether scoring is for the symphonic or the marching band. Detailed study and comparison of these examples will help to point up two primary considerations which are invariably linked to instrumentation choices. First, marches scored for concert programs usually have some wind instruments playing afterbeats as a contrasting relief from the continuous use of the percussion section. Second, the multiple part divisions regularly found in symphonic band scoring provide a rather rich texture, but they also cut down on the band's potential volume—a matter not seriously considered until the advent of the marching band opened up new horizons. Both styles of scoring are useful. The final choice of instrumentation for scoring marches naturally must remain the prerogative of each individual band scorer. However, the student should have the experience of scoring for both symphonic and marching bands. Source material is provided for this in the author's *Workbook for Band Scoring*.

The exercises and illustrations developed in this chapter have shown that the usual breakdown of the various component parts are as follows: melody, rhythm parts, and the bass with optional harmonic figurations, *obbligatos*, and sustained harmony parts.

It should be noted here that the scoring of popular songs and "show" tunes for the wind band distributes these elements in much the same way that they are distributed for the march. The big difference is in the style or manner in which the instruments are treated, either as solo or in combination. Here the scoring style reflects and aims to approximate the current trends in arrangements for dance bands.[1] Although the coloristic treatment of the instruments varies from that used for the marching band, the basic ingredients remain the same—melody and rhythm generously seasoned with harmonic spices.

[1] The bibliography lists several books on scoring for the dance band.

∞∞∞

CHAPTER TWENTY-EIGHT

BAND TRANSCRIPTION OF ORCHESTRAL MUSIC

Considerable attention has been given indirectly to band transcription of orchestral music in many of the preceding music examples. In considering this subject now as a work project, it is important to recognize that not all orchestral music is adaptable to band scoring. Source materials and scoring methods must be chosen carefully. Transcriptions should be based on what is best for the band, not on trying to make the band sound like an orchestra.

A student attempting transcription should have a good working knowledge of orchestration, particularly a knowledge of how to handle the orchestra's strings. It can be a serious mistake to assume that orchestral string parts are interchangeable with those for the band's wind instruments. Many modifications are required. Anyone familiar with the art of orchestration will comprehend the distinctions which must be made in scoring for the string and the wind sections, either separately or collectively. These scoring differences are discussed and fully illustrated in the author's *Orchestration: A Practical Handbook.*

Actually, the two sections have little in common other than range compass. The strings are a homogeneous family grouping, while the wood winds have three distinct timbre divisions. Furthermore, these sections vary, not only in tonal qualities, but in the means of tone production. Thus, the chief difficulty in this form of transcription is finding suitable modifications of orchestral string parts. Notwithstanding all differences in tone quality and production, the band's wood-wind instruments are usually regarded as the band's equivalent to the orchestra's strings.

The following chart shows the sectional ranges of the orchestra and the band. *Note:* The contrabass range given in Fig. 57 is the four-string model. The lowest note given for the wood-wind range in Fig. 57 applied to the instrumentation listed in Table 1.

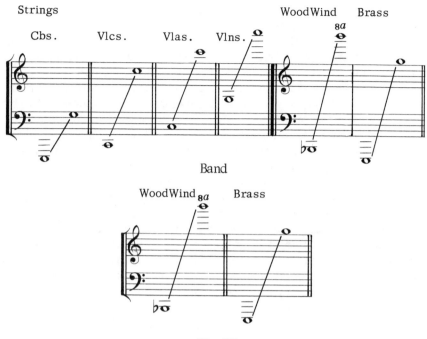

Fig. 57

The band, without a string choir, must be given sectional subdivisions which alter both the sound of adapted string parts and the manner in which they must be played by wind instruments. One has only to compare the tonal possibilities in the extreme high and low registers of both media to understand the inevitable problems arising from this single consideration. For example, the highest wood winds (piccolo, flute, and E♭ clarinet) are no match for the orchestra's first and second violins, nor can the tenor and bass reeds (alto and bass clarinets, alto, tenor and baritone saxophones, and bassoons) serve as equal representatives of the violas, cellos, and basses.

Another difficulty concerns the unpredictable number of reeds in the band, as compared to the usually well-planned balance of the orchestra's strings. For example, consider the large number of B♭ clarinets ordinarily available for most bands as balanced with the relatively few alto and bass clarinets. Obviously, the differences in instrumentation must be understood before suitable modification of string parts can be carried out successfully.

To reiterate, the orchestra is essentially a body of strings. Wind and percussion parts are added as each individual orchestrator determines. The band scorer, on the other hand, usually starts his scoring with a predetermined instrumentation dictated by practical as well as artistic considerations. With this preliminary information, it is possible to study in detail certain scoring techniques for band transcription of orchestral music.

The first step is to examine generalized voice allocations for the two media, as shown in the following listing. Numbers in parentheses for the orchestral instruments indicate both the number of players and the divisions of the parts. Roman numerals in parentheses give optional placements of divided parts. They also indicate the division of parts but not the number of players, which is indeterminate. Instruments in parentheses show alternate second registers that are to be encountered rather frequently. Asterisks are placed before instruments found only in the largest symphonic ensembles. *Note*: Although many important orchestral composers, such as Bizet, Prokofiev, Ravel, R. Vaughan Williams, and others, employ the saxophone to good advantage in their scores, the instrument has not as yet become standardized in the instrumentation of the symphonic orchestra.

TABLE 7

ORCHESTRA	BAND
Soprano	*Soprano*
Piccolo (1)	C and D♭ piccolos
Flutes (2)	Flutes I-II
Oboes (2)	Oboes I-II
*D or *E♭ clarinet	E♭ clarinet
Trumpet (1st)	B♭ clarinet I
Violins (1st)	E♭ alto saxophone I
	B♭ cornet I
	B♭ trumpet I
Alto	*Alto*
Clarinet (1st)	Oboe (II)
*English horn	B♭ clarinet II
Horns (1st and 3rd)	E♭ alto saxophone II
Trumpet (2nd)	B♭ cornet II
Trombone (1st)	B♭ trumpet II
Violins (2nd)	*B♭ fluegelhorns I-II
(Viola)	Horns I-III
	Trombone I

398

Tenor	Tenor
Clarinet (2nd)	*English horn
Horns (2nd and 4th)	B♭ clarinet III
Trombone (2nd)	*E♭ alto clarinet
Viola	B♭ tenor saxophone
(Violoncello)	B♭ cornet III
	*B♭ fluegelhorn (II)
	Horns II-IV
	Trombones I-II
	(Baritone)

Bass	Bass
*Bass clarinet	B♭ bass clarinet
Bassoons (2)	*B♭ or E♭ contrabass clarinet
Trombone (3rd)	Bassoons I-II
Tuba	E♭ baritone saxophone
Violoncello	B♭ bass saxophone
Bass	Trombone III
	Baritone (euphonium)
	Tubas
	String bass

Before proceeding further with this subject, it will be helpful to reconsider and correlate the details of instrumentation as they pertain to band transcription of orchestral music.

1. The orchestrator plans his scores with the reasonable assurance that his selected instrumentation will be carried out. On the other hand, the experienced band scorer knows that his instrumentation demands cannot always be met. Hence, he wisely scores for either the basic-band instrumentation, building up to the symphonic band on a supplementary basis, or he scores directly for the symphonic band, relying on an elaborate system of cuing and cross-cuing to take up the slack for missing instruments.

2. Because the band has many more instruments with heavier timbres than the orchestra, it is capable of far greater volume and power. Conversely, it follows that the band is less flexible with soft dynamics, for it cannot match the *pianissimo* of the orchestra's strings. (The clarinet family is the best group for this purpose.)

3. In the matter of combined ranges, it is significant that the string section traverses the entire range of musical expression, whereas the brass choir cannot comfortably maintain *tessituras* above the treble clef. This fact in itself is sufficient to cause a distinctive idiomatic style of band scoring in dealing with the high registers found in much orchestral music. *Note*: The instruments

given in Table 7 show the more usual relationships of the instruments in the orchestra and the band, based upon their ordinary usage. On occasion, almost every instrument of either group is employed in voice ranges other than those given. This is particularly true of those instruments having compasses spanning more than one register.

4. Other earlier comments concerning the predominately heavy instrumentation for the band's middle register are equally valid here in dealing with this form of transcription.

5. The bass register presents a real problem when a uniformity of timbres and tonal strengths is a consideration. The bass reeds cannot match the playing characteristics of the cellos and basses of the orchestra, nor are they always available for most medium- or small-size bands. A realistic approach to this problem requires that some mixing of reed and brass timbres is usually necessary, which, in turn, affects the tonal balance of these parts. For example, three-part writing for reeds coupled with a bass part played by a baritone is quite different in sound from the same part played by a bassoon, bass clarinet, or baritone saxophone—or a combination thereof.

6. The string's *pizzicato* can only be approximated by the wind's *staccato*. When this effect is used, it is important that the notation for the winds be written so that it will be similar to the real sound of the *pizzicato* (half notes become quarters, quarters become eighths, and so forth).

7. A major problem concerns working out idiomatic wind parts which give the effect produced by the strings. This often requires considerable ingenuity on the part of the scorer because of certain disparities in playing techniques.

8. Fortunately, many basic textures of much orchestral music can readily be modified for the band's wind instruments. The greatest difficulties arise in rearranging idiomatic string parts as equally playable parts for wind instruments. It is well to recall that wind players need breath breaks if their parts are to be played capably.

9. Most band transcribers of orchestral music work on the theory that a full complement of clarinets in the band can function similarly to the orchestra's strings. Although this premise is essentially workable and practical for most passages of concert music for the band, it should not overshadow the fact that the brass instruments form the band's basic choir. The wood winds are given preference over the brass for the execution of most string parts, chiefly because of their superior flexibility and delicacy of tone. Nevertheless, some string parts can profitably be

scored for the brass when such modifications seem appropriate and desirable. Muted brass is particularly effective in rendering passages adapted from strings at soft dynamic levels in all registers.

10. Many idiomatic playing styles and techniques of string instruments — repeated notes, *arpeggios*, various bowing styles, tremolos, harmonics—cannot be literally reproduced by the wind instruments. The scorer's taks is to seek instrumental combinations of wind instruments which, when scored idiomatically, will produce the *effect* of the string parts.

11. Band transcriptions of orchestral music should include timbre contrasts in proportion to the capacities inherent in the instrumentation. Obviously, band scores are more limited in this respect than are those for the orchestra.

Attempts have been made from time to time to synthesize the instrumentations of the orchestra and the band as guides to transcription. These equivalent groupings can be both helpful and practical as basic generalizations, but instrumental compromises must be made constantly if transcriptions are to be successful.

The following table lists two instrumentations arranged to show their interchangeable relationships. The order given for the orchestral instruments is that used in full-score publications. The asterisk used before the name of an instrument indicates its occasional use in most Classic and Romantic scores. This table is included here primarily as a guide in scoring when instrumentations for band do not include double reeds.

TABLE 8

ORCHESTRA	BAND
Classic Instrumentation	*Basic instrumentation*
Flutes and *piccolo	Flutes and piccolo
Oboes (1st and 2nd)	Flutes, E♭ clarinet, B♭ clarinets I, Alto saxophone I, cornet I
Clarinets (1st and 2nd)	B♭ clarinets II, cornets I-II
Bassoons (1st and 2nd)	Alto saxophone II, tenor saxophone, baritone, tuba
Horns (1st and 2nd)	Horns I-II
*Horns (3rd and 4th)	Trombones I-II
Trumpets (1st and 2nd)	Cornets I-II
*Trombones (1st, 2nd, and 3rd)	Trombones I-II-III
	Baritone
*Tuba	Tuba

401

Timpani and percussion	Timpani and percussion
Violins (1st)	Bb clarinets I, cornets I
Violins (2nd)	Bb clarinets II, cornets II
Violas	Bb clarinets III, alto saxophone II
Cellos	Tenor saxophone, baritone
Basses	Tubas

A second and more elaborate set of instrumentations of contemporary symphonic proportions appears in Table 9. Here the band instruments in parentheses indicate second-choice replacements in their preferred order, doublings, and cues. These suggested band choices are based primarily on similarities of range, with timbre considerations applied as prescribed by standard scoring practices. When the name of an orchestral instrument appears without numerical identification, only one instrument of this type is used.

TABLE 9

ORCHESTRA	BAND
Symphonic Instrumentation	*Symphonic Instrumentation*
Piccolo	Piccolo
Flutes, 1st, 2nd, and 3rd	Flutes I-II-III
Oboes, 1st and 2nd	Oboes I-II (Flutes, Eb clarinet, Bb clarinet I, cornet I, trumpet I)
English horn	English horn (alto clarinet, alto saxophone)
Eb clarinet	Eb clarinets (flutes)
Clarinets, 1st and 2nd (Bb, A, or C)	Eb clarinet (Bb clarinets I-II, cornets I-II)
Bass clarinet	Bass clarinet (alto clarinet, tenor or baritone saxophone)
Bassoons, 1st and 2nd	Bassoons (alto or bass clarinets, tenor or baritone saxophones, baritone, tuba)
Contrabassoon	Contrabassoon (contrabass clarinet, baritone or bass saxophones, tuba, string bass)
Horns, 1st and 2nd	Horns I-II (alto saxophones, fluegelhorns, cornets, trombones
Horns, 3rd and 4th	Horns III-IV (alto and tenor saxophones, trombones)
Trumpets, 1st, 2nd, and 3rd	Cornets I-II-III (trumpets I-II)
Trombones, 1st, 2nd, and 3rd	Trombones I-II-III

402

Tuba	E♭ and BB♭ tubas
Timpani and percussion	Timpani and percussion
Harp	Harp (piano)
Violins (1st)	B♭ clarinets I (flutes, E♭ clarinet, cornets I)
Violins (2nd)	B♭ clarinets I (alto saxophone I, cornets II, horns for afterbeats)
Violas	B♭ clarinets III (alto clarinet, alto saxophone II, horns for afterbeats)
Cellos	Bass clarinet (tenor or baritone saxophones, baritone)
Basses	Contrabass clarinet, baritone or bass saxophone (tubas, string bass)

The first illustrative example of the above tables is of particular interest in view of the discussion of bass register problems earlier in this chapter. The scoring has a baritone-tuba combination playing a *pizzicato* cello part with a reed quintet. Notice that Brahms' scoring has one string part combined with a reed quintet. Also observe the compensating dynamic of *pianissimo* for the heavier tonal weight in the bass part of the band score.

Obviously, a scoring entirely for reeds, with the bass clarinet and baritone saxophone substituted for the baritone-tuba parts, would prove to be less heavy and more homogeneous with the higher reeds.[1] The arranger of this work wisely refrained from padding the original texture with fillers or doublings, thus preserving the character of the composers' scoring, which employs the small Classic instrumentation.

[1] In this connection, it is to be noted that the military bands of most European countries are the concert bands as well. Some of them use the American basic instrumentation, with a single oboe and bassoon added.

Brahms, Op. 73

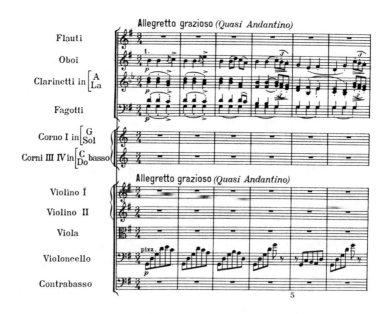

Brahms, Op. 73
Arr. for military band by Arthur Hibbert

Allegretto grazioso (*Quasi Andantino*)

The next excerpt from the second part of this movement is equally instructive. Notice how the antiphonal effect of the wind and brass choirs is arranged two measures before A. Also study the source and distribution of the parts for the *tutti* starting at A. Likewise observe the manner in which some brass instruments are retained five measures after A, thereby continuing the tonal firmness of the entire phrase.

EX.218a. *SYMPHONY No. 2, Third Movement*

Brahms, Op. 73

Brahms, Op. 73
Arr. for military band by Arthur Hibbert

Presto ma non assai ($\bullet = \bullet$)

B.& H. 8781

There are other styles of orchestral music for a small instrumentation which benefit from expanded textures when transcribed for the band. This fundamental change is often applicable to operatic overtures, post-Classical suites and dance forms, to name but a few.

The following excerpt illustrates the manner in which relatively few voice parts of an orchestral score can be expanded and developed to fit the part requirements of the symphonic band. Notice how middle-range resonance is built into the scoring, how the rhythm is emphasized at 9, and how the measured tremolo for the first violins is discarded. It is likewise important to examine the way a full complement of high wood winds is permitted to carry the melodic line in the first two measures without support from the brass and the way it is reinforced by the cornets after 9, when the figuration is less rapid.

EX.219a.   *ITALIAN IN ALGIERS, Overture*

EX. 219b. *ITALIAN IN ALGIERS, Overture*

Rossini
Trans. by Lucien Cailliet

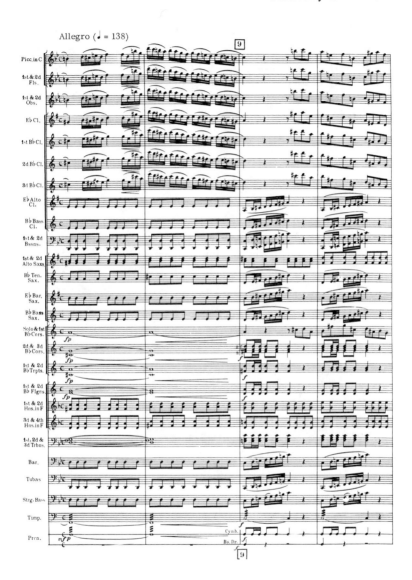

409

The two following band transcriptions have been derived from orchestral instrumentation given in Table 9. In Ex. 220, the transcriber's decision to retain the original key of D major should be noted, as it demonstrates that all band music need not be written in flat keys. (Actually, the sharp keys of G and D do not constitute impractical tonalities for well-trained bands.) Examination of the band scoring here discloses that the transcriber adhered rather closely to the orchestral plan of building up the *crescendo*. Note that the eighth-note rhythm is kept intact, without assistance from the percussion section. Compare the voice allocations of this scoring with those given in Table 8.

EX. 220a. *SYMPHONY IN D MINOR, Third Movement*

Franck

EX. 220b. *SYMPHONY IN D MINOR, Third Movement*

Franck
Trans. by James R. Gillette

411

The final example is a tour de force for the band as well as for the orchestra. The scoring for the brass in the band version is obviously intended for experienced players, as the extreme high registers are used most conspicuously. Note that the part writing for the band adheres closely to the structural textures of the orchestration. This reference is to a point made earlier, namely, music which is horizontally conceived and executed rarely requires harmonic fillers to increase its sonority or brilliance.

EX.221a. *SIEGFRIED'S RHINE JOURNEY*

from Die Götterdämmerung

R.Wagner

EX. 221b. *SIEGFRIED'S RHINE JOURNEY*

from Die Götterdämmerung

R. Wagner
Trans. for symphonic band by Lucien Cailliet

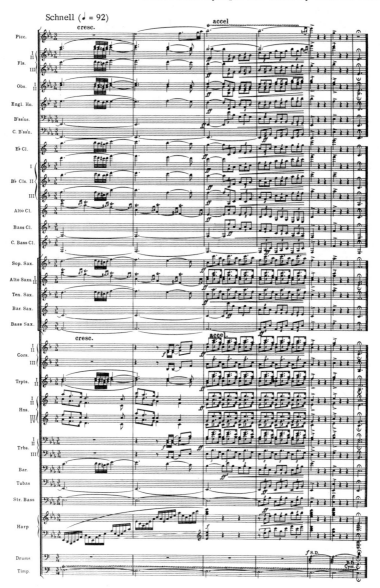

It has been said that some band transcriptions of orchestral music are bad, that others should never have been attempted, while still others sound better than their original orchestral counterparts. These statements could, of course, apply equally well to transcriptions of piano and organ music. No doubt the reason for the difference of opinions lies primarily in a basic but technical fact: music which utilizes the maximum idiomatic resources of its medium is usually the least accessible and workable for transcription in a different medium. These considerations, if applied to the band, need not be based on its inability to cope with technical modifications. Rather, it is a matter of avoiding transcriptions which could bring about the loss of artistic standards set by the original source material. Obviously, the band transcriber has won half his battle when he chooses source material which lends itself to restatement in a new medium.

Finally, the student should make use of the lessons in the *Reference Chart of Keyboard Idioms and Patterns* when planning band transcriptions of orchestral music.[1] An analysis of full scores for orchestra and band listed in the final pages of this book will provide further material for measure-by-measure comparisons, which can be of inestimable value in developing a scoring technique for band transcriptions of orchestral music.

---

[1] This study plan can be profitably coordinated with the work projects in the author's Orchestration: A Practical Handbook.

CHAPTER TWENTY-NINE

CONCLUSION

Solo Instruments with the Band - Chorus with the Band
Conducting Technique for the Band Scorer - Score Reading
Rehearsal Numbers - Cuing - Selected Listings of
Band Transcriptions

SOLO INSTRUMENTS WITH THE BAND

The band repertory is noticeably weak—in quality, not quantity—in works for solo instruments with band accompaniment. Everyone familiar with the old band concerts in the park can remember the ornate cornet solos, usually in variation form with very dull accompaniments, and the showy clarinet fantasias, often based on operatic melodies with equally uninteresting accompaniments. Perhaps no other part of the repertory offers such challenging and rewarding opportunities to the symphonic composer who is willing and able to work in this area.

There is a wide variety of instruments and combinations which are available as solo possibilities with the band. In fact, practically every instrument of the band's symphonic instrumentation could be considered as a possible solo instrument, including such percussive ones as the xylophone and the piano. This void can be remedied only when experienced composers will experiment and explore the marvelous potentialities awaiting them with the same spirit they display for rare and unusual combinations of orchestral instruments.

BAND ACCOMPANIMENTS

The scoring of band accompaniments does not actually involve any techniques which are new or different from those previously examined. Many of the illustrative excerpts contain accompanied solo passages which can serve as models for more extended passages and even for whole movements. The one extremely important factor is the scorer's ability to keep the solo or *soli* instruments from being covered by the accompaniments. This most

415

certainly does not mean that accompanying parts must be color-less or uninteresting, with endless stretches of afterbeats or *arpeggios.* It is a phase of scoring which demands a knowledge-able combination of instruments in styles that have tonal balance as well as part interest.

The weakness in most solo pieces for the band has not been in the exploitation of the solo instrument, but in the musical qual-ity of both solo and accompaniment materials and in the way they have been used. There seems to be no logical reason why music in this category cannot reach the high standards of composition and scoring craftsmanship found in many twentieth-century ori-ginal works for the band. Part of this transformation can be brought about by writing accompaniment and *tutti* parts so that they will by symphonically conceived and executed—parts which will have thematic developments with organic relationships. Well-mixed passages in the contrapuntal style, varied with thematically ar-ranged phrases of style mixtures, can work wonders in reducing the boredom of playing or listening to stereotyped accompaniments too long associated with music in this category. The very few pub-lished full scores of this type are listed at the end of this chapter.

CHORUS WITH THE BAND

Another form of band scoring—scoring for chorus and band—still awaits extensive exploitation. Here too, it would seem that artistic efforts would be rewarded. Several orchestral composers, notably Stravinsky and Milhaud, have experimented with choral compositions having single wind- and percussion-instrument ac-companiments. Their efforts have shown that a selective and nu-merically limited instrumentation can combine and blend well with human voices. The American composers Don Gillis and Ro-bert Kurka have both written operas with band accompaniment. With these beginnings, adventuresome composers and arrangers can continue to seek new and challenging combinations.

The technicalities of scoring for band with chorus are essen-tially the same as those already indicated. There are, however, several unpredictable factors which usually require the judgment of experienced conductors. These deal with the size and balance of the chorus and the band, the style and character of the music, and the place of performance—indoors or outdoors. Here too, the problem is one of achieving balance between the choral and in-strumental forces. These factors require special consideration in scoring. The band scorer must be able to calculate accurately the distribution of timbres for well-arranged textures.

416

Choral accompaniments ordinarily can be divided into two types. The first and most simplified form is that which doubles the vocal parts in unisons and octaves with little or no change, as in the setting of chorals. A second and more musically interesting variety has independent musical structure which supports vocal parts without necessarily doubling them.

We have seen sectional and full-band settings of *America* used to illustrate literal doubling, in unisons or octaves, of vocal parts. Scoring independent accompaniments presents many new and challenging problems, since adequate instrumental support must be achieved without destroying tonal balance between two dissimilar media.

Accompaniments which have complex voice textures and/or harmonic idioms often require doubled vocal parts superimposed on independent accompaniments. This is usually necessary if any of the following factors is present:

1. Significant extended passages with difficult vocal intervals needing instrumental support
2. Parts which demand bold melodic profile
3. Vocal parts written in weak *tessituras*
4. Involved *fugatos* of significant length
5. Peak climaxes calling for maximum power and brilliance

The selection of doubling instruments will be dependent upon the dynamics, ranges, and the musical character of each phrase. The notation for wind instruments so employed is idiomatic when note repetitions in the vocal parts, caused by the prosody, are eliminated from the doubling part.

Notes extraneous to the accompaniment can be introduced as pitch cues for choruses, especially after long periods of rest, or to anticipate tricky entrances. They are both helpful and necessary in music with advanced harmonic idioms or complex contrapuntal textures.

The band scorer interested in writing for the choral-band combination is advised to study representative works in full score in the choral-orchestral repertory. The final movement of Beethoven's Ninth Symphony, Verdi's *Requiem*, and the *Symphonie des psaumes* by Igor Stravinsky are works suggested for this study.

The *Reference Chart* can be helpful in the arrangement and scoring of band accompaniments for vocal or instrumental groups. Its application to the development of accompaniments as complete units to which doubled vocal parts may be added as needed, offers a wide variety of solutions to scoring many keyboard idioms and patterns. The very few published full, vocal-band scores available are listed at the end of this chapter.

417

CONDUCTING TECHNIQUE FOR THE BAND SCORER

The prospective band scorer should make every effort to become familiar with all of the instruments of the band, either through study and playing experience and/or through attendance at rehearsals and performances where music can be studied and followed in score form. Also, many band recordings are now available for private study purposes. In addition, it is highly desirable for the student to hear his own scores in rehearsal or performance, for mere notations then become associated and identified with timbres of real living sound. Obviously, all band scoring will remain tentative and doubtful until the scorer is able, with his inner ear, to hear what he has written.

Another helpful experience may be had through practical courses in conducting. Such courses not only demonstrate baton technique but also help the student to understand the conductor's objective and impersonal approach to concerted music making. This kind of experience is equally indispensable to the successful band scorer, for he too must be able to appraise his work at the professional levels of both conductors and publishers. Conducting discloses scoring weaknesses and strengths which might otherwise remain mysteries. The conductor's art transforms lifeless notation to living sound; the band scorer must provide the material for the transformation. The Bibliography lists several books on conducting which are of interest and value.

SCORE READING

Score reading is another subject which no longer need be omitted from the potential band scorer's background and experience. A course in band-score reading, combined with illustrative recordings, offers opportunity for timbre identification and objective appraisals of instrumental combinations in many styles and forms. Full scores of original works and transcriptions, along with many band recordings, are now available in sufficient quantity to ensure the success of such classes at most academic levels. The subject is as indispensable for the experienced band conductor and scorer as are its counterparts in the field of orchestral music.

REHEARSAL NUMBERS

The importance of providing well-placed rehearsal numbers or letters in both full and condensed scores and in all parts cannot be overestimated. They are the one practical means of permitting a director to stop and start during rehearsals without causing undue confusion or delay. These rehearsing aides are usually inserted at intervals varying anywhere from ten to fifteen measures, at the beginning of *tuttis* and difficult passages, or after many measures of thin scoring. In short, rehearsal numbers or letters are placed and spaced to simplify repetitions during rehearsals.

We have seen the use of rehearsal numbers and letters in many of the excerpts throughout this text. It should be observed that rehearsing aides must also be *placed in all parts* exactly as they occur in the full score. Cues of easily distinguishable instruments are sometimes also inserted in parts preceding entrances which follow long periods of silence. Their purpose is to assure the player of his correct count of measures.

CUING AND CROSS-CUING

There have been numerous references in earlier chapters to the importance of cues and cross-cuing and the necessity for including these performance aides in parts for instruments most likely to be missing from some bands. Actually, cues often serve a double purpose. They act as a practical means of providing alternate substituting instruments without necessitating transposition by the players. *Note*: The band scorer makes all transpositions for cues and cross-cuing in the parts of the full score. Cues are also sometimes used by directors to strengthen passages in regular parts which are unusually difficult tonally and technically.

The intervals of transposition for cued parts are determined by adjusting the interval difference between the original part, if any, with that of the substituting instrument. For example, E♭ alto clarinet parts (written a major sixth higher than they sound) will be written a perfect fifth lower for B♭ clarinets (written a major second higher than they sound).

419

Fig. 58

Cuing is generally planned on the premise that certain reeds, the third and fourth horns, and a few percussion instruments may not be available and/or may be the weak parts of some bands. It is highly desirable in cuing parts to select instruments which have similarities of range and timbre. Muted brasses represent the closest timbre substitutions for the double reeds, although their individual ranges and the dissimilarities of their playing techniques remain important factors for consideration. By way of illustration, a muted trombone makes a good substitution for a bassoon, providing passages remain interchangeable for the two dissimilar systems of technique—keyed fingerings versus slide positions.

Table 10 lists the instruments most apt to be cued in American editions of published concert music for the band. The accompanying list of cues should not be considered conclusive, since other choices may be more desirable, as determined by tempos, dynamics, ranges, styles, and the many other factors pertinent to all scoring plans.

TABLE 10

Wind Instruments	Suggested Cues
Oboes I-II	Cornets - trumpets (muted), flutes, E♭ clarinets, B♭ clarinets
English horn	Cornets - trumpets (muted), trombone (muted), E♭ alto clarinet, E♭ alto saxophone

Bassoon I-II	Trombones (muted), E♭ alto clarinet, B♭ bass clarinet, B♭ tenor saxophone, E♭ baritone saxophone, baritone, tuba
Contrabassoon	B♭ or E♭ contrabass clarinet, B♭ bass saxophone, string bass
E♭ clarinet	Piccolo, flute, B♭ clarinet
E♭ alto clarinet	B♭ clarinet, B♭ bass clarinet, E♭ alto saxophone, B♭ tenor saxophone
B♭ bass clarinet	B♭ tenor saxophone, E♭ baritone saxophone
E♭ baritone saxophone	B♭ bass clarinet, B♭ or E♭ contrabass clarinet, baritone, tuba
B♭ bass saxophone	E♭ baritone saxophone, B♭ bass clarinet, B♭ or E♭ contrabass clarinet, tuba, string bass
Fluegelhorn I-II	Cornets, trumpets, horns, trombones, baritone
Horns III-IV	E♭ alto saxophone, B♭ tenor saxophone, cornets, trumpets, trombones, baritone

Percussion Instruments	*Suggested Alternative Instruments*
Chimes	Bells (glockenspiel)
Timpani:	
Rolls, separated accents	Bass drum
Rhythmic figures	Tenor drum, snare drum
Xylophone	Bells (with high woodwinds optional)
Temple blocks	Wood blocks (different sizes)
Tom-tom	Snare drum (muffled), tenor drum (shallow)

The band scorer will find that it is quite helpful to write all cued parts in a colored ink after the full score is completed. Cued parts have all stems pointing upward, regardless of their positions on the staff. In cross-cuing, simultaneous notation for original parts have all stems facing downward. Should a cued part be given to an instrument without a part of its own, full-measure rests are then placed below the staff. Numerous examples have shown cues in full and condensed scores in small type, in parentheses or brackets, or in a combination of these styles. Names of more than one instrument have indicated that the original part has been cross-cued, which permits the director to make a choice when necessary. The band scorer should fully understand that

421

cued parts are functional in character and that their use may alter both tonal color and balance. They are, at best, makeshift substitutions, but highly important in scorings intended for publication.

SELECTED LISTINGS OF BAND TRANSCRIPTIONS

Finally, the band scorer's attention is directed toward the following selected lists of published full-band scores covering all forms of transcription discussed in this text. There is much practical knowledge to be gained from the study of a note-by-note analysis of these scores, since all the details of changing *tessituras*, spacings, doublings, and fillers can be minutely examined in context and compared to the original source material. This study can be a ready-made corollary to the application of all entries discussed and examined in the *Reference Chart of Keyboard Idioms and Patterns.*

FULL-BAND SCORES REPRESENTING SEVERAL
FORMS OF TRANSCRIPTIONS

Piano or Organ to Band

Composer	Transcriber	Medium	Title (Publisher) [1]
Albéniz	Campbell-Watson	Piano	Tango(W)
Bach	Abert-Weiss	Organ	Choral and Fugue(S)
Bach	Cailliet	Organ	*Fervent Is My Longing* (EV) Fugue in G minor(EV)
Bach	Gillette	Organ	*We All Believe in One God*(W)
Bach	Goldman, R. F.	Organ	*In Dulci Jubilo* (S)
Bach	Leidzen	Organ	*Jesu, Joy of Man's Desiring*(CF)
Bach	Moehlmann	Organ	Prelude and Fugue(R)
Bach	Wellington	Piano	Fugue No. 4 from *Well-tempered Clavier*(S)
Bartók	Leidzen	Piano	*Bear Dance*(A)
Bartók	Leidzen	Piano	*An Evening in the Village*(A)

[1] See key to publishers at the end of this table.

Composer	Transcriber	Medium	Title (Publisher)
Beethoven	Kilbert	Piano	*Two German Dances* (S)
Bendel	Campbell-Watson	Piano	*Sunday Morning at Glion* (W)
Brahms	Guenther	Organ	Two Choral Preludes(S–B)
Franck	Wagner	Organ	*Pièce héroïque* (S)
Guilmant	Schmutz	Organ	*Allegro vivace* from Organ Sonata in D(A)
Moussorgsky	Leidzen	Piano	Part 1, *Pictures at an Exhibition* (CF)
Saint-Saëns	Cheyette	Piano	*Pavana* (S)
Schubert	Greissle	Piano	*Military March* (S)
Tchaikovsky	O'Neill	Piano	*Troïka en traineaux* (W)

Orchestra to Band [1]

Composer	Transcriber	Title (Publisher)
Beethoven	Safranek	Overture, *Coriolan* (CF)
Berlioz	Hemming	Overture, *Beatrice and Benedict* (CF)
Boieldieu	Zamecnik	Overture, *The Calif of Bagdad* (SF)
Borodin	Leidzen	First Movement, Second Symphony(CF)
Brahms	Hibbert	Third Movement, Second Symphony(BH)
Cherubini	Morrissey	Overture, *Anacreon* (W)
Cailliet	Cailliet	Variations on the theme *Pop! Goes the Weasel* (EV)
Copland	Beeler	*Lincoln Portrait* (BH)
Copland	Copland	*An Outdoor Overture* (BH)
Dukas	Winterbottom	*L'Apprenti sorcier* (BH)
Dvořák	Leidzen	Finale, *New World Symphony* (CF)
Falla	Greissle	*Fire Dance* (C)
Franck	Gillette	Finale, Symphony in D minor(W)
Franck	Harding	Excerpt, *Psyché and Erós* (K)
Franck	Malone	First Movement, Symphony in D minor(S)
Glinka	Hemming	Overture, *Russlan and Ludmilla* (CF)
Glinka	Lockhart	*Valse fantasie* (B)
Glinka	Winter	*Jota* (BH)
Goldmark	Laurendeau	*Bridal Song* and Intermezzo from *Rural Wedding Symphony* (CF)
Gounod	Godfrey	Overture, *Mirelle* (BH)
Gounod	de Leonard	Overture, *Mirelle* (S)
Gomez	Clarke	Overture, *Il Guarany* (CF)
Gould	Gould	*Cowboy Rhapsody* (MM)
Hadley	Weiss	Overture, *Alma Mater* (B)
Handel	Cailliet	Overture, *Messiah* (BH)
Hanson	Maddy	Second Movement, Symphony No. 1(CF)
Humperdinck	Maddy	*Prayer* and *Dream Pantomime* from *Hansel and Gretel* (R)
Harty	Brown	*Field* Suite(BH)

[1] Orchestral scores are available for these works.

Composer	Transcriber	Title (Publisher)
Haydn	De Rubertis	Overture, *Orlando Palandrino*(R)
Kleinsinger	Roach	*Tubby, the Tuba*(S)
Mozart	Lake	Minuet from Symphony No. 39 (D)
Moussorgsky	Leidzen	*Coronation Scene* from *Boris Godunov*(CF)
Moussorgsky	Winter	*Persian Dance* (BH)
Offenbach	Greissle	Overture, *La Belle Hélène*(S)
Pierné	Beeler	*March of the Little Leaden Soldiers*(BH)
Rimski-Korsakov	Duthoit	Polonaise from *Christmas Night* (BH)
Rimski-Korsakov	Harding	Overture, *The Tsar's Bride* (K)
Rimski-Korsakov	Sartorius	*Dance of the Buffoons*(W)
Rimski-Korsakov	Winter	Overture, *The Maid of Pskov*(BH)
Rossini	Britten	*Soirées musicales* (BH)
Rossini	Brown	Overture, *The Silken Ladder* (BH)
Rossini	Cailliet	Overture, *La gazza ladra*(SF)
Rossini	Cailliet	Overture, *Italian in Algiers*(SF)
Saint-Saëns	De Rubertis	Finale, Symphony No. 1 (W)
Saint-Saëns	Lake	Overture, *Princess Juane* (CF)
Saint-Saëns	Winterbottom	*Marche heroïque*(BH)
Schubert	Leidzen	First Movement, Symphony in B minor (CF)
Schumann	Taylor	Adagio from Symphony No. 2 (abridged) (P)
Shostakovich	Richter	Finale, Symphony No. 5 (BH)
Sibelius	Richardson	*Alla Marcia* from *Karelia Suite*(BH)
Smetana	Grabel	Overture, *Libussa*(CF)
Smetana	Overgaard	Overture, *Hubička*(S)
Strauss, J.	Brown	*Emperor Waltz*(BH)
Strauss, J.	Cailliet	Overture, *Die Fledermaus*(BH)
Strauss, R.	Cailliet	Waltzes from *Der Rosenkavalier*(BH)
Suppé	Zamecnik	Overture *Jolly Robers*(SF)
Thomas	Safrenck	Overture, *Raymond* (CF)
Wagner, R.	Cailliet	Excerpts from Act 1, *Lohengrin*(R)
Wagner, R.	Cailliet	*Siegfried's Rhine Journey* from *Die Götterdämmerung* (R)
Wagner, R.	Cailliet	*Invocation of Alberich* from *Das Rheingold*(SF)
Wagner, R.	Drumm	Introduction to Act 3, *Lohengrin*(CF)
Wagner, R.	Drumm	Prelude, *Lohengrin* (CF)
Wagner, R.	O'Neill	*Entry of the Gods into Valhalla* from *Das Rheingold* (CF)
Wagner, R.	Winterbottom	*Homage March*(BH)
Weinberger	Bainum	Polka and Fugue from *Shwanda the Bagpiper*(A)
Wood	Brown	Overture, *Manx* (BH)

Band to Orchestra

Composer	Transcriber	Title (Publishers)
Crist	Crist	*Vienna 1913*(W)
Handel	Harty	*Water Music*(BH and P)
Holst	Jacobs	Suites Nos. 1 and 2 (BH)
Schuman	Schuman	*Newsreel in Five Shots* (S)
Williams	Jacobs	*Folk Song Suite* (BH)

Solo Instruments with Band

Composer	Transcriber	Title (Publishers)
Cowell		Little Concerto for piano and band(A)
Gershwin	Grofé	*Rhapsody in Blue* for piano and band(NW)
Grieg	Bain	First Movement, Concerto in A minor for piano and band(S)
Handel	Malin	*Concerto Grosso* (with two solo flutes and solo B♭ clarinet) (R)
Wagner, J.		*Concerto Grosso* (with three solo cornets and solo baritone)(W)

Chorus with Band

Composer	Transcriber	Title (Publishers)
Berlioz	Goldman	*III. Apotheosis* from *Grand Symphony for Band*(M)
Bergh	Campbell-Watson	*Honor and Glory*(R)
Teague		*Hail to Our Flag*(A)

Key to Publishers

(A)	Associated Music Publishers	(MM)	Mills Music, Inc.
(B)	C. C. Birchard Co.	(NW)	New World Music Corp.
(BH)	Boosey and Hawkes, Inc.	(P)	Theodore Presser Co.
(C)	J. and W. Chester, Ltd.	(R)	Remick Music Corp.
(CF)	Carl Fischer Co.	(S-B)	Summy-Birchard Publishing Co.
(D)	Oliver Ditson Co.		
(EV)	Elkan-Vogel Co.	(S)	G. Schirmer, Inc.
(K)	Neil A. Kjos Music Co.	(SF)	Sam Fox Publishing Co.
(M)	Mercury Music Corp.	(W)	M. Witmark and Sons

BIBLIOGRAPHY

BAND SCORING

Adkins, H. E.: *Treatise on the Military Band,* Boosey and Co., Ltd., London, 1931.

Clappe, Arthur A.: *The Principles of Wind-band Transcription,* Carl Fischer Inc., New York, 1921.

Dvorak, Raymond F.: *The Band on Parade,* Carl Fischer, Inc., New York, 1937.

Fennell, Frederick: *Time and the Winds,* G. Leblanc Co., Wisconsin, 1954.

Gallo, S.: *The Modern Band,* C. C. Birchard Co., Boston, 1935.

Goldman, Edwin Franko: *Band Betterment,* Carl Fischer, Inc., New York, 1934.

Goldman, Richard F.: *The Concert Band,* Rinehart & Co., Inc., New York, 1946.

Lake, M. L.: *The American Band Arranger,* Carl Fischer, Inc., New York, 1920.

Lang, Philip J.,: *Scoring for the Band,* Mills Music, Inc., New York, 1950.

Leidzen, Erik: *An Invitation to Band Arranging,* Ditson ed., Theodore Presser Co., Bryn Mawr, Pa., 1950.

Skeat, William J., Harry F. Clarke, Russell V. Morgan: *The Fundamentals of Band Arranging,* Sam Fox Publishing Co., New York, 1938.

CONDUCTING

Earhart, Will: *The Eloquent Baton,* M. Witmark & Sons, New York, 1931.

Gehrkens, Karl W.: *Essentials in Conducting,* Ditson ed., Theodore Presser Co., Bryn Mawr, Pa., 1919.

Grosbayne, Benjamin: *Modern Baton Technique,* Harvard University Press, Cambridge, Mass., 1957.

Rudolf, Max: *The Grammar of Conducting,* G. Schirmer, Inc., New York, 1950.

Scherchen, Hermann: *Handbook of Conducting,* Oxford University Press, London, 1933.

Weingartner, Felix: *On Conducting,* E. F. Kalmus, Inc., New York, 1905

ARRANGING FOR DANCE ORCHESTRA

Cesana, Otto: *Voicing the Modern Dance Orchestra,* Modern Music Publications, New York, 1946.

Diamente, Carlos: *Arranging Latin-American Music Authentically,* King Band Publications, New York, 1948.

Miller, Glenn: *Glenn Miller's Method of Orchestral Arranging,* Robbins Music Corp., New York, 1949.

426

INDEX

427

428

Effects, special *(cont.)*
  slap tonguing, 262
  tremolos, 250–255, 376–380
  trills, 247–250, 376–380
E. F. G. Overture (*see* James)
El Amor Brujo(see Falla —Greissle)
Elégie, Op. 38, No. 6, Grieg, wood
  winds unit for, 120
Elephant from *Carnival of Animals,*
  Saint-Saëns — Cray, tubas,
  soli for, 189
English horn, 12, 13, 15, 85, 90–95
  examples for, 92–95
  range, 85
  range divisions, 91
  reference to, 12, 15, 90
  transposition, 85
English Suite in D minor (*see* Bach)
Enharmonic changes, application
  and definition, 23
Erik the Red (*see* Hallberg)
Eulogy (*see* Wagner, Joseph)
Euphonium (*see* Baritone)
Evening in the Village, An, Bartók—
  Leidzen, clarinets unit, 63

Falla, Manuel de, *Serenata Andaluza,*
  two- three-part music (ho-
  mophonic), 344
Falla —Greissle:
  Ritual Fire Dance from *El Amor
    Brujo,* piano used in, 244
  trills for wood winds, 251
Fanfare from *West Point Suite* (*see*
  Milhaud)
Fanfare and Allegro (*see* Williams,
  Clifton)
Fantasia on the Dargason (*see* Holst)
Fantastic Dance, Op. 1, No. 3, Shos-
  takovitch, two- three-part
  music (style mixtures), 353
Fauchet — Campbell-Watson:
  Symphony in B♭, *Nocturne,* refer-
    ence to, 164
  solo horn, 152
  for trombones, 167
  Scherzo, baritone, arpeggios for,
    181
  for tenor saxophone, 71

Fauchet —Gillette:
  Symphony in B♭, Finale, for bass
    saxophone, 79
  for cornets, 146
  for trumpets, 146
  Overture, for baritone saxo-
    phone, 76
  for bass clarinet, 60
  for English horn, 92
  for flute, 38
  for horns, 153
Fennell, Frederick:
  Time and the Winds, quotation
    from, 5–7, 13
  reference to, 12
Field drum, 216
Fiesta Mexicana, La, Reed,
  reference to, 100
Fiesta Mora en Tanger, Turina,
  repeated notes, 335
Fillers, application and definition,
  14, 115–117, 267–268
Finale from Symphony in B♭ (*see*
  Fauchet — Gillette)
Finale from Symphony in D minor
  (*see* Franck —Gillette)
Fischer — Wilson:
  *Le Journal du Printemps, Cha-
    conne,* for cornets, 129
  Gavotte, double reeds unit,
    101
  wood winds unit, 103
  Overture, brass (contrapuntal),
    198
  wood winds unit, 107
Five Chorals, Bach — Frackenphol,
  reference to, 60
Fluegelhorn, 126–127, 141–142
  parts for, 141–142
  range, 126
  range divisions, 127
  transpositions, 126
Flute, in C, 33–39
  parts for, 35–39
  range, 33
  range divisions, 34–35
  in E♭, 21
  in G, alto, bass, 15, 33
Flutter tonguing, 255–257, 376–380
Fogelberg, Maurice (*see* Ravel —
  Fogelberg)

431

433

435

438

440